An Unlikely Herc

Esther Cailingold's Fight for Jerusalem

For Frances

For Frances

with best wishes

[signature]

MAY 2000

'I HAVE PLACED WATCHMEN ON THY WALLS, O JERUSALEM'
Isaiah LXII:6

An Unlikely Heroine

Esther Cailingold's Fight for Jerusalem

ASHER CAILINGOLD

With a Foreword by
YITZHAK NAVON
Former President of Israel

VALLENTINE MITCHELL
LONDON • PORTLAND, OR

First published in 2000 in Great Britain by
VALLENTINE MITCHELL
Newbury House, 900 Eastern Avenue
London IG2 7HH

and in the United States of America by
VALLENTINE MITCHELL
c/o ISBS, 5804 N.E. Hassalo Street
Portland, Oregon 97213-3644

Website: www.vmbooks.com

British Library Cataloguing in Publication Data:

Cailingold, Asher
    An unlikely heroine: Esther Cailingold's fight
    for Jerusalem
    1. Cailingold, Esther 2. Women soldiers – Jerusalem –
    Biography 3. Soldiers – Jerusalem – Biography
    4. Jerusalem – History – Siege, 1948
    I. Title
    956.9'442'052'092

ISBN 0-85303-409-5 (cloth)
ISBN 0-85303-408-7 (paper)

Library of Congress Cataloging-in-Publication Data:

A catalog record for this book is available from the
Library of Congress

Printed and bound in Great Britain by
MPG Books Ltd, Bodmin, Cornwall

TO AVI, OUR ELDEST SON OF BLESSED MEMORY

This book was to have been dedicated to Edna, my beloved wife and life partner. As I wrote it, however, we received the dreadful news that our son Avi had suffered a heart attack. He lingered unconscious for the next 17 days, surrounded by family, colleagues and caring doctors and nurses at the Hadassah Hospital on Mount Scopus, where his aunt Esther had walked in her white coat 50 years earlier, bringing books and kind words to the patients.

Avi died on Holocaust Memorial Day. Our visit to his grave at the end of the seven-day *shiva* (period of mourning) was on Israel's Independence Day. And we unveiled his tombstone on Jerusalem Day. These national anniversaries were landmarks both in his short life and in that of the aunt he never met, Esther.

Avi's life followed that of Esther in many ways, although he was spared for twice as long and has left us Michal, his widow, and four wonderful grandchildren to comfort us in our grief. Like Esther, he sought out life's challenges: he spent several years in the battered northern border town of Kiryat Shmona; two years in the Upper Galilee kibbutz of Gonen, living an orthodox Jewish life in a secular society; and his last 11 years in Israel's prison service, working mainly in rehabilitation, where he was loved and admired by prisoners and prison officers alike, respected for his honesty and his dedication to the welfare of those who had rejected society and whom society had set aside.

The motifs of Avi's life were tolerance, fostering respect and understanding. He was the quintessential man of peace. May the example of his life be a beacon to future generations, as was that of his heroic aunt, Esther.

Asher Cailingold

Contents

PART THREE

PART FOUR

List of Illustrations

Between pages 16 and 17

1. Esther as bridesmaid, aged three.

2. On holiday in Bournemouth, aged eight.

3. Yaacov Eliyah Fenechal, maternal grandfather.

4. Feige Fenechal, maternal grandmother.

5. Naftali Cailingold, paternal grandfather.

6. Esther's mother and father, 1935.

7. At Myrdle Street Junior School, Whitechapel, London, 1932 (extreme right in front of teacher).

8. As a student at London University, 1944 (front row extreme right).

9. At the Bachad training farm, Thaxted, Essex, 1945.

10. Passport photograph.

11. The new teacher.

12. The old Evelina de Rothschild School on the Street of the Prophets.

13. The R.A.F. Zone Pass that enabled her to reach school.

14. The photograph of Esther in the Zone Pass.

Foreword

by YITZHAK NAVON, *Former President of Israel*

Esther Cailingold was a young London girl who came to
Jerusalem in 1946, a time of supreme historical significance to
the Jewish People. She volunteered for action and took part in
the battle for Jerusalem's Old City, where she succumbed to her
wounds on May 29 1948. She was 22.

It is hard to imagine how one person could cram so much
into such a short life. Esther was the sort who enjoyed a good
concert, appreciated beautiful scenery and took pleasure in
good company. Fun-loving by nature, she was idealistic and
very brave, passionately imbued with religious Zionism. She
practised what she preached and did not preach to others what
she was not prepared to do herself.

Sometimes, an individual's life can encapsulate an entire
period. Such was true of Esther. She bore witness to historical
events which she recorded in her letters to her family in London
with an accurate, witty and critical eye. To her it was a privilege
to take part in the War of Independence of a people who,
having risen from Holocaust ashes, now had to withstand the
furious combined attack of its neighbours.

Yet this book does not limit itself to the telling of Esther's life.
It has a wider vista, describing the political and military context
of the day: the British Mandate, the United Nations, the Jews,
the Arabs. It is a work which blends gripping history with the
life of a unique girl who lived through that history to the full,
and, at the moment of ultimate challenge, flung herself into the
fray and paid the ultimate price.

I commend this book as compulsory reading especially for

Jewish youngsters everywhere. For it is a very human and liter-
ary experience, a piece of living history in the struggle of the
Jewish people for independence and sovereignty. These are
what Esther's letters are about – a personal and historical testimony set against the unfolding events of her time and recorded
with a meticulous eye.

Nothing illustrates this better than her last letter to her family,
in which she writes, in part:

> We have had a bitter fight, I have tasted of Gehenem [Hell]
> – but it has been worthwhile because I am convinced that
> the end will see a Jewish State and the realization of all our
> longings ... I shall be only one of many who fell [sic] sacri-
> fice, and I was urged to write this because one in particular
> was killed today who meant a great deal to me. Because of
> the sorrow I felt, I want you to take it otherwise – to remem-
> ber that we were soldiers and had the greatest and noblest
> cause to fight for.
>
> God is with us I know, in his own Holy City, and I am
> proud and ready to pay the price it may cost to reprieve it
> ... Please, please, do not be sadder than you can help – I
> have lived my life fully if briefly, and I think that is the best
> way – 'short and sweet', very sweet it has been here in our
> own land ...

Can there be a more noble and braver testimony than this?

YITZHAK NAVON
4th Adar Rishon 5760/10 February 2000

Preface

In the harsh November of 1946, Britain languished in the dismal aftermath of the Second World War. The departure of my elder sister Esther for Jerusalem that month filled me with envy. A restless teenager, all I wanted was to join her in her adventure, far from the strictures of school and home, the endless shortages of food, clothes and heating fuel. She was escaping the misery of smog-filled London for the sunny climes of the Holy Land. But beyond that, she was actually going to the land of our dreams, fulfilling our Zionist beliefs. At our family dinner table, where our father regaled us with stories from his days as a young Zionist activist in pre-war Poland, a homeland for the Jewish people was the constant topic of conversation.

For the 18 months that followed Esther's departure, we shared her exploits through the vivid letters she wrote us, as often as three times a week. And what exploits! A year after arriving in what was then Palestine, she volunteered for the Haganah, the underground defence organisation of the nascent state. A few weeks after that, she exchanged her teaching post at a Jerusalem girls' school for the life of a full-time soldier.

After the death of our mother in 1992, my sister Mimi and I discovered Esther's letters in a suitcase, probably unopened for the best part of 50 years. Rereading those letters woke in me a feeling which I can best describe as a sense of debt to my long-dead sister. Through Esther's letters, supplemented by material collected from official and private sources, I have ventured to tell her story. It is the saga of a bright and adventurous young woman who found great happiness fighting for Israel's independence, and who died on the barricades of Jerusalem's beleaguered Old City weeks before her 23rd birthday.

In telling Esther's story, I have been greatly helped by her friends and colleagues, who plumbed their memories and allowed me to use their precious letters and documents. Special thanks are also due to the Israel Defence Forces Archives, and to Moshe Erenwald, a colleague of my son Eli, who shared with me his Master's thesis, which describes the battle for the Old City's Jewish Quarter in May 1948.

In addition, I would like to express my gratitude to Wendy Elliman for her skill and patience in editing this book.

Prologue

The long line of army trucks moved slowly through the quiet Jerusalem streets, each bearing its precious load of six flag-draped coffins. It was early September 1950, shortly before the Jewish New Year, and those who had died fighting for Jerusalem two years before were being brought to their last resting-place in the Mount Herzl military cemetery.

During the terrible months of siege and battle which heralded Israel's birth, there had been no time to prepare a military cemetery fit for the fallen soldiers of the Jewish people. They had been temporarily buried in a disused quarry below where the Supreme Court now stands, the many coffins stacked in two layers to save space. A tall stone monument stands there today in memory of over 1,000 men and women who died in Jerusalem during the brutal spring and summer of 1948.

A week before the trucks set out for Mount Herzl, my Uncle Reuven and I had watched the exhumations at the old quarry, in response to urgent pleas from my father. Unable to get to Israel himself in time, he desperately needed to know that his daughter was indeed dead and so bid her a final farewell.

The nightmare of my sister's death had begun for me two years earlier, on Sunday June 6 1948 on a London Tube train. Here I saw a 'Stop Press' item in the newspaper. Headlined 'TWO LONDON GIRLS DIE IN BATTLE', it reported that 'Esther Cailingold, daughter of a London publisher ... a Sten gunner, fell while blasting Arab positions round the Old City.'

I was due to leave for the three-week-old state of Israel in a few days. My mother had taken to her bed, sick with worry that the second of her three children was heading for a war zone. My father was on his way to the United States on business. I arrived home to find that my sister Mimi had already heard the terrible news.

The two years that followed were one long nightmare for our family. My father was racked with guilt at having taken Esther to Palestine in November 1946, and he developed a morbid fear that she might still be alive and calling to him for help. That terrible fear was not laid to rest until he reached Jerusalem, just in time for the reburial on Mount Herzl. Uncle Reuven and I gave him details of the exhumation, but that did not stop him climbing aboard the truck carrying Esther's coffin and tearing open its lid. He looked inside and cried out *'Techiyat hamaitim!'* (May the dead be resurrected!), before collapsing into my arms.

Father never stopped mourning his oldest child. But from the moment he saw Esther in her coffin he accepted that she, by making the supreme sacrifice, had helped create an independent Jewish state in the Land of Israel, a cause for which he and his family had fought since the early days of the religious Zionist movement in Poland.

The clang of shovels on the stony Jerusalem soil was the only sound heard that day on Mount Herzl, as Israeli soldiers helped hundreds of families cover the coffins of their loved ones. Psalms and the prayer for the dead were recited. Then an infantry platoon fired the traditional three shots. Silence fell across the newly consecrated ground, broken only by the sobs of the families gathered around the fresh graves. We wept for those who had gone. Little did we know of the rivers of tears that would be shed in that place after the battles of the years to come.

Twice each year, on Israel's Memorial Day for her fallen soldiers and on the anniversary of Esther's death, the family gathers at her graveside. She was our older sister, a 22-year-old girl who travelled alone to a strange land, who changed into a person we never knew, and who died happy to be part of the struggle to fulfil the Zionist dream.

PART ONE

1 Roots

Esther was born in London in the summer of 1925, seven years after the Great War had given way to the era of the Flapper and the Charleston. London was then the capital of a vast empire and a city of dramatic contrasts. For some, it was a good time to be alive and London the best of all places to be. But for the limbless veterans of the Flanders trenches sprawled on the city pavements, begging cups in hand and with 20 years to wait for the welfare state, the world looked very different.

Within this bustling, effervescent society, thrived a Jewish community of some 200,000 souls, two-thirds of all Britain's Jews, clustered around Whitechapel Road in London's East End. One of them was our mother's father, Yaacov Eliyahu Fenechel.

Yaacov Eliyahu came from a hamlet or *shtetl* known as Szediszow, near Cracow, one of two and a half million Jews who fled the starvation and pogroms of eastern Europe in the last years of the nineteenth century. He made his way to London in the last weeks of 1899, in the footsteps of his stepfather, who had emigrated some time before and was finding life in England more congenial than in Szediszow. Our grandfather docked at Tilbury on the River Thames, a youngster from a rural area without a penny in his pocket, a word of English in his head or the education or skills which would earn him a living. How thrilled he must have been to receive a dockside welcome from a group of bearded, Yiddish-speaking men. His joy was short-lived. They turned out to be proselyte missionaries, from whom he was saved at the last moment by a more worldly fellow passenger, who led him to the Jews' Temporary Shelter in Mansell Street, where half a century later his eldest granddaughter Esther would try to help young survivors of the Holocaust.

He soon made contact with his stepfather, found work in the fur trade and brought over his wife Feige to join the burgeoning Jewish community in Whitechapel. The first of their two daughters, our mother Anne, was born in 1901. Betty followed in 1904.

The Fenechels settled down to the hard-working, highly respectable life of a strictly Orthodox, yet open-minded family. Yaacov Eliyahu moved from the fur trade to household linens, selling goods on credit from door to door, and devoting his free time to voluntary work at the 'Oesstreichisher Stiebel' in Fieldgate Street, a small, custom-built replica of an east European synagogue. He eventually became its president, and, though he never achieved great financial success, he was known as a pillar of the community, honest to a fault and always willing to help others. Years later, on Shabbat (the Sabbath) and Jewish festivals, we would walk there proudly clutching the hand of the distinguished-looking gentleman who was our grandfather, resplendent in his silk top hat and black morning coat.

Yaacov Eliyahu was one of the two men who most influenced Esther as she grew up. We lived with our parents in the strictly Orthodox home of our grandparents, two elderly people who clung tightly to their Jewishness and their religious lifestyle when so many around them gave way to compromise. The currents of assimilation were very strong in Britain then, but the influence of our grandparents' home, with its deep love of Judaism and unusual broad-mindedness, produced both children and grandchildren proud of their Jewishness.

Our grandfather, or Zada as we called him, was probably the kindest human being I have ever known. He was never judgemental, always willing to listen to the problems of others and forever involved in sorting out difficulties. With all this, he was a very practical man, who helped out in the kitchen (he was expert at *gefilte* fish), repaired clothing on his sewing machine, fixed pipes, drains and fuses for neighbours and never ever accepted payment for his good deeds. He was a dearly loved role model to both his children and grandchildren, and he exercised a major influence on our lives and on our value systems as we matured.

While our mother was growing up in London, our father was still in eastern Europe. His father, Naftali, had been born in 1868 in Pinsk, in the part of town known as Karlin, an early hotbed of Zionism, where Chaim Weizmann went to school and from where the Shertok (later Sharett) family came. Karlin was a centre of the young 'Chovevei Zion' movement, the ideological forerunner of Theodor Herzl's political Zionism – and my father's family was thus immersed in Zionism long before Herzl.

In 1890 Naftali married and moved to Warsaw, where he opened a bookstore. Our father, Moshe Yehuda, was born there five years later, the third child and eldest son of the six children that Naftali and his wife Miriam were to have. They moved to Lithuania when Moshe Yehuda was nine, and he recalled Vilna schoolboys mocking his Polish-style velvet cap. The family returned to Warsaw five years after that, but Moshe Yehuda stayed on in Vilna to continue his *yeshiva* studies. It was there that he acquired his extensive knowledge of Hebrew, as well as what amounted to a virtual obsession with the Bible and its very special language. At 18 he was ready to return to Warsaw and embark on a career as a bookseller and publisher in his father's business. The year, however, was 1913 – the winds of war were beginning to blow across Europe, and the world and the lives of millions were poised to undergo a drastic change.

The German army captured Warsaw on 5 August 1915. German troops flooded the city, conducting themselves brutally and with blatant anti-Semitism. While the cruelty of the Russians and the anti-Semitism of the Poles were taken for granted by the Cailingold family, such behaviour from the apparently enlightened Germans shocked them deeply. Until then, their Zionism had been theoretical and ideological. Now it took on a more practical form. There was, they decided, no future for them in eastern Europe.

Naftali had the necessary connections. Alongside his business activities, he had helped establish the religious Zionist Mizrachi movement in Poland and Lithuania, he was a member of the

Jewish National Fund's board of directors and he was a frequenter of Zionist rallies and conferences. His six children shared his attachment to the Zionist cause, and Moshe was among the founders of Poland's Young Mizrachi, the forerunner of the religious Zionist youth movement.

In spring 1919 Moshe wrote an open letter, in perfect Hebrew, to Young Mizrachi and its Warsaw committee. The time had come, he declared, to talk less and do more to prepare young people for *aliyah*. 'Let's leave politics to the old people and get on with the practical work!' he wrote. 'Let's deepen their knowledge of Hebrew and their Jewish knowledge, and give them the training they need to contribute to the *Yishuv* [Jewish community] in the Land of Israel!!' (This letter turned up by sheer chance almost 70 years later. Moshe's grandson Eli was researching for his degree in Modern Jewish History at Bar Ilan University near Tel Aviv. He found the letter in a file documenting the early years of the Zionist movement.)

Perhaps because of this letter, Moshe was chosen to represent the Polish movement at the founding conference of Britain's Young Mizrachi in London. Addressing the conference in Hebrew, he was shocked to realise that few of those in the hall understood a word he was saying. His speech did, however, impact on at least one member of the audience: 18-year-old Anne Fenechel was profoundly impressed by this handsome, fiery young man.

Moshe returned to Warsaw, disillusioned with the British movement and at a loss to understand how young Orthodox Jews could lack all knowledge of spoken Hebrew.

A few months later, in spring 1920, Fate entered the story in the form of a drunken Polish soldier whom Moshe saw beating an old Jew on a Warsaw street. Like the biblical Moshe, without pausing to think, my father Moshe leapt on the soldier and threw him to the ground – no mean feat for a man barely five feet tall! A crowd gathered and police whistles blew.

Jews simply don't beat up Polish soldiers, whatever the provocation. Moshe ran literally for his life. That night, he crossed the border into Germany. With a British visa still in his passport from his visit of a few months earlier, he headed for London.

The story of our father's attack on the Polish soldier became part of our family folklore. For him, however, his flight to England was not simply the exchanging of one Diaspora for another, but a way-station en route to the Holy Land. Back in Warsaw, grandfather Naftali took it as an omen that the time had come for the Cailingolds to leave. His London-based son, he decided, would facilitate the move. He instructed Moshe to stay in London, apply for British citizenship and earn the money that would help his family in Palestine.

Moshe's brothers Reuven and Yaacov went to Palestine later that same year. Reuven started out as a labourer, helping build the Bikur Cholim Hospital in Jerusalem, before transferring to the new telephone service in which he eventually became deputy chief engineer. Yaacov joined the agricultural settlement of Moshav Kfar Hess, where his son still lives on the family smallholding. Naftali spent another five years in Warsaw, busy with both his business and Zionist activities, until he, too, left for Palestine with his wife Miriam and their daughters. Miriam fell seriously ill and died two years later. Naftali lived on another quarter-century, running his bookstore next to the main synagogue on Tel Aviv's Allenby Street until his death in 1951.

Meanwhile, in London, our father had opened a branch of the family book business, making a name for himself as a valuable resource in Anglo-Jewry – a man who not only published and sold Hebrew books, but also understood their contents. Soon after arriving in London and still knowing no English, he ran into a bearded gentleman in the post office and asked his help in sending a telegram to his family in Warsaw. The 'Englishman' invited the young man home that Shabbat – where his daughter Anne recognised the fiery delegate from the Young Mizrachi conference the previous year. Her father, too, was impressed by the young man, though more for the extensive Jewish knowledge he displayed and for his fine voice when he sang Shabbat songs. Marriage arrangements were soon being discussed and the couple was formally engaged, when Anne suddenly became ill. Tuberculosis was suspected, a disease then considered incurable. In an everlasting testimony to our father's love for our mother, he not only continued the engagement, but also paid for her convalescence in Germany's Black Forest. Mother returned to England with a clean bill of health and married father at the Spitalfields Great Synagogue on Tuesday, 19 August 1924.

The young couple moved into the Fenechel home at 18 Milward Street, behind the London Hospital, yards away from Whitechapel Road. Ten months later, on June 28 1925, to the joy and excitement of her parents and grandparents, Esther was born. Esther's birth was followed by that of Miriam and then of myself, Asher, children never known by any but Hebrew names.

The outside world was all Flappers and Charleston, but inside that small terraced house glowed a warm world of Jewish culture and tradition. The highlights of the year were Shabbat and the Jewish festivals, when the rich aromas and tastes of Jewish food tickled the palate, and the soul sang with the excitement of Jewish folklore and customs played out before the eyes of the young children.

To the intense Jewishness of my grandparents' home was added another dimension – that of our father's fervent Zionism. Our lullabies were about the Carmel and the Yarden, and I'm sure we knew *Hatikva*, the Hebrew national anthem, long before we learned *God Save The King*. A tapestry depicting Theodor Herzl on the balcony at the Zionist congress in Basel hung from our *succah* walls, and I still cherish a picture of Rachel's tomb and a wooden-covered book of pressed flowers that my Uncle Reuven brought from Palestine when he visited us in London in 1935.

With the perspective of time, it seems that we always knew our home in London was no more than temporary, and that our real home was across the Mediterranean in the Land of Israel. Esther was a Zionist long before she knew of any formal movement or heard her first Zionist speech. She imbibed her Zionism if not with her mother's milk then with the Hebrew songs our father sang to us.

Esther thus grew up with two male role models: grandfather (Zada) imparting his inherent kindness, consideration and love for mankind; and father with his respect for learning, his national pride and his sense of daring to fight for our fellow Jews.

2 Whitechapel

Esther grew up in London, the heart of the British Empire, on which the sun never set. In school, our teachers would point to the pink-shaded masses on the global map and our little chests would puff out in pride that most of the world was 'ours'.

Esther started school at the age of three, first at the Rutland Street Infants School and later the Myrdle Street Junior School. A classmate, Doris Haskel (née Rosenblatt), remembers Esther as 'a very bright girl, very clever, who always looked clean and tidy, the pleats of her navy school tunic always pressed. She was a friendly girl but a little bit distant.' A class photograph shows a neat, well-scrubbed eight-year-old Esther, with a very serious look on her face.

There must, however, have been a great sense of dissonance in Esther's young life. While her teachers told her that she lived at the heart of civilisation, father would talk of how primitive he found London in comparison with his native Warsaw where, for example, they had had a telephone at home for years, an item still considered a luxury in London. It was December 1926 before parliament passed the Electricity Supply Act, promising within seven years a national electricity grid to which half the homes in Britain would be linked. I remember gas lighting in the streets right up to the Second World War, lit each evening by men reaching up with long poles.

The greater dichotomy, however, was between our cocoon-like Jewish existence and the increasingly secular and permissive society within which we lived. Our Jewish community retained the atmosphere of pre-war eastern Europe. To reach his bookshop, father had no more than a five-minute

9

walk from our house in Milward Street, along Whitechapel High Street, and around two corners to Old Montague Street and his shop at number 6. Along the way, he would pass the bagel woman, with her shrill cry and her huge basket of *frischer bagelech,* and the two sisters who sold pickled herrings and cucumber straight from the barrel. The language of the street in those days was overwhelmingly Yiddish, and our cultural venues were the Yiddish section of the Whitechapel Library, the Jewish section of its art gallery, the area's thriving Yiddish theatres and the *cheders* where we studied after school. Even the local schools were so geared to the large numbers of Orthodox Jewish children, that on winter Fridays they ran to a system called 'double session', in which we studied through the lunch break so that school would end early enough for us to get home in time for Shabbat.

In the early 1930s, when we were all quite young and still living in London's East End, our paternal grandfather, Naftali, came with our Uncle Reuven from Palestine to visit us. They brought wonderful gifts from the Holy Land and left a deep impression of the mysteries to be found out there. Even then, the idea of Eretz Yisrael (the Land of Israel) as our true home was imprinted on our young minds.

When I think back about my sister and wonder how she chose her unusual path, I think of how she grew up, immersed in the obstinate Zionism of our father and the warmth of our Orthodox Jewish home. I think too of what was happening in Britain during her childhood. In the years after the First World War, the huge numbers of single women in the country were becoming a major force, with issues such as women smoking in public the focus of heated discussion. (Esther was to become a heavy smoker, much to the anguish of our father, who believed that women shouldn't smoke!) The Pankhurst ladies had won their battle for women's suffrage only in 1918, and it was not until 1928 that the voting age for women was reduced from 30 to 21. But perhaps more than all this, it was the exploits of Amelia Earhart and Amy Johnson that inspired young women of those days to seek out new frontiers.

The Cailingold household was one in which national and international events were discussed around the dinner table. In August 1929, Esther certainly heard her parents' views on the declaration of martial law in Jerusalem after 60 people were killed in riots. In 1930, there was rioting in Britain too, when many of the nation's two million unemployed took to the streets. In 1933, Oswald Mosley set up the British Union of Fascists. Joan Cooley (née Weiner), a schoolfriend of Esther, recalls going with her to a Mosley rally in London's East End, 'because Esther wanted to show me how hatred of the Jews was being spread'.

> Mosley and his Blackshirts were marching, and we joined a protest rally. The reality and the closeness this engendered of horrendous menace and anxiety seemed disparate (as indeed it was) and far beyond my immature coping. I felt Esther to be braver, and more aware [than I]; she became for me a symbol of this threatening adult protest.

In January 1933, Adolf Hitler had come to power and young Esther heard our father voice dire concern about this monstrous dictator. By November 1934, Tory backbencher Winston Churchill was warning parliament that Germany was rearming out of all proportion to its peacetime needs – an argument firmly rejected by fellow Tory Stanley Baldwin. October 1937 saw Adolf Hitler welcoming the Duke and Duchess of Windsor to Berlin, and in the following year, British Prime Minister Neville Chamberlain sacrificed Czechoslovakia for 'peace in our time' in a pact which pledged that 'Britain and Germany will never go to war with one another again'.

Moshe Cailingold, meanwhile, was travelling to and from Poland several times a year to buy books from his uncle who still ran the family business there. The business in London was doing well, and a second office was opened in the West End, opposite the British Museum, itself an enthusiastic client of M.L.Cailingold's Judaic and Hebraic expertise. Any spare cash was sent to Palestine to help his struggling family survive.

As the business flourished, Whitechapel grew more stifling,

and the house at 18 Milward Street too small for its multi-generational seven inhabitants. The decision to move was finally made when Esther graduated from elementary school with results so outstanding that she was awarded a scholarship to London's most prestigious girls' high school, the North London Collegiate School in Camden Town on the other side of the city.

It was time to say goodbye to England's version of a Polish *shtetl* with all its warmth and sense of community. More and more of the migrant Jews of London's East End were ready to enjoy the fruits of their labour in the fresher air and wider streets of the north and north-west of the city, and the Cailingolds eagerly joined that flow.

3 North London Collegiate

The move from the East End to north London in summer 1936 was a turning-point in the lives of the whole Cailingold family, and particularly that of their eldest child, Esther. Although Milward Street was only 30 minutes away by clanging electric tram from our new home in Heathland Road, Stamford Hill, in lifestyle it was light-years distant.

Our two-storey East End home had comprised four box-like rooms and a kitchen. It had shared a narrow cobbled street with a pub and a stables, housing the horses of a local brewery. The clattering of heavy-hoofed dray horses is a lasting memory. Going back years later, everything seemed so tiny. Synagogue and school were a stone's throw away. The corner grocery, the kosher butcher and Grodzinski's bakery all looked like part of a nineteenth-century European film set.

Contrast that with our new home at 30 Heathland Road, a three-storey, 12-room house, with bay windows and parquet floors, gardens back and front, hedges and rose bushes! Esther, Mimi and I each had our own bedroom, and our grandparents had a two-room suite! A sign on the house's side door read: 'Tradesmen's Entrance', and a notice on a lamp post in front of the house announced that 'Anyone allowing their dog to foul the footpath or their child to play on the street will be liable to a fine of 40 shillings.'

Amid the turmoil of the move, 11-year-old Esther was outfitted in the various summer and winter uniforms of her new school, brown velour hats for winter and beige straw for summer, all very compulsory and probably very expensive. But the honour of a place in this famous school was more than enough

13

compensation for our parents, and we younger children were constantly admonished to follow Esther's shining example.

North London Collegiate School had been founded by Frances Mary Buss in April 1850 'for the daughters of middle-class families', a full 20 years before the 1870 Act provided elementary education for all in Britain. The school was not only a pioneer venture but quickly developed standards of excellence under a series of brilliant principals. By the time Esther started there in 1936, Mary Drummond, its third principal, had been at the helm for some 18 years, proving herself an outstanding administrator and bringing the school to new heights. She crowned her efforts by acquiring the Canons Park estate in Stanmore as school playing fields and turning it into the new school campus in June 1940.

The school was a major influence on Esther. It exposed her to the best in academe, art, music and theatre, and developed in her a passion for English literature. It also transmitted a revolutionary message: that its students could attain the highest levels of success in their studies and aspire to positions of importance in their chosen professions.

There were other Jewish girls at the school and even a Jewish teacher, Miss Senator, who taught languages and supervised Jewish students whose parents did not want them to attend the school's Christian services. This was probably Esther's first testing-ground as regards her faith. From the warm Jewish embrace of the East End, she now spent long days in an all-encompassing and very non-Jewish environment, in which scarcely another girl was even passingly interested in a Jewish way of life.

Not that the move to north London was devoid of all Jewish advantage. Stamford Hill, where we now lived, had become home to hundreds of German Jews, who had fled to Britain in the path of the rising Nazi monster. Followers of Rabbi Samson Raphael Hirsch, they combined strict adherence to Orthodox Judaism with involvement in the life of the country, in sharp contrast to the Polish Jews in Britain. Outwardly conforming with their Christian neighbours in both dress and conduct, even German Jews who strongly observed their faith went hatless in public and at work. They had brought with them to Stamford Hill a vibrant Jewish educational life, which opened its arms to girls as well as boys. In place of the Old World East End *cheder*, it comprised a system of formal Hebrew classes, informal *chaverim* groups and meeting-places for young adults, under the leadership of Rabbi Avigdor Schonfeld, head of Britain's Adath Yisrael congregation, and later his son, Rabbi Dr Solomon Schonfeld.

Esther was introduced to this educational world by a close friend, Hannah Lindenberg (née Goldschmidt), who came from one of Stamford Hill's German Jewish families. 'Esther was very religious,' recalls Hannah. But she was also a fierce feminist: 'I'll never forget how angry she became when she learned of the custom among the Hindus of the widow throwing herself on her husband's funeral pyre!'

For us youngsters in Stamford Hill, these were halcyon days. We lived along wide clean streets and had three big parks to play in. The most popular was Clissold Park, with its deer enclosure, peacocks and other exotic birds and animals, its swings and slides, cricket pitches and tennis courts. We took glorious seaside vacations at Clacton, Margate and Eastbourne, playing in the sand, eating ha'penny ice-creams (making sure they were kosher, of course) and surrounded by loving parents and grandparents, mother's sister Aunt Betty, Uncle Asher and cousins Gene and Geoffrey.

We were a small family but to us it seemed quite a crowd. As well as our own household of parents, grandparents and us three children, our only other close relatives in England were Betty and Asher Preger and their two children, and we took holidays together with them and other Jewish families, comfortable in our shared Jewishness and with no need to explain or excuse our way of life. Good as Stamford Hill was, it was not the East End. School was now very un-Jewish. We were forever explaining why we were going home early on Fridays or staying away on Jewish festivals. I doubt the undercurrents of anti-Semitism that Mimi and I experienced in our junior schools were manifested within the refined atmosphere of North London Collegiate, but outside events were soon to sharpen the lines that divided Jews from so many of their non-Jewish neighbours in those days.

For London Jews, Cable Street was to have a resonance similar to that of the Munich beer halls for the Jews of Germany. Situated deep in the poorest section of east London, close to its Jewish areas, Cable Street became the rallying site for the British Union of Fascists before the war. (Heavily bombed during the war, after 1945 the rallies moved to Ridley Road, closer to Stamford Hill.)

Cable Street had particular significance for our family because at number 198 lived and practised Dr Hannah Billig, our family physician and a dearly loved and respected figure in our lives. For us, as for many London Jewish families, her calm, kind, supportive manner made a visit to her Cable Street clinic something of a pilgrimage, which may explain why we children more than once ran into Mosley's rampaging Blackshirts. The memories haven't faded: charging police horses, the red banners of competing communist rallies, bands of non-communist Jews jeering from the pavements and, most vivid of all, the menacing tramp of jack-booted marchers, declaring to the world that we Jews were the root of all evil. The anti-Jewish riots reached their climax on a Sunday in 1939 in what is known as the Battle of Gardiner's Corner (a crossroads on Whitechapel Road), when full-scale combat raged between the Blackshirts and thousands of Jews and communists who tried to stop them marching. That this memory is with me still indicates that our parents must have brought us down to the East End to see that we Jews had very tangible enemies, even in liberal democratic Britain.

Through all this, Dr Billig stood out as a true heroine for us children – and later for many other people, too. She received the George Medal for her bravery during the London Blitz, saving lives as she scrambled through the rubble of bombed buildings to help victims of the German air raids (on one occasion, with a broken leg), and she was again honoured for her services as a medical officer with the British army in India. After the war she worked on in the slums of east London until the 1970s. Even retirement failed to halt her: she spent her last years in Israel, working with the newly arrived Soviet 'mountain' Jews in the development town of Or Akiva.

Esther as bridesmaid
aged three.

On holiday in
Bournemouth,
aged eight.

Yaacov Eliyah Fenechel,
maternal grandfather.

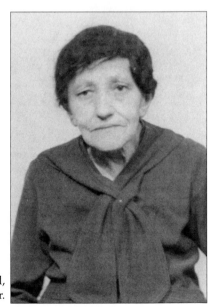

Feige Fenechel,
maternal grandmother.

Naftali Cailingold,
paternal grandfather

Esther's mother and father, 1935.

At Myrdle Street Junior School, Whitechapel, London, 1932, (extreme right in front of teacher).

As a student at London University, 1944, (front row extreme right).

At the Bachad training farm, Thaxted, Essex, 1945.

Esther's passport photograph.

The new teacher.

The old Evelina de Rothschild School on the Street of the Prophets.

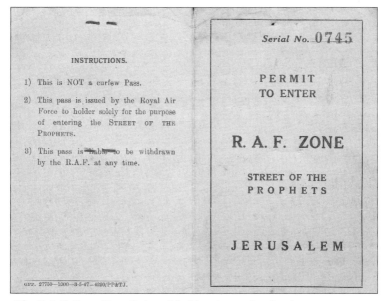

Signature of holder _Ester Carli..._

Ht. _5'4½"_ Eyes _HAZEL_ Hair _brown_

Distinguishing marks _NIL._

Permission to use car:

Reg. No. _____ Make _____

Type _____ Colour _____

Date Pass issued _18·9·47_

Date for renewal	Date Renewed	Signature & stamp of Issuing Officer
16·12·47	1·12·47	_F.O._
18·3·48		

AIR HEADQUARTERS   AIR HEADQUARTERS   LEVANT

Name (Blocks) _MISS C AILINGOLD_

Address of residence _59 RavziaN Road_

(Blocks) _REHAVIA._

Community _JEWISH_

Signature of Issuing Officer _____

for R.A.F. Commander

Serial No. _0745_

PERMIT
TO ENTER

R. A. F. ZONE

STREET OF THE
PROPHETS

JERUSALEM

The R.A.F. Zone Pass that enabled her to reach school.

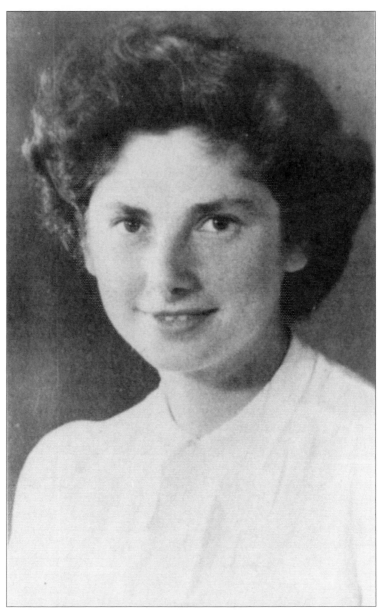

The photograph of Esther in the Zone Pass.

Hannah Billig was someone whom Esther much admired. Long before the bombs began falling on London, this remarkably brave, diminutive lady was an island of calm and common sense in a sea of anti-Jewish hatred. She was a beacon for teenage Esther, who was beset by confusion over mixed loyalties to her British and Jewish heritages. What so profoundly disturbed Esther's keen sense of social justice was that Oswald Mosley was embraced not only by 'the great unwashed', but also by factions within Britain's aristocracy – principally, the so-called Cliveden set.

Esther's faith in Britain's fair play and respect for its culture which she was taught daily at school were sorely tested by what she read in the newspapers and saw in the streets during those last years before the war and the Holocaust it brought on her people. One autumn morning in 1938, as we walked past the convent at the end of Heathland Road, we found splashed across its walls in red and blue: 'JEWS! GO BACK TO PALESTINE!!' Neither the convent nor the city seemed bothered by the hate message – nor did the Jewish community make any effort to erase it.

This graffiti appeared at the same time as the British cabinet was abandoning its plans for partitioning Palestine and thus making good its 1917 promise of a Jewish homeland. On 7 February of the following year, Britain convened the St James Conference in London to discuss the future of Palestine and of Jewish immigration. Arab delegates declared their regular refusal to sit with Jewish negotiators, and both sides rejected the British proposals out of hand. In May, parliament published its infamous White Paper, nullifying its commitment to a Jewish national home in Palestine, harshly reining in Jewish immigration and land purchase, and aspiring to a Palestinian state with an Arab majority within a decade.

While all this was happening, we three children were being admonished to 'Go back to Palestine' every time we turned the corner of Heathland Road. Ironically, the graffiti remained in place until one night in 1940, when a German plane dropped a bomb on the convent, destroying the building along with its wall and its Jew-hating message.

Esther, meanwhile, had settled down to the demanding routine of life at North London Collegiate. I remember her sitting for hours at the table in our living room, deep in her seemingly endless homework, her finger constantly stroking the space between her eyebrows. Mimi and I quickly learned not to disturb her. Not that it would have made much difference: her powers of concentration were prodigious, and life at home bustled on around her. She devoured books at an alarming rate. To my young eyes they all seemed to be a thousand pages long and either in Latin or staggering under titles like *The Rise and Fall of the Roman Empire*. According to classmates, she was not much interested in sports, although hockey sticks and tennis rackets were part of the kit that she took to school.

Although we had left the rich Jewish life of the East End, our family still clung to the small *shtiebl* type of prayerhouse, rather than the large synagogues favoured in north London. So while we obtained our Hebrew education in Rabbi Schonfeld's Adath Yisrael congregation, we attended services in the home of Mrs Marguiles in Dunsmure Road. The atmosphere was cosy, many of our fellow worshippers were familiar faces from the East End, and most important of all, our *shtiebl* was graced by Rabbi Eliya Lopian, who went on to become a rabbi and teacher of great eminence.

Our father, however, had a passion for cantorial music, and every now and then, he would gather up his three children and sneak off to the synagogue in Egerton Road to hear Cantor Goldstein and his magnificent choir. One Friday evening in spring 1939, dressed in our finest, we headed for Egerton Road to hear the famous actor Eddie Cantor, who was in Britain to raise funds to bring Jewish refugee children into Palestine

It is probably true to say that we Cailingold children were more aware than most of the gathering war clouds. During 1937 and 1938, father became obsessed with what was, for us, the mysterious activity of 'signing affidavits'. We understood he was deeply involved in getting Jews out of Europe, in any way possible. He was still travelling several times a year to 'the Continent' (as the British call everything on the other side of the

English Channel), importing and exporting books from Europe, the US and even as far afield as South Africa and Australia. But he always had time for what is known in Yiddish as *rutteven Yidden*, the holy commandment of saving Jewish life, incumbent on every Jew. For him, this began long before November 1938's *Kristallnacht*, which finally brought home to German Jews their mortal danger. We children were used to seeing our father welcome to his home and his store strangers who had come, not to buy books, but to obtain the precious signature that enabled them to 'buy' a relative free from what was shortly to become the slaughterhouse of continental Europe.

Father's 'signing affidavits' became tangible for us for the first time one day in 1938 when Moshe Schul, his wife Hannah and their two sons arrived from Hannover in Germany. Hannah was my mother's cousin and here on our doorstep were our first real-life refugees. The Schuls were enterprising people and found their own apartment while they awaited the precious visas which would take them across the Atlantic to Bridgeport, Connecticut. They were in the category of the 'lucky ones'.

That same year, US President Franklin Roosevelt called a conference at Evian in France to discuss the growing refugee problem. The response of Australia, one of the more liberal and enlightened nations which attended, typified the conference response to the desperate pleas of German and Austrian Jews. 'As we have no real racial problem', intoned the Australian delegate, 'we are not desirous of importing one.'

The year 1938 was one of confusion and impending crisis. In January, the British government decided to issue all children with gas masks. Soon after, the three of us were taken to a local church hall to be fitted out with the horrible rubber devices (a memory starkly revived for me in Israel 52 years later during the Gulf War). In September, Prime Minister Chamberlain returned from Munich brandishing his umbrella and his piece of paper. Our father, however, entertained no illusions about Chamberlain's policy of appeasement, and continued to welcome refugees, who were now arriving daily. From our grandparents, we children knew sufficient Yiddish to communicate with the newcomers, and we played with their children and often translated for them in school.

19

As war grew closer, the tension at home increased. In August 1939, father decided to go to Warsaw in a last-ditch effort to bring out the relatives who still lived there. Over the years, he had obtained visas to Palestine not only for his parents, brothers and sisters, but also for his uncles, aunts and cousins. The exception was Uncle Aharon who, influenced by anti-Zionist rabbis, had stayed behind in Warsaw with his wife and seven children, running the Polish branch of the family book business.

So, that fateful August, Moshe Cailingold took the boat-train from Victoria to Hamburg, boarded a train to Danzig on the Polish border, then changed trains for Warsaw. Not only was he the sole Jew from Hamburg onwards, he was also virtually the only civilian. His travelling companions were, to a man, German stormtroopers, then being massed on Germany's eastern border. Nonetheless, in a spirit of bravado (clearly passed on to Esther), Moshe bribed the train guard for a few minutes' private use of his compartment, where he put on *tefillin* and recited the morning prayers. In his pocket was his precious British passport and the priceless Palestine visas for his Warsaw relatives.

Aharon Cailingold's bookstore was at 32 Ulica Nalewki, a street shortly to be swallowed into the death-trap of the Warsaw Ghetto. Uncle Aharon greeted father's rescue mission with scorn and anger. 'Zionist, get out of my house!' he shouted. All that father succeeded in saving on that fateful trip to Poland was a one-ton consignment of books published in eastern Europe – the last volumes of Hebraica to be saved from the Nazi flames. All we have left of Aharon Cailingold and his family are the biographical Pages of Testimony that we filed in the Hall of Names at the Yad Vashem memorial in Jerusalem.

That first Shabbat after father returned from Warsaw, he broke down and wept while reciting Kiddush at dinner, to our great distress as children, who had never seen our father cry. Thereafter, Kiddush was always difficult for him, particularly on festival evenings when the *Shehecheyanu* blessing is added, thanking God for keeping us safe and bringing us to this day. A world he had known and loved was to be destroyed. Father knew beyond all doubt that it was going to happen, and that the Zionist lifeline had been shunned by the masses of European Jews.

4 War Years

It was the last week of August 1939. Continental Europe stood on the edge of an inferno. While many Europeans believed that their brave armies would withstand the German Blitzkrieg, bumbling, appeasing Britain was quietly preparing for war. Protected from invasion by the 22-mile-wide 'tank ditch' between Britain and France, air attack was England's most immediate danger. Air-raid shelters had been in preparation since November 1937. By the following summer, all children had been issued their gas masks, and in July the government ordered construction of 1,000 Spitfire fighter planes – much of this a result of Winston Churchill's campaigning. A less visible preparation for war was an elaborate plan to evacuate children from urban centres at the outbreak of hostilities.

That last week in August thus found all three Cailingold children trailing off each morning to the North London Collegiate School in Sandall Road, Camden Town. Our parents had decided that we should stay together in case of evacuation, and rely on Esther to ensure that her younger sister and brother remembered their Jewish prayers and customs. The all-girls secondary school accepted a few younger brothers in special cases, so there I was, one of five boys in a school of 600 girls, turning up each day, like all the others, complete with gas mask, label on my coat and bag of emergency rations in my hand. These rations consisted of tinned meats and army biscuits, all of a decidedly unkosher variety, so mother made sure that we also had a good supply of thick egg sandwiches to keep us going.

Looking back, I suppose it was an embarrassment for Esther to bring her younger sister and brother along each day. For Mimi and me, there was fear of the unknown war mixed in with the excitement of adventure. As it was still school vacation, a special programme had been devised to keep us occupied. I remember a long list of subjects read out at morning assembly, from which we were invited to select what would interest us. The list began with Astronomy and must have ended with Zoology, but since my mind wandered off almost at once, I found myself attending dull sessions about firmaments and galaxies – much to the amusement of my sisters. More deeply engraved on my memory from those days are the magnificent hymns that the school sang each morning.

The fateful day came on Friday, 1 September 1939. At 4.45 a.m., Hitler's troops poured across the Polish border while his planes dive-bombed Polish troops and civilian targets. One of the first responses of the British government, preceding its declaration of war by over 48 hours, was to set in motion a well-rehearsed programme of civilian evacuation from the country's cities. With their cool efficiency, the British excel at this sort of undertaking. In three days, 1,500,000 children, pregnant women and mothers of small babies were taken to safety via Britain's railways.

We were among the first to be evacuated. Early on the Friday morning, we shouldered our backpacks, checked that our labels were firmly tied to our coats, grabbed our gas masks and marched out in military formation to the nearby railway station and the train taking us to our 'secret' destination. Miss Hedges, North London Collegiate's music teacher, had composed a marching song especially for the occasion:

Strap your pack to your back,
With a sandwich for a snack,
For North London is marching along!

After what seemed like an endless rail journey, we reached Luton, a small industrial town known for its hat factories, and which today provides London with an additional airport. For us youngsters, Luton might as well have been at the other end of the world, it seemed so far from home. I remember the three of us lining up in a large hall with the other evacuees, so that local families could choose which of the strange Londoners dumped on their doorstep to take home. We were constantly passed over: no one wanted a threesome, but Esther was under strict instructions from our parents to keep us together at all costs. We were, in fact, left to the very last. Mimi finally volunteered to go to one family, while Esther and I went to another nearby, an elderly childless couple called Minnie and Walter Parrish. Our hosts turned out to be wonderful people, and when they heard about Mimi's predicament, they went to collect her, too, so we could all be together.

Fourteen-year-old Esther proved as mature and responsible as our parents expected, and we younger children were in no doubt that she was in charge. In short order that strange first day, she had us organised, ensuring that we said our prayers and had some semblance of a Friday-evening atmosphere at the table. The Parrishes were strictly observant Wesleyan Methodists, who had no idea at all about Jewish dietary laws or our other religious idiosyncrasies, but they were so kind and understanding that memories of the weeks we spent with them are only happy ones. I spent hours helping Mr Parrish on his allotment, where he grew the family vegetables – and which, in our efforts to keep kosher, became our dietary staple.

Knowing more subsequently about the evacuation operation which eventually involved some 3,500,000 children, it's clear how lucky we were to have been taken in by kind and understanding people. Surveys showed that some 75 per cent of people in Britain at that time were, to some degree, anti-Semitic. Some Jewish children reported that their hosts searched them for the horns they were convinced grew on all Jewish heads. Although Mrs Parrish took us along to the church hall for social events, I think it was purely because she enjoyed showing us off. Unlike some of the other host families, the Parrishes never made any attempt to involve us in Christian practices.

On the morning of Sunday, 3 September, we huddled round the radio with the Parrishes as Neville Chamberlain, having given Germany 15 minutes' grace after expiry of the 11.00 a.m. deadline, announced to the world that Britain was at war with

Germany. That declaration of war was soon followed by the dreadful wails of the air-raid siren in a false alarm that panicked the country: we were fully expecting a German attempt to wipe us out with a massive air attack of poison gas.

During that terrible weekend, when the fate of Europe and its Jews was sealed, the Royal Navy fired Britain's first shots of the Second World War in another part of the world altogether. It fired neither in defence of civilian shipping nor in pursuit of German U-boats. The target was a refugee ship named *Tiger Hill*, bringing 1,400 visa-less Jews to Palestine. Some had embarked at Varna, Bulgaria, six weeks earlier; others had joined the ship at Constanza. British naval police opened fire on *Tiger Hill*, killing three of its passengers, wounding 12 and interning the remainder in the Sarafand detention camp. Thus, Britain's declaration of war on Germany encompassed war on Jewish immigration to Palestine. All immigration certificates issued to German Jews were cancelled on the grounds that they were enemy aliens! Britain's policy towards the Jews was not apparent to us at the time. Later it become a major factor in our Zionism.

Life in Luton settled into a pleasant routine at 141 Alexandra Avenue, with the Parrishes proving the kindest of people and the most caring of hosts. Mother came up from London about once a week. Unswerving in her loyalty to our father, she was overshadowed by him at home. In Luton, her weekly visits became our lifeline. An attractive woman with auburn hair which did not fade even in her 90s, she was the consummate Jewish housewife, a homemaker in the truest sense of the word. Her cooking and baking were superb, and our clothes and shoes were bought exclusively in the West End.

Her first visit to us in Luton was a colossal surprise, as I really think we never expected to see our parents again. A week was as long as a year to me then, and our artificial way of life at the Parrishes seemed to be how we would live the rest of our days. Mother came on Sundays, bringing goodies with her from London. Our favourite was a freshly cooked chicken, and after she left, we would rendezvous outside the Parrish home with Sheila Kritzler (née Oster) and her brother Norman, another of the five boy evacuees at North London Collegiate, trading a leg of our chicken for some of their salami.

Eight days after our evacuation, Esther wrote to her friend, Hannah Goldschmidt:

> We are not with Jewish people unfortunately, but we don't eat the meat and our Jewish teacher sent a message saying what we mustn't eat, to our hosts ... We are very happy here except for the food question. We are in a nice little modern house with a very nice old man and lady in the new suburbs of the town, on the hills where the air is very fresh and we go for long walks in the hills ... From the news tonight it seems we might be here a jolly long time. The wireless said that the economical [sic] policy will be based on the idea that the war will last three years or more! Though that doesn't mean to say that it will.

There was a small Jewish community in Luton, and we began going to synagogue on Shabbat, which was the most difficult day of the week for us, doubtless presenting a sorry picture of orphaned waifs. About three months after we were evacuated, our parents took a house in Luton, together with our grandparents and the four Pregers. The main purpose of their move was to ensure that we children had a Jewish home and that our Hebrew lessons continued, despite the war. Father spent the week in London, nursing his dying business. Who wanted Jewish books with a war raging in Europe and the news getting worse by the hour? Strict rationing had been imposed. All able-bodied men and women were conscripted, and many families were struggling with a drastic cut in income as they adjusted to a soldier's salary. Nor was there much chance of acquiring paper to print new books, so even everyday stock like the Hebrew Bible and prayer book were soon thin on the shelves – and we children experienced economic distress for the first time in our lives.

I was enrolled in a Luton elementary school, while Esther and Mimi attended the relocated North London Collegiate, which shared premises with a local girls' high school. Esther's classmate, Joan Weiner, has:

distinct memories of jocular teasing and fun exchanges when we were evacuated, sharing Luton High School. Maybe we needed to let our hair down to balance the difficulties of those times. In the break, we would tease Esther by picking up the skin of our hot chocolate to dangle before her. I think she put on an exaggerated show of repulsion to entertain. Also, with Sylvia, Thelma, Olive and myself as audience, Esther would demonstrate her unique skill when, standing without bending her knees, she could press her flattened palms entirely on the floor … This all seems so foolish now, yet it recalls … a fondness and pleasure in Esther's company.

On weekends, in our rented house in Luton, Esther would organise us five children, to relieve the tension of two families in one cramped house. I remember her producing a play about country life, and spending hours coaching four-and-a-half-year-old Geoffrey Preger to say in broad Somerset: 'Ye be right Gaffer Jarge, this be main rare beer.'

By March 1940, our parents had had enough of Luton, with its minuscule Jewish community, 11 of us in a small house and father in London all week. North London Collegiate announced it was moving back to London and to its new campus in Canons Park, Edgware. London was, in any case, unscathed and the panic about devastating air raids demonstrably unfounded. So back we went to Heathland Road, arriving a couple of weeks before the Passover festival. What a relief to be home!

Esther and Mimi began their daily commute to school in Edgware and life settled down, marred only by the increasingly alarming news of German victories across the Channel. Then in May, London suffered its first air attack of the war. Thinking we would be safer nearer the girls' school and away from the more densely populated part of the city where we lived, our parents decided that we should sleep at the Pregers' apartment in Edgware. This proved a bad mistake: the Royal Air Force Fighter Command was headquartered just up the road in Stanmore, and the noise of the anti-aircraft guns was unbearable. The first German attempts to send bombers over London were met with

26

such tremendous ground salvos that we were actually in far greater danger from flying shrapnel than from the bombers! So after a couple of sleepless nights, we moved back to Stamford Hill, reinforced our own basement air-raid shelter, and awaited the real onslaught of Hitler's Blitz on London in the summer of 1940.

The Luftwaffe gathered 2,669 aircraft for the assault on Britain, which it launched on 5 August. Night after night, we went resignedly down to our air-raid shelter to try and sleep while the battles raged overhead. (In Esther's letters from besieged Jerusalem in 1947/8 she wrote that the shelling reminded her of the Blitz.) Father became a fire-watchman, on duty one night a week in Heathland Road and one night near his shop in Whitechapel. I remember him limping home once, his leg gashed with shrapnel. And I remember Esther organising us when father was fire-watching, ready to extinguish any bomb that fell close to home.

All through the Blitz, we children continued going to school, my sisters making the long trip across town to Edgware. We witnessed air battles more than once, and on one occasion even had to dive for cover when a low-flying enemy pilot decided to machine-gun pedestrians. Britain's motto was 'Business As Usual' and it is a lasting testament to British tenacity that children were educated and did exams in these near-impossible conditions. Esther's class at North London Collegiate sat their matriculation in an air-raid shelter.

Slowly news began coming in of the loss of fathers and elder brothers in battle, and there were terrible occasions when we arrived at school to hear a classmate had been badly hurt or killed in an air raid during the night.

For all that, spirits among us youngsters remained high. The new girls' school campus at Canons Park boasted a giant cedar tree in its grounds, which posed an irresistible climbing challenge. Esther, it seems, climbed too high one day, got stuck and missed one of her lessons – an incident which placed certain cedar branches 'out of bounds' thenceforth.

Esther's passions remained reading, classical music and theatre. 'She went to the library frequently and was a great reader,' remembers Sylvia Ball (née Rose). 'She would purposely mispronounce new words, much to our amusement.'

While her interest in music was passive, Esther loved to act, as did our father, who was a great mimic and storyteller. If not for her strict adherence to Orthodox Judaism, she might have headed for the professional theatre. Meantime, she threw herself into school productions, often competing for parts with classmate Leatrice Levine (née Jacobs).

> In 1942, when we performed *Pride and Prejudice*, Esther was Lady Catherine de Burgh whilst I was Mrs Bennet. The following year, when *The Dumb Wife of Cheapside* was performed, I was the husband whilst Esther had the much coveted part of The Wife … She was an enthusiastic contributor to all activities and a person who gave the maximum of help with the minimum of fuss.

The conflicting influences on the young Cailingolds took on a new dimension with the arrival in staid, prim, middle-class Stamford Hill of its first authentic Chassidim, led by the Shotzer rebbe. Dressed in the full regalia of long shiny black coat or *bekkische*, trousers tucked into long white socks and velvet *shtreimel* trimmed with fox tails on his head, he had the disconcerting custom of spitting and muttering curses whenever he passed the church in Dunsmure Road. This stopped only when he moved to Lordship Road and became a virtual hermit in his own castle.

Our comfortable little *shtiebl* had closed with the outbreak of war, and father decided to join the Shotzers. So we became part of that closed Chassidic world, albeit retaining European dress and working and studying like other Londoners. A fellow congregant was Victor Hochhauser, the London impresario, who recalls trading kicks with me under the table when we two lads got particularly bored. So it was that at the end of 1942, the family gathered one Shabbat in the Shotzer rebbe's Bethune Road *shtiebl* to hear me recite my Barmitzvah portion. I was wearing my first suit with long trousers, bought with the whole family's clothing coupons, saved for me all winter.

Being wartime, there were strict limitations on social gatherings and festivities, so we made do with a family lunch at home after the service. Then Esther came up with the brilliant idea of going to the theatre to celebrate my Barmitzvah. A few days after Shabbat at the Shotzers with herring and *lokshen kugel*, the family was thus seated in the stalls of a West End theatre watching Vivienne Leigh perform in George Bernard Shaw's *The Doctor's Dilemma*.

Our romance with the Shotzer rebbe did not survive. My father left the congregation some years later, disgusted with the rebbe's virulent anti-Zionism – triggered, I fear, by my appearing one Shabbat with a blue-and-white 'Zionist' *kippah* on my head, rather than the regulation black *yarmulke*.

That summer, in July 1943, Esther graduated from high school with distinction. A congratulatory letter from the principal exempted her from London University's Intermediate Examination, and allowed her to go straight into a BA degree course. A second letter from the principal informed Esther 'she has been awarded the Prance Scholarship for a very good result in higher school. Do let me congratulate you most warmly and send you my very best wishes. I enclose a cheque for four pounds, three shillings and fourpence'.

That same summer, first I, then Esther contracted jaundice, a disease hardly known in England at the time. She languished long after I recovered, and pressed on me her unused season ticket for the Albert Hall promenade concerts. I was unenthusiastic, but she was relentless, and her powers of persuasion quite changed my life. From the first concert that summer, I joined Esther in a love affair with classical music. When she recovered, she introduced me to lunchtime chamber music recitals at the National Gallery (which were later to move across the road to St Martins in the Field), and we began a collection of classical records – the old 78s – beginning with Beethoven's Egmont Overture. I wasn't the only one whose ears she opened to classical music. Joan Cooley (née Weiner) says: 'It was with Esther that I attended a wonderful recital at the Friends' Meeting House in Euston, with Peter Pears and Benjamin Britten.'

From concerts, Esther led me on to opera, ballet and theatre, with which London was replete even in wartime. She also had a particular talent for choosing well-written light literature. I remember a book called *Antigua Penny Puce*, whose title scared me away. But Esther said it was well written, so I gave it a try and ended up with a thoroughly enjoyable read.

With the end of school, Esther's childhood was over, and she prepared herself for university and life away from home. Father considered service in uniform unsuitable for an Orthodox Jewish girl, and encouraged her to seek a career in education, because women teachers were a priority profession and thus exempt from wartime duties. (Four years later, Esther's letters from Palestine described her efforts to obtain a semblance of military dress, even as the British arrested anyone suspected of bearing arms.)

So, in autumn 1943, our clever elder sister travelled north to her college's evacuation venue in Nottingham, leaving Mimi and me to continue in our respective London high schools.

5 College Girl

Esther left home for university at about the same time that the war reached its turning-point. On 23 October 1942, Allied forces at El Alamein had fired 1,000 artillery pieces in a 15-minute barrage, launching the attack that turned the tide in North Africa. January 1943 saw the Red Army defeat the Nazis at Stalingrad in the war's largest land battle. Goering's Luftwaffe had been crushed in the Battle of Britain, and it was Germany that now cowered under aerial bombardment: in three devastating nights in July 1943, the RAF dropped over 7,000 tons of bombs on Hamburg alone, 40,000 people lost their lives and a million terrified civilians fled the city. In September, Italy surrendered to the Allies.

At home in Britain, rationing of food and clothing tightened, Oswald Mosley was released from prison on grounds of ill health and Winston Churchill was cured of pneumonia with a new wonder-drug called penicillin.

All this we read in the newspapers. What we didn't read was what was happening to our fellow Jews across the water in occupied Europe. The 'gentlemen' who met at Wannsee in January 1942, many of whom had doctoral degrees, had 'inventoried' some 11,000,000 Jews for slaughter, a figure which included the 334,000 of us in Britain and Ireland. By the end of 1942, an estimated 1,900,000 Jews were already dead – and that was before the Nazi death-factories embarked on their industrialised slaughter.

When we sat down to our Passover *Seder* in April 1943, we had no idea that our brethren in Warsaw were rising from the sewers to take on the Nazi might, choosing for themselves the

31

way they would die. It took General von Stroop six weeks to subdue these lightly armed youngsters; four years earlier, the entire Polish army had been defeated in half that time. Though our father still wept when he recited Kiddush each week, even he could not imagine the enormity of the tragedy overtaking European Jewry.

In London University's wartime home of Nottingham, Esther found lodgings with the Munches, a family of Seventh-Day Adventists, together with Hannah Goldschmidt. Hannah and another London friend, Joan Weiner, were studying at London University's Goldsmiths College like Esther, but in the College's non-degree programme which aimed to cram as much as possible into a shortened course, and thus replace the large numbers of male teachers recruited into the armed forces.

Esther was 'very much the dominant partner, very ambitious and always willing to try new ideas,' remembers Hannah. 'Even in those days she was always talking about coming to live in Palestine. Her outlook on life was very idealistic, which she seems to have got from her father, to whom she was very attached.'

Because of her excellent school results, Esther was one of a small group enrolled in a two-year BA programme, with a Diploma in Education in the third year – a regimen, as made clear in Esther's letters home, that was intensive and challenging. She was also the only Jewish girl in this group. Fellow student Betty Dawson (née Wake) had, until then,

> never knowingly met a Jew ... I was very much a country girl, born and brought up in the Isle of Wight and educated at a small mixed Grammar School. I had not travelled at all (partly because of the war) and at 18 had been just once to London. So Esther was a series of surprises to me!
>
> I ... knew just a little, from books, of what an Orthodox Jewish background might entail. However, during those first few months, we were thrown together, and I think enjoyed one another's company immensely. Esther was very proud of her family and its scholarly traditions. I had never been looked at so objectively before, and I found it extraordinarily stimulating to have to marshal my thoughts

about my Christianity and my culture when we engaged in long discussions. In most ways we were as different as we could be, but I remember our relationship as wonderfully open and refreshing. We went several times to concerts. The Hallé Orchestra visited Nottingham – on Saturdays, of course – and I think I remember being given money to buy Esther's ticket. We then met at the concert hall, to which she walked ...

Esther held herself somewhat aloof, but I feel that was a deliberate choice. Her 'specialness' was important to her. She had a great respect for scholarship, imposed on herself a strict discipline in thinking and action, and seemed often indifferent to others' opinions. But she had a wonderfully clear mind, a sharp sense of humour and a great feeling of purpose in life. Knowing her was a real part of my growing up.

Nottingham's Jewish community was very small, comprising mostly people who had gone there because of the war. Local families were hospitable, however, particularly regarding Shabbat meals. And although boyfriends were not part of the life of an Orthodox Jewish girl living away from home, I do recall a young Jewish soldier from Nottingham coming to our house every now and then.

Esther kept up her Jewish studies when she was at university, with the Bet Yaacov educational network for girls in both Nottingham and, during vacation, in London. She also went to Rabbi Schonfeld's Ben Zakkai society, largely, I think, as an outlet for her acting skills. I remember her giving a terrific performance in *The Passing of the Third Floor Back* at the Stoke Newington Town Hall.

She was also increasingly involved with the religious Zionist youth movement, Bnei Akiva (as were Mimi and I), which young Jewish refugees had brought with them from Germany on the eve of the war. Bnei Akiva's adult section, Bachad, had set up in Britain, as in Europe, a series of *Hachshara* or training farms, whose purpose was preparing Jewish youngsters for life in Palestine's kibbutzim. Esther went to these *Hachshara* centres

33

as often as she could, doing the farm work there, sharing Shabbat and debating, until the small hours, issues such as the meaning of socialism in the light of the Torah.

The founder and focus of what we simply called 'the Movement' was Arieh Handler. He was primarily responsible for importing Bachad and Bnei Akiva into Britain, and he arranged for many young German refugees to join *Hachshara* groups. The atmosphere in these training centres, and even in the youth groups, was definitely foreign. It once took me a while to realise that a lecturer expounding on 'Zionist sinkers' really meant thinkers!

Handler remembers Esther as

> one of our first so-called 'English' members ... I remember conversations with her on the future of Eretz Israel – none of us believed at that time that the State would be declared in 1948, but I remember so well her view that the future of Jewry in the Diaspora will only be assured provided the majority will go to Eretz Israel and will establish a State there. I also remember her attitude toward her fellow members – always pleasant, always helpful and always stressing the educational task of our youth movement activities. She was really an example to all of us.

Hannah Tennenhaus (née Faust), a war refugee from Germany, met Esther in the movement:

> She was a very pretty, vivacious young girl during those London years ... She was carefree, with an insouciance at variance with the more sober personalities of those of us who were refugees, while she had enjoyed a carefree childhood in England.

Many of us – and especially Esther – nursed guilt about our 'carefree childhood in England', and were uncomfortably aware of the 'more sober personalities' of our young friends, who had left parents and family in Europe to be swallowed up in Hitler's inferno.

As the war continued, Stamford Hill and even staid suburban Heathland Road were changing. Large numbers of houses had stood empty during the Blitz (more than once we rushed our stirrup pumps and sand buckets into abandoned properties nearby to douse incendiary bombs), and many of their residents had chosen not to return. These homes were now being bought by Jewish families in search of a friendly community. Opening *shtiebls* and *yeshivot*, they brought to Stamford Hill the *shtetl* life we had left behind in the East End. Among the newcomers was the Gross family, who moved into our road after their home was destroyed in the bombing. Esther and their elder daughter Ida became close friends, and Esther was to live for a short while with Ida (by then, Yehudith) and her new husband in Jerusalem, three years later.

The year 1944 brought new hope and renewed danger for Londoners. Operation Overlord, the long-awaited Allied invasion of continental Europe came on 6 June. For two days, we couldn't get to school as the endless convoys made their way south through London towards the embarkation ports. The end of the war was finally in sight and we thrilled to the news of Allied successes and the liberation of lands in enemy hands for over four years. The invasion was scarcely underway, however, when we Londoners became the targets of a new weapon: Hitler's V1 pilotless planes, the 'doodle-bugs'. Without military value, their purpose was to shatter morale in the civilian population. They killed 5,500 people and destroyed 25,000 homes. Worse, however, was to come in the form of the V2 rocket, a 12-ton monster, which flew at 3,600 mph and devastated entire city blocks. After a couple of these landed too near us for comfort, our parents decided it would be best for us to leave London. Esther stayed in Nottingham, and Mimi, our grandparents and I joined the Pregers up in Buxton, where we took long and marvellous walks in the nearby Peak district, one of the loveliest parts of England.

The upheaval, the separations and uneven education of the war years were accompanied for our family, as for many others, by considerable financial stress. I recall Shabbat meals when we had neither meat nor fish, and made do with concoctions of potatoes and tinned pilchards. And, of course, we spent night after night in our basement shelter.

As we were soon to discover, however, we were living in paradise compared with what was happening to our fellow Jews in Europe. As the unimaginable slowly became known, people reacted in different ways. Esther burned with a fierce inner rage, fuelled not only by what had happened in the death camps, but also by the refusal of the civilised world to help the refugees, either before the war or after it. She became an activist with a cause: the only response to the horror and bloodshed, she firmly believed, was for the Jewish people to have national independence in their own land.

6 The Survivors

On 8 May 1945 the war in Europe was over and the monster was dead in his Berlin bunker. Britain rejoiced, and none more so than its Jewish community, so close to the enslaved European continent. The times were crazy, and we went to all-night parties and danced around pavement bonfires – things that respectable Anglo-Jewish youngsters (even those of us in Zionist youth movements) rarely did. Through the joy, however, our father sounded a sombre note. Dark times were ahead for the Jews, he insisted. We didn't understand what he meant, but reality was soon to catch up with us. Typically, it came to Esther first of all.

By the summer, she was busy collecting clothing for the survivors of Europe's death camps. But, as she wrote to her friend Hannah on 15 July 1945, she had

> something bigger afoot, which will surprise you. I have written to College to ask if I can postpone my third year in order to go abroad to do relief work with the Jewish Relief Committee … I do not want much said about it, because I may not get permission, knowing our own conservative, procrastinating authorities.

It was our father, however, not the authorities who stopped Esther volunteering in Europe's Camps for Displaced Persons. Esther was furious and stomped out of the house one day in August without telling any of us where she was going. We soon found her in Windermere in the Lake District, where a reception centre had opened for 300 child camp-survivors, rescued by the Central British Fund.

Windermere was a turning-point in Esther's life. (Sir Martin Gilbert devotes a full chapter in his book *The Boys* to that traumatic first day of the child survivors in Windermere.) The youngsters with whom she volunteered to work, some of them about her own age, had spent a third or more of their lives in extreme conditions, and were aggressive, distrustful and antisocial. As her heart went out to them, Esther choked on the realisation that their fate could so easily have been hers.

That same month of August 1945 saw two atom bombs dropped on Japan and, with them, the end of the Pacific war. It also saw the Labour Party's landslide victory over the Tories and the descent from power of the war hero, Winston Churchill. British Jews largely supported Labour, with its promised fairer deal for all and championship of the welfare state. How bitter then was our disappointment over government callousness towards Holocaust survivors and its forgotten promise to establish a national homeland for the Jews.

With the end of that summer, Esther returned to Nottingham and began her practice teaching of young children, which she seems not to have enjoyed too much. In May 1946, Goldsmiths College moved back to London.

Esther wrote to Hannah:

> Last Thursday I went to New Cross for the first time. At the gate, I came face to face with the Warden and he practically fell on my neck in a sort of Welcome Home. The place is still in a shocking mess, frightfully cold, frightfully depressing. However it's only for one and a half days a week. An awful journey too ... I may go with Ida [Gross] to the Farm again for a weekend. We are also planning to go abroad for the summer! Palestine comes first of course, but since I am afraid that will be impossible, Switzerland or France is next choice.

The 'Farm' in Esther's letter was the *Hachshara* training centre in Thaxted, Essex, which had become a mecca for movement youngsters. We spent long weekends and school vacations there, helping with the farm work and enjoying a rich mixture of Jewish culture and fun.

Of major excitement in our family was father's discovery that Palestine was now an accessible business destination. Before the war, he had travelled extensively, but always in Europe, buying books from his uncle in Warsaw and selling them throughout the continent. With Europe in ashes, he began going to Palestine, where he not only bought books, but also saw his father, brothers and sisters. And with several large Jewish book companies newly established in the United States (New York, in particular, boasted an active market in old and rare Hebrew books), the US too featured on his travel itinerary.

Our family life was returning to normal. Father was energising a business that had barely got by during the war years. Our grandparents were back home with us, the Pregers, too, were back in London, and we three children were continuing our education, preparing ourselves for a conventional middle-class Jewish life.

This apparent normality, however, was short-lived. The legacy of war was with us. In June 1946, Esther began working with a group of young survivors from Prague in the Jews' Temporary Shelter in Mansell Street in London's East End – ironically, the same Shelter where our mother's father had been taken half a century earlier, when snatched from the clutches of Christian missionaries on the dockside. This Prague group was the eighth and last transport of child survivors brought to Britain by special Home Office permission. Of the quota of 1,000 children, only 732 ever arrived, including three groups brought in by Rabbi Dr Schonfield. One and a half million Jewish children had perished in the Holocaust, many of the surviving youngsters were trying to get into Palestine in defiance of the British blockade, and there were simply not enough children to fill the British quota.

This last group of child survivors reached the Shelter as Esther was completing her university studies, and she divided her time between exams and the youngsters. She graduated with First Class Honours, but it was her work at the Shelter that consumed her.

Etta, a survivor of Theresienstadt, remembers

numerous kind people visiting us at the Shelter, trying to express their sympathy. It was a difficult situation for our visitors, not knowing how to react to us, as they felt uncomfortable, being aware of the horrors we had gone through. We in turn did not feel happy at being the objects of pity. One who was different from all others was Esther Cailingold. There was an air of calm about her. She said very little, but we felt she was there to be friendly and ready to listen if we cared to talk or not, depending on us. As we became more acquainted, she chatted to us about many subjects young girls were interested in and gave us useful information about life in England. Her visits were a joy to me. She put me in a buoyant mood every time she came.

Geoffrey Paul, later editor of the *Jewish Chronicle*, volunteered to work with the boys, at Esther's request. He recounts:

Some of the children screamed out at night in their dreams or moaned the dark hours through. Others wanted to go out into the streets and punch every passing policeman as a protest against the actions of the Palestine Police. There was a most provocative recruiting poster for the Palestine Police right opposite the Shelter and the kids had to be restrained from defacing it. I remember that Esther spent as much time trying to comfort me as our not surprisingly unruly charges. In fact, my overwhelming memory of my encounters with her is of someone with immense inner calm, a maturity and responsibility beyond her years and a smile that eased tense situations.

That summer, Esther recruited Mimi and me to socialise with the young survivors and try to involve them in our lives. This was a very hard job. They were filled with anger, which expressed itself in violence towards us who had been spared the deportations and the death camps. How shocking it was for us sheltered religious youngsters to encounter young Jews who truly believed that 'God died at Auschwitz'. For me, this was a massive challenge to my faith, and I must assume that Esther's own intensified involvement with her Judaism resulted, at least in part, from her emerging from this confrontation with renewed religious belief.

7. A Dream Come True

During that summer of 1946, as Britain struggled through the aftermath of war, life for British Jews remained fraught. With the country's economic situation catastrophic and food and fuel in short supply, British fascists set out to convince the nation that 'the Jews are to blame'. The response of the Jewish community, however, was no longer passive. The Jewish Ex-Servicemen's Association, together with its militant arm, the 43 Group, were beginning to inflict broken heads in fascist ranks.

Nonetheless, there was a strong sense of betrayal among British Jews, whose hopes had soared under Churchill and his clearly indicated support for a Jewish state in Palestine. In August 1942, he had written to US President Roosevelt, 'I am strongly wedded to the Zionist policy, of which I was one of the authors.' On 18 April 1943, he had told the Lord Privy Seal (Clement Atlee):

> I cannot agree that the White Paper of 1939 [virtually halting Jewish immigration into Palestine] is 'the firmly established policy' of His Majesty's present Government. I have always considered it a gross breach of faith committed by the Chamberlain Government in respect of obligations to which I was personally a party.

In 1947, though out of power, he was still calling on the Labour government 'to quit Palestine as quickly as possible'.

Labour's position, however, was diametrically opposed. On 29 June 1946 the government ordered the arrest of Palestine's Jewish leadership. The following Sunday, Britain's diffident, mannerly Jews took to London's streets in their first large-scale public protest. The government, they charged, had reneged on its 1917 promise of a Jewish homeland and was now showing soulless indifference to the plight of Holocaust survivors. Led by uniformed Zionist youth movements waving blue-and-white flags (the three Cailingold children striding in their ranks), the protesters set out from Gardiner's Corner in the heart of London's East End, marched through the City of London and ended with a mass rally in Trafalgar Square. Questions were later asked in parliament about the 'paramilitary' nature of our uniforms.

This march was our first opportunity to demonstrate to ourselves and to the world that our first loyalty lay with Zionism and Jewish independence – even if this relegated to second place our loyalty to Britain, the land of our birth. For Esther, it was a moment of truth. Within a year, face to face with the British army in Palestine, she would be forced into a direct choice between her Jewishness and her Britishness.

As we marched in Britain, events far more tragic for the Jews were unfolding in Poland. In the town of Kielce, where four years earlier the Nazis had machine-gunned the Jewish old, young and infirm into a hastily dug pit, Jews were being slaughtered in a new blood libel. A group of survivors had returned in search of family and possessions before leaving for Palestine. A Christian child had gone missing and townspeople accused the returning Jews of killing the child for his blood. On 4 July 1946, 42 Jews were massacred in Kielce, while police and militia stood by. There could be no future for the Jews who survived the Holocaust in central and eastern Europe.

In Palestine, however, British mandatory authorities, backed by 100,000 troops, stood implacably in the way of Jewish immigration and a Jewish state. On 22 July, fighters of the breakaway Etzel bombed the mandate secretariat in Jerusalem's King David Hotel, killing 41 people. With the decision the next month to deport 'illegal' Jewish immigrants to detention camps in Cyprus, British troops began dragging Jewish death-camp survivors off boats and onto prison ships, to confine them again behind barbed wire. Cries of 'Free Immigration!' and 'A Jewish State!' resounded in the streets of Palestine.

By now, Palestine's Jewish leadership saw a Jewish state as inevitable. Secretly, they set out to acquire arms by any means possible, and encouraged the population to learn how to use them. The second priority was settlement: the borders of the new state, they believed, would be largely decided by the existing Jewish settlements. For years, the name of the game had been 'od shaal' (one more piece of land), and groups continued trying to establish new communities. One such settlement had been attempted at Biryah near Safed in the Galilee by Bnei Akiva members, but the British had driven the settlers off the land and arrested their leaders. In response, youngsters flocked to Biryah in their thousands from all parts of Palestine to re-establish the settlement.

The fight for Biryah became a *cause célèbre* for the movement in Britain. One of its leaders, Shalom Marcovitch (later Maagan), had been in Palestine and visited Biryah, and he returned to Britain inspired by this example of Jewish courage and determination. That summer of 1946 saw the biggest-ever Bnei Akiva camp. Held in Flixton, Yorkshire, it was a jamboree, taking as its name and theme *Biryah*. The story of the Galilee settlement ignited the hundreds who came. We sang songs around campfires and re-enacted the drama that had taken place. Esther, then working at the Shelter, brought some of the child survivors with her to Flixton.

Esther must by then have been actively preparing for life in Palestine. She went regularly to the *Hachshara* training farms in Buckingham, Bromsgrove and Thaxted in Essex, farming the land by day and studying Bible and ideology by night. It was at Thaxted that she got to know Gubby Haffner (now Yehuda Avner), whom she met up with again in Palestine. Five years after Esther's death, Gubby married my sister Mimi, thus becoming my brother-in-law. He went on to advise several Israeli prime ministers, and became a senior member of Israel's foreign ministry, serving as ambassador to Britain and Australia.

Gubby recalls the first time he and Esther talked at length, in the dining hall at Thaxted, and remembers being struck by the interest that she took in the lives of the people she met:

She was a great interviewer and gave people her undivided attention. She was a totally authentic person who wore no make-up and didn't seem to need any. She had a roundish face, pointed obstinate chin, brown eyes and thick brown hair. When I met her later on in the Haganah, in her over-sized battledress, she looked a little absurd, yet very attractive. She caught the fellows' eyes without meaning to. She had a soft, husky voice, very appealing and with an easy laugh, although she was really a very serious person, with great spiritual depths.

Towards the end of that summer of 1946, Esther saw an advertisement in *The Jewish Chronicle*: the Anglo-Jewish Association (AJA) was looking for an English teacher for one of its projects, the Evelina de Rothschild School in Jerusalem. Esther leapt at the opportunity and applied at once, filling in many forms and submitting to a lengthy interview, during which she was careful not to appear 'too Zionist'. The AJA at that time was strongly pro-British, running its Evelina school in Jerusalem in order to produce British-educated ladies to serve the mandatory authorities. As far as Esther was concerned, however, the job was a way to get a visa and work permit for Palestine at a time when the entry of Jews was strictly circumscribed.

All that summer, an explosive resentment had been building inside Esther. The full horror of the Holocaust was now known, and her months with the tortured child survivors personalised for her the slaughter of a full third of the Jewish people. Her measureless distress was compounded by what she saw as the treachery of the country of her birth: instead of honouring its promise and compassionately giving the survivors a homeland, Britain had taken a few hundred youngsters within its gates – and sent its armies to keep the surviving homeless thousands out of the Promised Land. By the autumn, she could think of little else.

She waited eagerly for a reply to her job application. Perhaps working in Jerusalem would provide both the creativity and fulfilment that she was seeking, a life which would satisfy her craving for Jewish identity and national pride.

45

The answer came just a few weeks later during the Succot festival, when a registered letter from the AJA informed Esther she was hired. She was immediately the talk of Bachad and the envy of her friends, many of whom had been waiting for visas to Palestine since fleeing Germany on the eve of war. Clothing was still rationed, so preparing Esther for her trip wasn't easy, but within a month she was ready.

She was to make the long journey by road, rail and sea in the company of father, who was combining the trip to Palestine with business. Early on the morning of Sunday, 17 November 1946, we all got up to see the two of them into a taxi outside our home in Heathland Road. Neither Mimi nor I can remember any farewell party nor, in fact, any proper parting from our sister. Of course, we had no way of knowing we would never see her again. Our last physical image of Esther is that of a very bright and very forceful 21-year-old, climbing into the taxi, her whole life ahead of her.

For the next 17 months, we followed that life through a stream of letters, the first of which was written only hours after we said goodbye. It was a postcard, penned in haste that same Sunday morning:

Dover, November 17, 1946, 10.20 a.m.

Dear Mummy,
Just a line from the station to say journey safely negotiated so far. Raining here. Love to all from Daddy and myself,

Yours, Esther.

PART TWO

8 A Beautiful Land

It took Esther and father 11 days to reach Palestine. They travelled by ferry to France, journeyed overland to Marseilles and there boarded the SS *Providence* to Haifa. Six days after leaving England, Esther wrote to us from aboard ship:

> There is such a mixture of languages on the boat that I do not know when I am talking French or German or Yiddish, or trying to hear Hebrew. The woman in my cabin insists on talking a mixture of Russian and Polish to me which is very awkward. I have mostly been reading or talking ... I wish you could share the weather.

The *Providence* docked at Haifa early on Thursday, 28 November. Esther wrote to us that same day, from the Bat Yam home of our grandfather and his daughter, Aunt Leah. 'Well, all I can say for the moment is that it is lovely – a beautiful, beautiful land. There are so many impressions and experiences in the four hours I have been here, but it is all wonderful.'

Bat Yam, then a pastoral seaside village, now part of Greater Tel Aviv, was to become a second home for Esther. We children had never met any of our father's large family, other than on our grandfather's fleeting visit to London in the 1930s with his son and daughter-in-law, Reuven and Yaffa. Esther met them all – Uncle Reuven, Aunt Yaffa and their four children in Tel Aviv; Uncle Yaacov, Aunt Miriam and their four children on Moshav Kfar Hess; and in Bat Yam, grandfather, Aunt Leah, Uncle Leibel and their daughter Rivka. Rivka was the same age as Esther, very bright and at that time already an intelligence officer in the

Haganah, the underground Jewish defence organisation which, after statehood, became the Israel Defence Forces (IDF). (She was later assistant to Chaim Herzog when he headed IDF intelligence and she went with him to Washington where he was posted as military attaché. It was in Washington that she married, became pregnant and tragically lapsed into a coma from which she never recovered, giving birth to a healthy daughter before she died.)

During those first weeks in Palestine, Esther's two concerns were settling into her teaching job at the Evelina de Rothschild Girls' School and finding a suitable place to live.

She wrote to her friend Hannah Goldschmidt, in London:

> We came to Jerusalem on the Sunday morning and I was then in the school right away. I started full teaching on the Wednesday … The Palestinian children – the 'sabras' – are just bursting with vitality and bumptiousness, so that they need disciplining to some extent. The very real problem is to get these kids ever to shut up and give you a chance to teach them something!

If teaching presented a challenge, finding accommodation was harder still – particularly in Jerusalem where the British had severely restricted any kind of building. For the first six weeks, Esther lodged with Mrs Levy, Evelina's principal in her apartment on the school premises. ('I think the only times I am the least bit moody is in the company of the school Principal's family, who are so depressingly English,' she wrote to Hannah. 'Not that I mean anything against them, but you see, to perfect my process of complete assimilation, I do not want any immediate contacts with the past.') By January, she had found a room on King George Street, one of the city's main thoroughfares, next door to the British officers' club. Three weeks later, the British evicted her along with every tenant in the building. Three weeks after that, on 1 March 1947, a break-away Etzel unit bombed the club.

Esther never solved her housing problem. She moved ten times during the 18 months she lived in Jerusalem, but so happy was she to be in Palestine, that nothing seemed to worry her. In early January she wrote to Hannah:

> Let me beg you to do all you can to come out here in the summer, if only to see it for yourself and so that I can talk to you again. I was so pleased to hear that Ida [Gross from Heathland Road] is really coming, and soon too. She will not regret the sacrifices involved, and neither would you … I had not consciously made up my mind from the first moment to love it all – so however thrilled and impressed I am by everything I see and do – all of it, I say frankly, is biased, seen by me through rose-coloured spectacles, maybe. But I am happy, so very, very happy, that I can see that at only very rare intervals, had I ever known before what happiness means, certainly not as a continuous state of mind and being, as it is with me now.

Even in Esther's more prosaic letters home, her joy erupts. On 2 January she wrote to us:

> All is quiet here, with the military busy with its [New Year] festivities, I suppose, since we have not even been stopped for our passes these evenings. Work has gone fairly smoothly this week as I get the hang of things … Tonight I am going to a concert given by the Palestine Symphony Orchestra, and looking forward to it very much … Now that I am settling down more, I have time to think about the people and places I left, although I cannot think of any place as home but here, where I feel really at home. All that went before seems now only a temporary phase, and not really living at all – but now it is all just beginning … If anything unpleasant should occur here it would be worthwhile the suffering because one can feel that this is part of the struggle for a great cause and a great aim. I think none of you will have any regrets in changing your old lives for this one, however strange and difficult it will seem at first. Well, I am lucky, so very lucky, and I am now waiting only for you all to share it with me.

Everything about Palestine pleased Esther. She wrote to Ida Gross:

> Jerusalem, despite the feeling of strain and tension in the air deliberately aroused by the tanks and trucks dashing through the streets, the stacks of barbed wire and the swarms of English soldiers, is an interesting, varied place. Here there is history and an Oriental beauty, and the twisting, hilly streets are themselves interesting. Here there are also the fine, modern buildings of the wealthy residential quarter, with the Jewish Agency headquarters, but nearby there is the intricate network of old streets, courtyards and alleyways which make up the Mea Shearim, or 'Hundred Gates', where all the Chassidim live. And what Chassidim! Here one sees what *peyot* [side curls] really mean, and *streimels* [fur hats] and silk *bekeshes* [long coats] even on the little boys ... Only when I look at the great ancient hills among which Jerusalem stands, which sweep down in ridge after ridge of neatly terraced stone, nothing but brown sand and bleak white stone, that I see what it meant to establish colonies on the peaks of those hills, as is being done continuously. How they ever got up there or got down again I cannot imagine.

After the rationing and austerity of post-war London, Jerusalem's then still plentiful and kosher food was an unexpected delight. 'I saw a wonderful concoction in a confectioner's, of chocolate and pink icing – really a work of art,' she reported to Ida. 'The cafés here are fine, so neat and fresh, and, just as we learnt, you can sit down and read a large selection of newspapers.'

'I have had some felafel', she informed us, 'which is some vegetable mince boiled in little balls in oil and served with raw salad stuff, sauce and red peppers in a sort of half-moon pocket of Arab bread called "Peter". Anyway it's delicious.'

While Esther was settling in, the political drama continued to unfold. In Geneva on 12 December, the first post-Holocaust Zionist congress met. Missing from that congress, as Chaim

Weizmann, its president eloquently described, was an entire generation of murdered European Jews. Delegates argued heatedly over whether to attend a London conference, convened by the British to discuss Palestine's future. Underlying the argument, however, lay the real conflict: whether to accept partition of Palestine between Jew and Arab, which would mean establishing a Jewish state in only part of Eretz Yisrael. The majority view was a state at any price, even if that price entailed what we now call territorial compromise.

Meanwhile, schools in Palestine closed for the Hannuka vacation, and Esther spent late December 1946 exploring the country. She headed first for Tel Aviv. She wrote to Hannah:

> You know, on the way [to Palestine], I was told what a wonderful sensation it is to walk along the streets of Jewish Tel Aviv and feel yourself a free person. I listened and nodded and thought to myself: 'Yes. I can imagine just what you mean. You came from the Continent, perhaps 20 years ago, but even then the Jew was never really secure there, look how it has always been in Poland. But', I thought, 'after all, in England we are used to walking openly and freely on the streets, so the wonderful feeling just won't strike me as it did you, as a marvellous novelty.'
>
> This is what I was thinking, but I was all wrong. I had really no idea what it means to live in one's own land, among one's own people, to be and to feel at home, without having to apologise to somebody every minute for being an outsider. Yes, even we who lived in a tolerant land, or what was once so, also had to be careful not to make ourselves conspicuous, not to cause too much inconvenience – at school, at work – by observing our own ways of living. But here *we* set the standards, we live according to our habits and our culture, even where there are non-Jews, who are themselves outsiders here ... This feeling of living in one's own right, this freedom from personal embarrassment in little things or big, is worth any sacrifice, any effort, any danger – believe me! And so I am happy, when I little expected happiness to come so easily to me.

From Tel Aviv, Esther went north to Kibbutz Tirat Zvi in the Bet Shean valley, which to us in the movement at that time was legendary, as the first religious kibbutz. Founded in June 1937, its first settlers were youngsters trained on *Hachshara* in Germany, determined to show that religious pioneers were as tough and capable as any. Isolated from other Jewish settlements in a climate whose summer temperatures reached C45° and on soil containing up to 60 per cent lime, they withstood bitter Arab attack, and received a special citation of honour after the War of Independence.

Esther wrote to us from Tirat Zvi, bubbling with enthusiasm:

> The kibbutz is really fine, much bigger and more developed than one would have thought, with lots of lovely babies and youth. They have fine houses of four nice rooms, sausage factory, market-gardening, fruit, chicks and so on. The first thing one sees inside the gate is a circular lawn, with water and a laid-out plot, avenues, a grass amphitheatre ... fishponds and a good irrigation system, a remarkable achievement for only 10 years work. The scenery is beautiful, with the hills of Transjordan on one side and the Bet Shean Valley on the other. I have been eating oranges today with juice like – well, if I say like honey, you will think I just mean honey, or if like nectar, that I am being poetic – but I have never tasted such before. At night it is pretty cold with jackals howling. Today has been a real holiday.

From Tirat Zvi, Esther went on to Yagur near Haifa, a non-religious kibbutz, from where she wrote to Hannah:

> This, you will remember, is the kibbutz so thoroughly searched and raked-up in the summer by the British. Now just get rid of any ideas you have of a kibbutz. I had pictured the soldiers breaking into a little camp of a few scattered houses and upsetting the isolated settlers – well by those standards, Yagur is a gigantic place of 1,300 people, living in a completely independent community

which, at this size, amounts to a small township. Their lands stretch just about as far as one can see. They live in very nice rooms in three-storied houses, have, of course, laundry – all electric – hospital, school buildings, beautiful dining hall and kitchens. There is a proper library building and cultural centre, that is being added at the moment.

A few days later, Esther was back in Jerusalem:

It is very warm today, a hot wind, and the air is very close – according to Auntie Leah a *hamsin* that I have heard so much about, but of course not too bad because this is 'winter' … So now I am back and school starts on Sunday … It seems that mine was the only labour permit issued in the past six months. How we all hope that the position will change soon. That is what one hears all the time. I must admit it does not worry me though, I am too happy all the time.

In the short weeks since we had seen Esther, we already sensed enormous change in her. In a letter to Hannah, she wrote:

I really have determined to change myself along with my way of life – that is, the bits that needed changing, even though some of the good things may have to go too. Actually, people here are inclined to occasional moodiness. You hear a lot spoken of one's *matzav ruach*, which means a mood, usually bad, and everybody kindly explains that this is a term you must learn as you will hear a lot about it! But this is only because of the worry of the political situation and the general unrest and uncertainty, felt particularly in Jerusalem – because otherwise one just cannot help feeling happy and content here.

I really seem to have undergone a process of re-birth, from which I am only now very slowly emerging. From the time we landed I somehow became half lost to the world. I could not take in the vastness of what was happening to me. I really did not know what people were saying and seemed to walk around in a daze for weeks. I simply could not get to grips with reality, because it was such a wonderful reality. Now the impressions of that time come back to me, and I begin to make firm contacts with life, and to get down to living it normally. I somehow wanted to get over all the 'firsts' – the first time I went on a bus, the first time I bought myself a cup of tea in a café, the first time I posted a local letter with a local stamp, the first time I went to the pictures here. All these little things made me feel I belonged, that I was acclimatising myself, that I was now a genuine Jerusalemite and Eretz-Israelite. All this probably sounds very silly, but I am writing down for you what up till now have been only half-formed sensations for me ...

We must each shoulder our individual responsibility to improve what we see to be wrong in the way we honestly think best, and as best we can. This is a brand new country, though so old, and if one only stops to think of, and to look at what has been made of it in a mere 50 to 70 years, it is so astounding that all criticism must die on the lips, because there you have the answer. The pioneers did their job, a fine job and wonderfully. But do not expect to come here and find a perfect state. Our wonderful Holy Land is in its raw infancy as a modern state – not so very raw, mind you, on the surface, but still with a lot of body-building and training to do. It has been born – that is the wonderful and important thing. Now it has to be brought up and educated. First, however, the trials and dangers of babyhood have not yet, unfortunately, passed. The dangers of birth have been survived, but the child is still weak and it may be some time before it is firmly on its feet and growing fast. The worst of it is, it has been born into an unhappy and uncomfortable world, a war-baby on a losing side. But, as you know, Jewish people only live for their children, because in them and with them lies the future, and this little Land is the only future we have. So whether you like it or not you will have to adopt it sooner or later, but the sooner the better, for it and for you – and when you do so, you should be proud and keen to nurture it and foster it with all you have. I am writing this in the plural 'you' but also in the singular 'you' for your benefit. As you may realise, I am at the moment considerably frustrated in this desire to play my part, and yet one can do it in small ways, if only for one's own satisfaction, by buying things only that are manufactured here, by speaking Hebrew, and simply by being here.

9 A New Teacher

Esther was eagerly embracing her new sense of identity and the Jewish struggle for independence. Her pupils, however, saw her as simply one more British teacher, sent to Jerusalem to teach them English; and her colleagues saw her as the newcomer on the staff, to be given the hardest schedule, invariably including the last hour of the day between 1.00 and 2.00 p.m., when everyone was tired and drowsy in the midday heat.

One of Esther's pupils, Naomi Hadari, took pity on the new young teacher, and would bring her flowers to cheer her up – much to the disgust of the other girls! (Naomi's grandfather, Mr Mandelbaum, owned the house which became the crossing-point between Israeli and Jordanian lines following the War of Independence – the Mandelbaum Gate; her future husband is today head of the Western Wall *Yeshiva*, or Yeshivat HaKotel, opened in the Old City's ruined Jewish Quarter shortly after its recapture in the Six-Day War of 1967.)

Deep divisions ran between staff and students at Evelina in those days, both religious and political. While the administration upheld traditional Jewish Orthodoxy in school, most Evelina pupils came from non-religious homes and resented the daily prayer and ritual. When, in fact, heavy fighting forced the school to relocate from its fine old building on Shivtei Yisrael Street to the Rehavia neighbourhood, many students transferred instead to secular schools in the city.

A wider chasm still gaped between staff and students over their attitude to the British. The school principal and governors were vociferously pro-British at a time when Whitehall policy was increasingly anti-Jewish. However, the general feeling in

Palestine's Jewish community was that British behaviour towards the Jews during the past decade had been shameful: not only had Britain turned a blind eye to the peril faced by Europe's Jews with the issue of its infamous 1939 White Paper, virtually halting Jewish immigration to Palestine, but they were now compounding their crime. They were holding Holocaust survivors in detention camps in Cyprus. They were arresting Haganah members on the street and confiscating their arms. They were raiding kibbutzim in search of arms, imposing curfews on Jewish areas and imprisoning the leaders of the Jewish community in Palestine in the Latrun fortress.

Despite this strong anti-British feeling in the wider Jewish community, however, Evelina's principal and governors happily entertained British officers to tea at the school, and while it's highly doubtful that Evelina staff were actively disloyal to the Jewish cause, Esther was caught in an awkward situation. Her pupils perceived her as British establishment, while in reality her heart was in the struggle for Jewish independence. Her quiet disappearance from school some months later, her re-emergence as a Haganah fighter and the manner of her death turned her into a heroic, almost mystical figure for her fiercely Zionist former pupils.

That, however, was still ahead. Esther was still settling into teaching and into Jerusalem. On 8 January 1947 she wrote:

> At school we are having a big inspection in a fortnight's time, so there will be some excitement. I got my Identity Card today and tomorrow we are going to have the inoculation done at last .... There is a Road Safety programme on here now, as in London, which is quite ridiculous since there are so few pavements here, and those are blocked by barbed wire. However, so far things have been very peaceful despite incidents elsewhere.

On 14 January, she sent a special note to our beloved grandfather in London for his 70th birthday:

> I am hoping very much that, as I had the great honour to come to Eretz Israel while I am 21, so may this year be a

doubly happy one, by bringing you too here, and Booba [our grandmother]. This is a very special time of life, and you have earned and deserve the great happiness more than I did. I am sure you would both be very happy here, and I think all the time of our being at home together here, all of us.

By the end of the month, Esther had her first real feel of the increasingly heavy hand of the British administration. 'Well, just so that I could see what it was like, we had curfew two nights running this week,' she reported. 'The first evening it was announced suddenly at 5.00 in the afternoon, but people were still about for half-an-hour, and the next night we knew it would be on from 5.30 p.m. until 6.00 in the morning.'

The curfew was imposed to pressure the Jewish community into turning two wanted men over to the British, which the Jewish authorities duly did. But, according to Esther, the British 'just continue to blame the community for things in which we have no part and no say – in fact the powers that be here must be quite disappointed as they were looking for a chance to impose martial law'. She had barely been in Palestine two months, but for Esther, the British were clearly 'they' and the Jewish community 'we'.

Her roots in the country were spreading rapidly. In the last week of January, a fellow teacher at Evelina introduced Esther to one of the Jewish managers of the Palestine Broadcasting Corporation (PBC). Set up by the British in 1936 to transmit in Hebrew and Arabic, many of the PBC's Jewish broadcasters secretly moonlighted for the Haganah's underground radio service. They were looking for English-language broadcasters at the time, and Esther, with her North London Collegiate accent, was added to the Haganah list.

Around the same time, Esther got her first glimpse of East Jerusalem, when she attended a memorial service for Evelina's late principal. She wrote:

I went along to the Mount of Olives. It was very cold and wet, but I think this first impression of the place, which is in people's hearts the world over, was well-suited to the steep, stony hillsides, scattered with the dull-green hardy olive trees. The wonderful view was obscured, but it was still a thrill to look down to the Old City of Jerusalem, seeing the wall that shuts it in, and inside, the one remaining wall of the Temple, and the big, squat mosque in its compound on the holy site.

The first two weeks of February found Esther, newly evicted from her King George Street apartment, frantically looking for housing. Because of the British decision to create security zones in the city, she was in company with about half the Jewish population of the city. 'The evacuations are extending', she wrote, 'yet everybody seems to have found a roof to sleep under, nobody quite knows how. For me it was easy enough, I had so many offers of accommodation from all the staff and the children too.'

On 11 February, after several nights on a camp bed in temporary premises, she moved to a room in the home of one of Evelina's teachers, Dr Rieder and his wife, at 59 Ramban Street in Rehavia, where she stayed for the next eight months. She wrote:

> They have made a very comfortable room for me. Nice furniture, balcony, central heating, complete use of the kitchen, and generally a good home, and for only six pounds a month. It is in a beautiful house of flats. I wish you could see the way they live here, so different from English homes, not on a grand scale but comfortable and clean, as things have to be here. It is the last house in the road, right out on the Jerusalem hills, with a wonderful view, but also a good bus service, and only a few minutes from the town centre, because the city is not very big, after all.'

Today, that wonderful view can only be imagined. Number 59 is no longer the last house on Ramban Street. High-rise housing intrudes to the right, and the Knesset (parliament) building and the trees of Sacher Park cover the valley floor.

The school inspection Esther wrote of earlier did not take place,

> because the British cannot move around without armed escort, and as they themselves say, are kept confined to their places of work in 'ghettos'! Tanks patrol the streets at night, but as we expected, there is no martial law. On Tu B'Shvat (Arbour Day), we had a planting ceremony in the school garden and I planted a rose bush. It was really a halcyon day, warm sunshine and a heavy scent of eucalyptus as we stood around the bushes. Then we had doughnuts, freshly baked in the school, and plates of fruit and nuts, followed by a little concert. Sunday evening I went to a meeting for English-speaking students to arrange a series of tours and other activities. We are starting next Tuesday by seeing the educational and social work done among Yemenite children in the Old City. This evening I am going to give my first private lesson – I shall probably take about 35 piasters, which is equal, nominally to 7 shillings.

Meanwhile, back in London the British government was anxiously casting around for a solution to the 'Palestine Problem'. Foreign Minister Ernest Bevin presented a plan aimed at averting the establishment of a Jewish state: he proposed allowing 100,000 Jews into Palestine over a two-year period at the rate of 4,000 a month; establishing cantons, instead of dividing the country into autonomous areas; and appointing an Advisory Council to assist the High Commissioner in place of the Jewish Agency. This proposal was, of course, in blatant contradiction to the British commitment to a Jewish homeland given 30 years earlier in the Balfour Declaration, and it aroused resentment and anger among Jews in Palestine and beyond. Tension between the British and the Jews escalated, and Britain's efforts to subdue and intimidate Palestine's Jewish population intensified.

Esther made light of the increasing tension in her family letters, but she was more open with her friends. On 17 February she wrote to Hannah:

I don't like to start off like this, but there is something I am very anxious to make known, only you must promise not to pass this on to my mother because she will only worry about me. This will give you some idea of the humiliation and the frightening insecurity that one experiences here in our own Holy Land. Last Friday night I had been out to supper and it so happened that nobody was able to see me home all the way. Briefly, I came across a couple of thoroughly drunken soldiers holding up passersby with their guns – all the Military go about heavily armed – I got away alright after some argument, with the guns flourished at me all the time, and notified a tank crew in the next street of these dangerous soldiers. However in Sunday's papers it was reported that, a little while later, a Mr Wohlgelernter was seriously wounded by 'an accidental discharge while a gun was being unloaded'. Altogether there were four such 'accidents' on that one day, and it is *we* who are supposed to be the terrorists! Perhaps people from Germany knew the feeling of being menaced in this way, and being helpless to act or even appeal against it, but to me it was a new experience. These drunken louts are our own self-appointed masters, swarms of them, and patrols of tanks every night crawl through the main streets with great searchlights combing the balconies and house windows, or streams of jeeps tear through the traffic, causing pandemonium for no reason that anybody ever discovers. All our most beautiful modern flats are being made a shambles by having soldiers billeted in them.

One victim of drunken trigger-happy British soldiers was 42-year-old Pinchas Houminer, who was shot and killed crossing Strauss Street in downtown Jerusalem. His widow raised their six young children with no compensation from the British. One of the grandchildren Pinchas never knew was Shlomo, who grew up to be a careers officer in the Israel Defence Forces, and married my daughter Estie, named after her late aunt, Esther.

The letter continued:

Please don't get the wrong impression. I am so happy, with a happiness that I never knew existed, at least not for me, but now suddenly it is mine. All my new experiences, however unexpected, strange and different from the life I am used to, are a pleasure to me. The long hours I am working, the great care I have to take with money, the drawbacks of teaching in a private school, especially in this comparatively undeveloped and struggling country, the nervous stresses of life here at present, all count for nothing to me. I am still overpowered with the privilege, the wonder and the novelty of being here. Every day there are new experiences. Now there are the first signs of spring. The children bring me flowers at school and my room is thick with the smell of honey that exudes from the almond blossom which now flaunts its delicate pink over the barbed wire and sentry posts of Jerusalem ...

I have made many friends here and I am so sociable now, I can't help it! I eat in cafés and straight away somebody wants to know where I come from, and I have to tell the whole story, and sometimes it's quite difficult to call a halt!

This was not the reserved, reticent Esther we had known in London. People who met her in those days describe her as a flower opening its petals to the warm sunshine.

She had, she wrote to us in February,

more friends and acquaintances than I know what to do with, so I always have plenty of company... I am invited out tonight and tomorrow, and had two bunches of flowers sent today for my new room. (Yes, from young men but not terribly interesting.) I went to a concert last night for I have a season ticket for the series – not bad, but I am afraid I am getting used to lower standards – it included Shostakovitch's Fifth symphony. We are having a long weekend for Purim. Reports have to be ready for next week, so I am very busy as usual. I received this week a request to come for a wireless [radio] audition.

And a week later:

> Everybody goes around quite freely in the evenings, more
> so in fact than when I first came, when it used to be very
> quiet. At one of the concerts I went to, which had been
> postponed because of curfew, and then took place on a
> very critical day, Mrs Goldie Meyerson [Golda Meir] spoke
> to the audience, and stressed the significance of their
> coming to enjoy music and live normally as civilised
> people, though we have so many troubles. You know all
> the talk of morale and so on during the war. Well, it is even
> more important here to keep sane and calm, because there
> is a sharp tendency for people to get very depressed or
> excited. I am enjoying life to the full and am determined to
> do so, despite the difficulties. There has been a lot of hard
> work lately with reports and so on, acquiring passes to get
> into school and my private lessons – I am giving three a
> week now. I am very happy and all is worthwhile.

By the end of February, however, three months after arriving
in Palestine, Esther was referring openly to the difficulties and
inconveniences of life under the British in her letters home:

> There is altogether very little governmental concern for
> public welfare here. Now of course, domestic troubles are
> the excuse for further procrastination in giving us a definite
> clue to our future fate. Things are however more cheerful
> here this week, with ships coming in still and life going on
> as normally as life ever does here, taking into account such
> things as walking literally miles in a circle, to get to a spot a
> few yards away, because there happens to be a forest of
> barbed wire in the way. The latest outcrop is in the road
> leading to the school, which is now barred. The girls are
> allowed through and the staff have to have passes.

One of the very few personal possessions of Esther that we
have is her pass. It reads: 'Serial No. 0745 - PERMIT TO ENTER
R.A.F. ZONE, Street of the Prophets, JERUSALEM.' The inside

pages include her details and her photograph, overstamped with the legend: 'Air Headquarters Levant. Community: Jewish.' Esther's letter continues:

> It seems that a bomb went off tonight somewhere in Jerusalem, so I wonder if there will be any further developments. The non-Jews here are in a mess – they are not allowed to leave their compounds, and have to ask their Jewish friends to do their shopping for them!

Despite the precarious, even dangerous situation in Palestine, however, some aspects of Esther's life were easier than ours in Britain. A *Palestine Post* headline of 9 February 1947 reads, 'FUEL CRISIS IN SNOW-BOUND BRITAIN: Government Blamed For Lack Of Foresight.' During that bitter British winter of 1946/47, with food and clothing still strictly rationed, fuel for transport and heating was also in desperately short supply. While we shivered in London, we received letters from Esther announcing: 'Here it is spring already – I could have sent you strawberries and the loveliest of flowers.' Who ever saw flowers in grim London in those days?

> We have had an exceptionally mild winter and it seems to be over already. I hate to think of what you have been having – but really the English national crisis is no more than they actually deserve, a real punishment for their callousness to us. I see now it is perfectly true that the tolerant, well-mannered Englishman is quite a different person abroad, where he thinks himself the master of inferior foreigners and subjects who have to be subdued and ruled. For them, democratic principles and decency do not have to be applied.

At midnight on Saturday, 1 March, the British launched Operation Hippo, deploying 10,000 First Infantry Division troops to impose a curfew on the quarter-million Jews of Tel Aviv, Ramat Gan, Bnei Brak and Petach Tikva. So effective was Operation Hippo that on the Sunday 'even the cats didn't dare venture out'. Only two of the city's 6,000 telephones were left connected and not even doctors and nurses were allowed to leave their homes. Jewish north-east Jerusalem also fell under Hippo, resulting in the total isolation of its 25,000 residents. Jerusalem's other Jewish quarters were under curfew from 7.00 p.m. Saturday until 1.00 p.m. Sunday.

Operation Hippo was the British response to the destruction of their Goldsmith Officers' club by the breakaway Etzel group on 1 March – the club next door to Esther's former home. Eleven officers and civilians had died in the explosion, and a further 20 British military personnel were killed and 27 wounded that same day in ambushes carried out by Jewish underground groups in different parts of the country.

At 7.15 on the Sunday morning, Esther wrote:

> Waited in for the first news broadcast because there is no indication of the curfew being lifted. I now hear that it is still in force and martial law is operating in two of the poorer districts of Jerusalem – Geula and Mea Shearim which are very crowded and will probably be carefully searched. Curfew may continue until the afternoon, many people think until they [the British] bury their dead. Meanwhile, we are outside it so I can go out to post this letter, although I don't know when it will be collected. We also have shops available and I have some reserves – eggs for supper and breakfast and preserves.

The following day, Esther reported that her landlord and fellow teacher Dr Rieder phoned the school, and spoke to the principal.

> Mrs Levy said we were to come – for just one lesson! She likes to boast that the school carries on. Well, we set out for a long walk in the heat, because no buses were running yet. One street we had to pass was still being searched and before we knew where we were, we had been taken inside a compound for 'screening'. There we remained standing for four and a half hours in the sun. I was only asked my

name and age – one always carries an identity card of course. There were over 300 others with us, so we had plenty of company, but nothing to do. I took the opportunity to write a letter relating my experiences as they happened, for the benefit of the Bachad members or anyone else interested. [That letter never arrived, nor has it ever been traced.]

When I got back home exhausted, I heard that there was a telegram for me at the school. Mrs Rieder had phoned the school very worried by then that we were not yet back home. She of course was even more worried when she learned that we had never arrived. The telegram was from Ida, saying that she had arrived in Haifa and was hoping to land. This was all yesterday, Sunday. Meanwhile martial law had been imposed, so nobody could have gone to meet her, and neither can I. I cannot phone Tel Aviv, nor do I know where to find her. I have heard nothing from her since, so I hope she can reach me. She came at the worst possible moment, I never expected her to arrive so quickly on a cargo boat. There was only about a third of the school present today, as so many live in the martial law area. School finishes an hour earlier, as the cook cannot get out, so there is no lunch.

It took Esther an entire month to locate her friend Ida. On 7 March, she wrote:

I decided on Wednesday [Purim holiday from school] to try and get to Yavneh [a religious kibbutz which served as an assembly point for Bachad pioneers] to see if Ida is there already, as I have heard nothing from her since the telegram on Sunday saying she had arrived. There were no taxis or buses going to Rehovot, through which one has to travel, but I found much to my surprise, that there was a bus going to Tel Aviv. It turned out that there were five or six buses going together, because the drivers were Tel Aviv men and had permission to get home, so I started off with a whole bus to myself, but on the way we picked up others who were going to try to get into Tel Aviv.

At the Tel Aviv [military] barrier we had to get out. The city was absolutely dead outside – it is usually just teeming with life and activity. At the barrier there were crowds of Arabs with nothing to do, though this is not unusual for them. One was apparently doing good business, because he had a little, shaky buggy and donkey, in which he took 10 people and a lot of luggage right round to the Jaffa side of Tel Aviv, where they could be passed in by the CID [British plainclothes police]. These, however, had already gone off duty, but with myself acting as interpreter we managed to get quite a crowd in, with army lorries provided for transport. So I have the distinction of walking in and out of sealed-off Tel Aviv without even having to show an identity card! After that I took a taxi to Bat Yam where Uncle and Rivka were very surprised to see me. Yesterday, we went to Rehovot but there is no bus service to get me back from Yavneh the same day and I wanted to be back because it is Purim. So I still do not know whether Ida is there, as there is no phone, but I hope I shall hear something from her soon. Transport is worse than ever at the moment and I do not know whether I shall get back in time on Sunday morning. I expected Ida to come to Jerusalem, or at least to phone me. There is a risk of martial law in Rehovot any day, so I could not risk being cut off, as Mrs Levy would never get over it.

This letter caused great consternation in our London home. Our parents were shocked that Esther had exposed herself to such danger, and argued at length about whether this was bravado or naïveté. Father tended to the latter, misreading, I believe, the true nature of his elder daughter. My own memories of Esther encouraged me to see beyond the prim and proper English facade to where lurked a keenly adventurous spirit and an insatiable curiosity.

Several days later, Esther reported that she had at last heard from Ida. Our former neighbour from Heathland Road had arrived in Haifa aboard a cargo ship, accompanying two refugee children. Unable to get to Yavneh because of the curfew, she went first to the family of one of the children she had escorted to Palestine, and then to Sdei Eliyahu, a religious kibbutz in the Bet Shean valley right next door to Tirat Zvi, to deliver a radio she had brought from England for one of its members. On Sdei Eliyahu, she met a young man named Chaim Safrai, the son of a respected Jerusalem family, who was responsible for the kibbutz's security and defence and for liaison with the British authorities – and married him the following year.

In Jerusalem, life under the British continued to worsen. On 12 March, Esther wrote:

> Last night, I was awakened by explosions. I thought, oh, another air raid [Blitz memories]! This time, our district is also under curfew, but apart from the fact that it cuts out my Hebrew lessons and the ones I give, it gives me a chance to catch up on my work and on letter writing ... Funny situations arise among it all – some soldiers have specific rates for passing things over the cordon. One of them said he wasn't having any 'monkey business', when somebody only had a two-shilling piece to give him, instead of the shilling he charged, and he carefully gave the correct change! As I passed, I heard one Jew saying to another in Yiddish – shaking his head at the two thick rings of barbed wire – 'die Yidden zollen nisht entlofen vun Eretz Yisroel!' (it's so that the Jews shouldn't escape from Eretz Israel)!!

> At the moment school is much easier, because so many are away, about one third of the school, which brings the classes down to just the right size for teaching. Most of my after-school lessons are off now, and school finishes at 1.30. Today I went to the pictures – saw *The Idiot* in French. It was very annoying to find that on the weekly hot-water night, there was suddenly no water – tank had run dry.

She continues in a more serious vein:

> Here thousands are unemployed – including Rivka and Uncle Leibel – because their jobs happen to be on the other

side of the barbed wire in whichever direction. It is most depressing for all. People aren't allowed to talk or pass things over the cordon via the sentry any more. Now they are told to keep moving, so they have to talk whilst walking up and down, shouting to each other across the street in the hours that they are allowed out at all. During curfew, none of us is allowed out even on our balconies, which in summer will be quite a hardship. In due course, one goes through, on a smaller scale, all the experiences of Continental Jewry – evicted from home with one's *pekelech* [bags], arrests, insults from soldiers, barbed wire, concentration camps, searchlight patrols – a taste of everything. Only here we are in our own right and the others are the foreigners.

On 16 March, martial law was lifted. Esther describes the euphoria:

What an exciting feeling of freedom it gave, what a relief so near to Pesach [Passover], even for those of us actually little affected by martial law. The kids rushed through the barriers on the stroke of 12.00, and came to school so excited and yet subdued and a bit bewildered, even the youngest. Nobody, not even the authorities themselves, realised it would be over so suddenly except, of course, the Jews in Mea Shearim from whom I heard it already on Shabbat. It must be all written down somewhere in some Kabbala, or somewhere – although it's the little children who bring all the information and they are always right! Jerusalem is a terribly small town as regards gossip and news, but it has its good uses. If there is curfew for instance, it is not usually officially announced, so people could get into serious trouble unwittingly. However, within two minutes the news gets around town, nobody knows from where, but all are safely in the know!'

My sister had become a Jerusalemite. This city, holy to three great faiths, fought over by empires, was – and is – one big village to those who live there. People pour into the streets to share good times and bad. And Esther, within just a few short months, was one of them.

10 Under the Mandate

Palestine in spring 1947 was tense. Dov Gruener, an Etzel member who had attacked a British police station in Ramat Gan a year earlier, was on trial.

'In the Yeshurun synagogue today, a boy came upstairs in the middle of the sermon, flung a bundle of Etzel leaflets and disappeared,' Esther wrote to us. 'It relieved the tedium of the speech!'

Later, on 25 March:

> We were expecting the results of the Gruener trial today, with possible trouble, but so far nothing has been announced. Patrols go around throughout curfew time, including soldiers on foot, snooping around in rubber-soled boots. You can't imagine anything more disgusting and ridiculous. Of course when they are drunk, they make such a row that the whole effect is spoilt.

The following month, Gruener was found guilty and sentenced to death. A Shabbat afternoon in April found Esther and fellow teachers from Evelina in the home of Dr and Mrs Rieder, with Dov Gruener's sister, a Mrs Feldman. She had come from America to plead with the British authorities for her brother's life. Her husband, an American citizen, had appealed the sentence, but was refused on the grounds that 'he had no direct interest in the case'. The British then rapidly amended their own 1945 Emergency Regulations to prohibit appeals against military court decisions.

On 14 April, Esther wrote:

Just about five o'clock this morning a tank came around announcing, in very bad Hebrew, that curfew was imposed until further notice, from 4.00 a.m. Fortunately, I bought a packet of toast last night, when I heard there was a strike on. I put it into Mrs Rieder's electric toaster to get crisp and hot. I have various tinned stuff, including milk, and I made porridge for breakfast. I have some bananas and young carrots to eat now, so I can picnic very happily on my own, even if they do not lift the curfew at lunchtime. Mrs Rieder is stuck in Haifa where she went yesterday, and now Ida will not be able to come today either. She will have had to turn back half-way if she started out ...

Well, this is the first time I have experienced 24 hours of continuous curfew and by now (evening) I am thoroughly fed-up. It has been pretty cold sitting around indoors, too. We shall see what the morning will bring. Presumably they cannot go on indefinitely 'preventing' – anyway, in case I can post this in the morning, I will finish now with love and best wishes to all, Yours, Esther

5.45 a.m. Thursday: curfew lifted till evening. Hurray! But so much for my concert tonight.

What Esther did not know when she wrote was why the sudden prolonged curfew had been imposed, and that it affected not just Jerusalem but Palestine's entire Jewish community. Two hours before dawn on Wednesday 16 April, Dov Gruener and three of his Etzel colleagues were taken from their Acre prison cells and hanged. The British were not chancing a violent response: the operation was conducted in secrecy and deceit, the families of the four men having been assured that the sentence would not be carried out pending a Privy Council decision on the case. In fact, that august body never got to discuss the case at all. The four men were executed while the matter was still *sub judice*. British justice in this case clearly owed more to political than legal considerations. The relatives of the condemned men were informed four hours after the executions, and then taken to Safad for the burials.

Back in London, open support for the Jewish struggle for independence was mounting. There were Sunday rallies in Hyde Park and the East End, with the blue-and-white flag prominently displayed and plenty of 'takers' in fist-fights that broke out with anti-Semitic rowdies and Arab League supporters. Covertly, there were occasional Etzel and even Lehi exploits: stories of an assassination attempt on Ernest Bevin; a Jew found in possession of a firearm in the Whitehall area, arrested and sentenced to a long prison term; and a bomb which turned up in the Dover House office responsible for Palestine's economic affairs, a mere 100 yards from 10 Downing Street.

The Haganah had also established itself in London and was conducting less dramatic but far more directed activities. Its aims were threefold: recruitment, both of senior members of Zionist youth movements to send to France for training, and of battle veterans, such as pilots, tank crew and gunners; acquiring vital equipment (the most dramatic incident being the 'confiscation' of two Spitfire planes which were secretly flown across the English Channel one night); and establishing a defence network to protect Jews and Jewish premises in Britain. Remarkably, young Jews in Britain, as in Palestine, easily imposed on themselves the intense self-discipline that enabled them to work in clandestine opposition to the British.

Despite the growing tension and uncertainty of that spring in Palestine, Esther continued trying to persuade the family to join her, and was still doing so when she became a full-time soldier. She wrote to us:

> The Rieders are going to America in June, and as they want somebody in the flat, what about you coming here for the summer, instead of waiting until Hanukah? I shall have the long holiday at that time and when it is over and the Rieders come back, you can go to Bat Yam. I mean it quite seriously, so please think about it; it would make a very good arrangement. I heard today that the summer holidays begin on June 19, and the Rieders are leaving a few days before that, so you have not got too much time to make plans.

75

And in a letter to our mother a few days later:

> Before anything else, I want you to write to me that you are
> going to come here in June. Of course we know that it will
> be very difficult for you to get permission and you may not
> manage, but I really think you should start working on it
> straight away. Although I want it to be a real holiday for
> you, I also think of the serious matter of learning
> household ways here – so very different! In September, the
> woman in the next flat is going to America for a year. She,
> however, wants 20 pounds a month, and there are some
> additional expenses, but I have already seen it as an ideal
> home for Booba and Zada [our grandparents] and myself,
> because I shall have to leave this room in September. So
> bring them with you. Everything would just fit in well, so
> let's see what Daddy can pull off this time. Much as I have
> thought of coming to see you all in the summer – I can't say
> coming 'home', because here is my only home from the
> moment I arrived – I feel I owe the first real holiday to the
> Land, to looking around this new home, and really getting
> to know it. Then, having spent a complete year here, I shall
> feel that I really belong, as I most undoubtedly do, of
> course. Quite apart from the fact that I might never be able
> to return if I left now, and I am not going to take any risk
> with that.

And some weeks after that:

> I received your letter yesterday, and was very disappointed
> that you do not have more hope of coming. I know the
> difficulties that are being made, but it is not entirely
> impossible – only this week I heard of nine nurses who are
> coming out with entry certificates. You should at least try.
> Ida has put in a good deal of work for her sister, and I have
> an appointment with a headmaster this week to see if it is
> possible to bring in teachers. I heard when we were up at
> the University on Friday that they seem to be disappointed

that nobody from England seems to make any effort to come, as the Americans do. There are lots of them arriving all the time, and a new one-year course for South Africans has begun, despite the difficult times.

(This was the first session of the Institute for Youth Leaders from Abroad, a programme that is still run today, and has trained many thousands of Jewish youth leaders from around the world, including my wife, my brother-in-law and myself.)

The Passover vacation that April must have come as a welcome relief for Esther, after her efforts to make her mark as a teacher in a school located in a potential battle zone. On the first day of the vacation, she took off for Bat Yam to spend the festival with the family there, and also at last linked up with her friend Ida, who had arrived a month before. Ida had had a difficult time settling in, and had written unhappy letters to her friends in London. Esther found her on Kibbutz Sdei Eliyahu, and wrote to Hannah:

Well, I arrived last night with some trepidation, and after a long and very bumpy journey, to find Ida looking magnificent and getting on very well. It seems that her main trouble was, that arriving in the terrible cir-cumstances here and not knowing what to do, she simply had nobody to talk to. Of course she had a hard time of it and it was a very trying experience. I still think she was very wrong not to have come to me in Jerusalem all this time – and what with your letter and her own vague but awful hints, I was seriously worried.

For Esther there were few worse sins than writing letters that criticised Eretz Israel and complaining about conditions there. That her close friend Ida should have done so was unacceptable, and it was only when they actually met that she overcame her annoyance. To this day, Ida is still unsure why Esther was so annoyed when she arrived in Sdei Eliyahu.

Her mood must have changed very rapidly, however, as her letter goes on to describe the young kibbutz.

In some ways it is even nicer here than at Tirat Zvi, although smaller. They had an artist who laid out the kibbutz and decorated the children's houses with Biblical murals ... I am enjoying myself very much here. This morning I went to see how the flowers are cut off the male date palms and then taken to the other palm tree grove to fertilise the sprigs of creamy little flowers of the female trees. They should bear fruit just before Rosh Hashanah. The country is very, very dry, but on the kibbutz there is plenty of water and electricity. They have many fish-ponds too. I went rowing on one of the ponds and saw them netting in the fish. After draining they are left in a tank overnight and collected in the morning by a lorry, also containing a tank, so that they are sold in town alive – small carp for the weekend market. They have 60 children here, all very beautiful of course. There are about 140 adults in the kibbutz, including a group of youth trainees.

The school vacation finished on 14 April:

Today we started school again and everything is as nearly normal as can be here. The school repairs are almost done, so that we shall have the dining room and kitchens in use again, and the hours as before ... Well, Pesach is well and truly over by now, and I hope you enjoyed it as much as I did. I wore my Nylon stockings and they were very nice indeed. Saturday night I ate strawberries and ice-cream, and thought how you would have enjoyed them Mummy.

Later that week, she continued:

Thanks for sending the University graduation ceremony invitation, although out here with the lifestyle and the pace of activities being so different, it is of little interest to me. In fact Ida has already 'performed' the ceremony for me. She arrived here yesterday and is staying with me for about a week. We are going up to the University and to the Hadassah Hospital on Friday, where I have not yet been.

Evening curfew is still continuing but Ida is keeping me very good company, and we are enjoying ourselves preparing lavish meals, and doing Hebrew lessons together. A government issue of Australian butter has begun again, two quarter-pound packets a month, much cheaper than Tnuva (locally produced), and the school gets a supply which is distributed among the staff, so today I got three packets!

I bought myself a nice little vase when I was in Tel Aviv, and in it I have some glorious roses that a friend brought me. So my room is really pleasant in the long evenings, especially after the tension and hurry of the streets before curfew, even though we have patrols rumbling and ranting furiously all round our corner throughout the night.

The spring of 1947 was only two years after the Jews had experienced the greatest tragedy in their long history of persecution and strife. But in Palestine, a new type of Jew had already emerged, self-confident sometimes to the point of arrogance, determined to become at long last the master of his own destiny after 2,000 years in exile. Within a very few months, Esther had made a quantum leap from the classic Diaspora mentality of keeping her head well down, to someone who took things in her stride, improvised and knew that she would pull through somehow.

At the moment there are rumours and speculations about the High Commissioner's talk with Ben Gurion, his sudden departure and, latest news this evening, his sudden return. There may be some troubles ahead but, whatever happens, you can be sure the *Yishuv* will take it in its stride and pull through somehow. It is no good worrying about it, either on our part or yours. People of long experience here say that the country has always made the greatest progress as a reaction to difficult times which seem to stimulate fresh effort, and also partly as a result of the help given by Jews in other countries. It is only in town where restrictions are imposed and people congregate that these things are felt more deeply, but in the settlements they just carry on growing and multiplying, even though a sudden curfew may mean that a supply of fresh vegetables or fish may go to waste.

Her comments on the troubled times were always interspersed with her own news. 'I heard Shulamit Shafir play today,' she wrote to Mimi and me. 'Quite good, a nice programme including Mahler's Fourth Symphony with a real *hora* in the third movement. Are you still buying records, Asher?'

Despite her job, the extra lessons she gave, the Hebrew lessons she diligently attended and the vagaries of curfews and violence, Esther was enthusiastically exploring her new home town. She wrote:

It was lovely up at the University, in beautiful grounds looking over to the Dead Sea and down on to the Old City. There is a fine open-air amphitheatre, and a beautiful building for Jewish Studies. They are adding new buildings and have most impressive plans for development into an entire university city up on Mount Scopus.

The Hadassah Hospital was even more amazing. It is a really finished work of art, complete in every detail of building and equipment, and lavish on the American scale. We were shown around very nicely and spent a thoroughly enjoyable day. I have arranged to go up every Thursday to distribute books to the patients and am looking forward to it very much. On Shabbat we were shown around the Old City by a friend of mine, who was born and lives there. In fact her family has been in the same house for over 200 years – if you can call it a house – a cluster of rooms around a courtyard at the top of a winding stone staircase. Her father, Weingarten, is the *mukhtar* of the Old City. [He and his daughters featured prominently in the desperate battle fought there a year later.] We went through the Arab *shuk* again, but this time we saw fascinating things – the way they make most wonderfully elaborate altar candles, dipping cotton into wax, so that at each coating it becomes gradually thicker, until they have massive great things which are painted, then plaited, twisted etc.

We saw oil being squeezed from seeds by a blindfolded donkey turning two great millstones, also the flat cakes of Arab bread called 'piter' being baked. The Arabs insisted on us tasting some straight from the oven. The Weingarten family use some Arab food and the next day the younger sister, who is in my class, brought me a parcel which felt like a leather handbag. Opening it, I found a huge piece of the 'piter' folded up. I quickly hid it before the class could see, but thoroughly enjoyed it afterwards thick with butter!

During our tour we saw the Church of the Holy Sepulchure, from the outside only of course, and naturally finished up at the *Kotel* [Western Wall]. En route, we went into Zedekiah's cave, or more accurately, King Solomon's quarries, by the Damascus Gate. This is a long cave leading into many tunnels under the Old City, where one can plainly see how Solomon obtained his blocks of building stone without using metal tools … The tunnel, through which Zedekiah fled, is also supposed to have led right to Jericho, although it is now blocked by falls of rock. At one point there is an overflowing pool of water from drips coming from above, which in the course of time have worn away a perfect funnel up which one peers without seeing the top. The story is that these are the tears from the 'Wailing Wall' above.

These places, to be battlefields within a few short months, bustled with friendly Arab shopkeepers and curious Jewish sightseers as Esther got to know her adopted city. She revelled in the freedom and sense of belonging, her natural curiosity pulling her ever deeper into Jerusalem, and making it for her more a state of mind than a geographic location.

11 Exploring Palestine

On Sunday 4 May 1947, three weeks after the British had put Dov Gruener and his three fellow fighters to death, Etzel units launched their reprisal. In a defiant and audacious attack on British authority, they breached the massive Crusader walls of the Acre prison, freeing 131 Arabs and all 120 Jewish prisoners. Fifteen people died in the attack, and 23 more were wounded.

As well as liberating 251 detainees from the grim fortress, the operation was a resounding propaganda victory, boosting Jewish morale in Palestine sky-high, and showing the world that the Jews were no longer prepared to be victims. While a majority of Palestine's Jews sharply opposed the violence of the breakaway Etzel and Lehi, there was a growing feeling that the mandate must end at all costs – even if that sometimes entailed giving the British lion a fierce shove towards the door.

Esther's Zionist background opposed the breakaway groups. British Bnei Akiva of the time, with its senior Bachad group, made very clear to its members that the movement aligned with the Yishuv's official leadership. In politics, this meant that the religious Zionists were aligned with the Mapai Party, and in defence, the Haganah. For Esther, however, the situation was not clear-cut. Our father, from whom our Zionism had sprung, was an admirer of the late Zeev Jabotinsky, ideologue of the Revisionist Party (forerunner of Herut and Likud) and inspirer of the breakaway defence movements. As her hatred for British policy in Palestine grew Esther could not help but admire the daring of the Etzel and Lehi. When the time came for her to make her own choice, however, it was to the Haganah that she made her way.

Her letters continued to arrive regularly. On 4 May, she wrote:

> Thursday afternoon I went to the Hadassah Hospital to help with the library books for the patients, which I shall do every week. It was very interesting. In the evening there was the last of the season's subscription concerts, which was the best yet. It was conducted by a very versatile young conductor from America, Leonard Bernstein, who has quite captivated everybody. He conducted a work of his own, *Jeremiah*, in which a passage from *Lamentations* is sung by a contralto. Then he both played and conducted a piano concerto by Ravel, at the same time! – and had to give an encore, which was, I think, Gershwin. Friday afternoon I went to see a good dancer – Deborah Bertonoff – and last night, after I had been to call on the Rakovsky's, we all went to the pictures together – a film I had seen ages ago called *Hurricane*. I seem to have packed into this weekend a great deal of pleasure-making, but somehow one needs the relief and escapism, when one gets the chance for it.

Lag Ba-Omer, a minor festival falling 33 days after Passover, provided further relief and opportunity for escapism. She wrote:

> Children lit dozens of fires all over Jerusalem, on the numerous bare plots in the city. (I did not go to Tel Aviv for the long weekend, as I go to the Hadassah Hospital on Thursday afternoons – you should see me in my white coat!). There were at least half a dozen fires, and the kids burnt figures of Hitler. Did I tell you I have another wisdom tooth growing?

This last sentence jolts me into realising that my big sister Esther was still only 21 years old when she wrote that letter.

In mid-May 1947, the political search for a solution to the problems of Palestine began to move forward. The United Nations, acting on an Australian proposal, appointed an

11-member Fact-Finding Committee on Palestine, charged with submitting 'such proposals as it may consider appropriate for the solution of the Palestine problem' by 1 September.

The atmosphere of uncertainty in the country went up several notches, with no one knowing who would be in control of what the following year – including its education system. On 22 May, Esther wrote:

> It has been a very strenuous week, right up to the end, as we have had the inspectors at school for the whole week. Even two British inspectors came (with their armed police escorts). The Jews had various comments and criticisms to make, but nothing very important. They were more concerned with the system of the school as a whole than with the teachers, as the Government must present an education plan for the whole country. The reason for this urgent inspection was supposed to be secret, but there was an article in the paper which made it fairly obvious that it had something to do with the UN Committee. We finished the week with a discussion about next year's programme … I do not think I shall ever become a good teacher with really young children, under the age of 11. Everybody on the staff has their own particular job and it's no use saying that I am in the wrong one. It's not so bad anyway and the children are very sweet at times.

She went on:

> Things here have been most unexpectedly peaceful these last few weeks, so there is nothing for you to be worrying about. Zada [our father's father] is going to Jerusalem not to Kfar Hess, because Uncle Yaacov's building there is not finished yet. Why can't you feel safe about buying a piece of land near him? Zada looks very well and it struck me when I went home with him yesterday evening that he walks more firmly than ever.

The choice of entertainment available in Jewish Jerusalem's enclave of 100,000 people (many of them ultra-Orthodox) was remarkable. In that pre-television era, people went out far more than now, and Esther seized every opportunity to enjoy what was on offer in theatre, concert hall and cinema. In late May she wrote:

> I returned from Tel Aviv yesterday, and have been busy giving and correcting examinations all day. On Sunday evening we went to a concert with a young conductor just arrived from Rumania, and heard Beethoven's Seventh, which always gives me much pleasure. I had my hair cut for the first time here yesterday. Has Daddy any further plans about travelling?

On 6 June:

> I have had lots of work this past fortnight, correcting exams and writing reports, though I have also been out a lot this week. Last night I went to see the Habimah theatre, which should have come to Jerusalem long ago, but there was curfew at the time. I saw *Oedipus Rex* produced by Tyrone Guthrie when he was here – I'd seen the same production in London, which made it very interesting and easy to follow – and I stayed on to see *The Dybbuk*. Both performances were wonderful, really thrilling. *Oedipus* was most impressive and majestic, and the rolling dramatic Hebrew suits the old Greek play very well. *The Dybbuk* was celebrating the 25th anniversary of its performance, and the original actress, Robina, who is really great although she is over 60, took her old part. The Hebrew is simpler, although I cannot follow all of it.
>
> Did I tell you that I now have a fourth Hebrew lesson every week, when we study Bible (Judges), which is very interesting. I also went to a wedding this week, a really Chassidic affair, in the extreme. The *chuppah* was on the roof of a house. The bridegroom was something like the type I saw next day in *The Dybbuk*, also attended by his fellow

yeshivah students. The poor bride was all wrapped around and pinned up and had all her jewellery removed. Tonight I am invited out to supper. I went to see *The Story of G. I. Joe,* a very good American war film.

And a few days later:

Today I was invited to a nice tea party at the Hadassah Hospital for one of the library workers. We are in need of books in Yiddish and Polish for the new immigrants, especially from Cyprus, who are now in the hospital – could Daddy perhaps spare something? On Thursday we have a holiday – the King's birthday! Yesterday and Shabbat we witnessed quite a parade of most marvellous new cars on the Jerusalem streets in preparation for the UN Commission. Now today we have seen the first disturbances for some time.

On 19 June 1947, the Evelina de Rothschild school began its ten-week summer vacation, which was to prove a watershed in Esther's life. The very next day she was off to get her first taste of secular Jewish culture at an event which became a landmark in relations between observant and non-observant Jews – the Dalia dance festival. The festival was held on a Shabbat, and as it entailed travel, use of musical instruments, spotlights and ticket sales – all proscribed by religious law on the Jewish day of rest – it became a *cause célèbre* in the struggle being fought for the character of the future Jewish state. It's a struggle that continues to this day: should the state be conducted according to *halachah,* the ancient Jewish legal system, or should its laws be secular, like the majority of its inhabitants? In 1948, David Ben Gurion papered over this dangerous ideological rift by insisting that the pre-independence *status quo* be maintained. It was events like the Dalia festival that threatened the delicate balance of that pre-state era.

Esther seemed unaware of the political controversy swirling around the festival as she made her way to Dalia:

Tomorrow morning I am going away for the weekend – first of all to Dalia, a kibbutz south of Haifa, where they have a big natural amphitheatre where a festival of dancing and music is being held in the late afternoon. I am going with some friends and we shall spend Shabbat at a nearby kibbutz …

Haifa, Friday. Just arrived – as always the journey to Haifa is beautiful. We left Jerusalem at nine this morning. Lovely weather of course, not too hot, especially in Jerusalem where some nights are quite cold when there's a wind. We have to bring a blanket each as everybody spends the night at the festival out in the open – they expect thousands there, as the first time it was held three years ago, it was said to have been a wonderful affair.

Writing from Jerusalem four days later:

We spent some hours in Haifa, and then, with the brother of one of the girls and two of his friends, we joined the enormous queue for special buses to Dalia, where the dance festival was held. Well, just the sight of an endless procession of buses, cars, motor-bikes, moving ever so slowly in single file, leading from roads on all sides through the beautiful hills overlooking the Jezreel Valley was alone worth seeing. It was impossible to see the beginning or the end of this long trek – 25,000 people were there, just think of that for this small land, and they came from all over the country.

In a way, I regretted going because it was not an affair for Shabbat, and yet it was worthwhile. It was held in an enormous natural amphitheatre outside the kibbutz, in darkness, with the stage illuminated by a searchlight projector. Although we were sitting far away, we could see and hear everything. We took a blanket each and everybody sat on the ground. The members of the UN Committee were not present, more the pity, but members of the Secretariat were, and commented that what impressed them was that so many people should come such a long way simply to enjoy a cultural experience. They had never seen anything like it.

The festival performances went on until four o'clock in the morning, different kibbutzim sending in teams of dancers and orchestras to perform their own particular dances and songs, some of which were very good indeed. The girls mostly wore lovely dresses with traditional Yemenite embroidery. The first item was performed with blazing torches on the opposite hillside, and was very impressive. There were two dances by Arabs. The worst of this is that when they start dancing they do not know when to stop. People say that they can keep it up steadily for 24 hours! The second time people started clapping them off, but it only encouraged them, until everybody was soon clapping in time to the music. At the end, in true Hashomer Hatzair [the non-religious left-wing pioneering movement] good-neighbourly policy, they asked them for an encore, and when we left at daybreak they were still going strong, Jews and Arabs together in impromptu style.

We walked over to Ein Hashofet nearby, where we spent Shabbat. It's a marvellous kibbutz of the Hashomer Hatzair, named in honour of Judge Louis Brandeis, the American Zionist leader. We had a letter of introduction to one of the women on the kibbutz, who received us very nicely. She is a part-time journalist, a former American, working at the moment with the UN Committee, but she is one of those who built up the place from scratch. It is the same age as Tirat Zvi, begun 10 years ago, but much more developed, as they get lots of money from America. She knew that we would not eat the food, and arranged for us to have salads, and a nice room for the night. We slept a lot and it was beautifully peaceful all day and we wandered around and saw everything.

Esther spent the next day in Haifa:

We all took a bus ride up to Mount Carmel, and I stayed there when the others went back to Jerusalem ... When you come, I rather hope that you will want to live in Haifa – the sea is wonderful and the bay! You can only tell sea from sky by the deeper shade of blue, and up on the mountain it is as fresh and cool as in Jerusalem, although it is hotter in the town. The place is growing rapidly, whole new quarters are going up. Building goes on in Jerusalem all the time too, but I am afraid that the British are succeeding in discouraging Jews from settling here. The place is not so good for business and whoever can, leaves. Even now, when things are comparatively quiet, there is an atmosphere of constraint.

Esther's championship of Haifa as a future home for our parents had more impact than we realised at the time. Although her letters lay untouched for so many years, much of what she wrote lingered in our memories. Some 11 years after she wrote that letter, my wife and I left Kibbutz Lavi with our first baby and made our home in Haifa for the next 24 years, looking out at the incredible view of sea and bayside from our balcony window. In 1967, 20 years after Esther's letter and shortly after the death of our father, our mother at last decided to make her home in Israel, and came to join us in Haifa.

Esther's marathon letter about her trip north filled three air letter forms. She went next to see her friend Ida on Sdei Eliyahu. 'Ida is getting on very well and seems to be fixed up with a boy, although it is not supposed to be official,' she wrote.

> She is not getting married for at least a year, as she is coming to the Seminary in Jerusalem in September. I at the moment have plenty of other interests and, for me, marriage can wait. After all, I have time, and I certainly have no intention of rushing into anything. Quite honestly, I have hardly had time to catch my breath. And as for an excuse for coming here, I hope that you are not going to wait for that!

Our mother, it seems, had been urging Esther to give her a 'good excuse' to make the journey to Palestine. The letter continued:

> We went over yesterday to Ein Hanatziv, the new, third religious kibbutz near Tirat Zvi and Sdei Eliyahu. They had

just had a robbery an hour before. We went over on the bread cart pulled by a donkey over a bumpy road, and came back in a lorry. Ein Hanatziv is still in a very raw state a year after it was founded, and it is interesting to watch how it is being built and developed.

A few days later, on Shabbat 28 June, Esther celebrated her 22nd, and last, birthday.

12 Standing Room Only

June and July 1947 were crucial months in that much disputed territory known as Mandatory Palestine. The Talmudic discourse of two men, each holding on to one *tallit* (prayer shawl) and claiming it as his was being played out on a grand scale along the eastern shores of the Mediterranean – along with a third player, the British Empire, which declared it had been given the *tallit* for safe-keeping, and wasn't going to let go. The United Nations had adopted the Solomonic role: it dispatched its Special Committee on Palestine (UNSCOP), which was now touring the country trying to formulate recommendations for a viable solution.

The Zionist movement had long ago given up on the territory east of the Jordan River. Despite its inclusion as part of Palestine in the Balfour Declaration's promise to the Jews, it had been granted entirely to the Arabs in 1921, when the Kingdom of Transjordan was formed there and the British appointed the Emir Abdullah as its king. Now the moment of truth had arrived: the fate of the land between the Jordan River and the Mediterranean Sea was to be decided. Jewish leadership in Palestine, backed by the Zionist movement's mainstream in the Diaspora, was ready for further partition. A Jewish state was desperately needed as a home both for Jewish Holocaust survivors from Europe and for the oppressed Jews in Arab countries. The justice and logic of renewing Jewish sovereignty in the ancient Jewish homeland seemed overwhelming.

On Friday, 5 July, Esther managed to get a ticket to the first public session of the UNSCOP hearings. She wrote:

It was a most impressive and interesting experience. We had good front seats and heard Ben Gurion, Rabbi Fishman (who, as usual, was unintelligible and speaks Hebrew just like Yiddish) and Mr Horowitz, a very able Jewish Agency authority on statistics of the country. I see the English newspapers do not report on the meeting at all. They always give exaggerated cover to terrorist incidents, but would never report on our fair chance to state our case against misrule here. I hope you get the chance to read how Ben Gurion put it. At one point he almost wept – it was like Yom Kippur.

Chaim Weizmann also took the floor, using his brilliant oratory and biting wit to plead the case for partition. He had been without an official role since the 22nd Zionist congress held in Geneva the year before – a forum where he had exhorted delegates to have faith in the British government (for which, he became, in his own words, 'the scapegoat for the sins of the British government'). At UNSCOP his failing eyesight prevented him from reading any prepared speech, but he spoke very persuasively nonetheless, producing the necessary documents to support his case, along with a warm message from the South African statesman, Field Marshal Jan Smuts. Weizmann's partition plan was based on the Peel Commission's recommendations of exactly ten years earlier, with the addition of the Negev to Jewish Palestine.

Esther wrote:

Weizmann spoke extremely well, of course – an interesting, good-humoured, sincere address. We really have some great men who can express themselves for us with dignity and ability. The only trouble is that the others are really not interested in our case on its own merits. However, if they do decide to act finally, it will be partition and some kind of Jewish State – only we won't be able to call it the *Yishuv* any more, because as Weizmann said, there will be standing room only! [A pun on *Yishuv*, which comes from the word to *sit*.] If you don't believe that Jews here have the will to find a way in every aspect of life, you should just see the buses we travel in – usually holding 70 and built for half that number. You would be surprised how many can squeeze in, with a little cooperation all round!

The UNSCOP members toured the length and breadth of the country, lobbied intensively by the Jews and largely boycotted by the Arab leaders, who were not prepared for any kind of compromise. Unrest continued while the Committee went about its work. British soldiers and police were targeted by the breakaway groups, and in reprisal for these bloody incidents, British soldiers attacked Jews on the streets, often concealing their identity by dressing in civilian clothes. The situation was exacerbated by a British decision to execute three men captured after the Acre prison breakout: UNSCOP's appeal to the British government for clemency was turned down, and Meir Nakar, Yaacov Weiss and Avshalom Habib joined the tragic list of Jews put to death by the British. Reprisal quickly followed with the kidnapping and killing of two British sergeants by breakaway groups, despite pleas from the chief rabbis and the Jewish Agency leadership for their release.

With all this tension and drama, life in Palestine continued, and Esther seemed undeterred by the danger in the streets. She went to a concert in the amphitheatre on Mount Scopus,

a great joy, with a most marvellous view across the desert as far as the Dead Sea and the mountains of Transjordan in the extreme distance. Sitting on the steps among the fir trees, with a mountain breeze blowing, was a sheer delight. When the concert was over, we discovered the buses were all full, so we walked home down the hill toward old Jerusalem, which by then was twinkling with lights. It was about an hour's walk, hot but nice, and I came across my first snake – fortunately I saw it before it saw me! One also sees lots of lizards of different sizes, running across the hot walls of the Arab mud-houses, exactly the same shade of grey, so that it is difficult to see them.

Staying again with her relatives in Bat Yam, Esther wrote:

> I have just spent the morning by and in the sea and it was glorious. The water was almost hot, although one cannot swim much as the waves are high. Living here is like one long holiday, except that one does not have that holiday crowd packing the beaches, especially on a weekday, so it is really delightful.

The holiday mood broke on Thursday 17 July 1947, a fateful day in the history of the Jews. On that Thursday, as the UNSCOP members visited the port city of Haifa, a sea battle was raging 25 miles off the coast, as yet another boatload of Holocaust survivors tried to run the British blockade and reach the shores of their Promised Land. Crammed aboard a rickety cargo boat renamed *Exodus 1947* were 4,552 refugees, crewed by volunteers, many of them American Jewish ex-servicemen. The boat's captain was Ike Aharanovitz, on whom Leon Uris later modelled the character Ari Ben Canaan in his novel *Exodus*. The British had shadowed the *Exodus* across the Mediterranean and, signalled by their naval HQ, attacked it with six warships in sight of Palestine. It was rammed and boarded at night, and in the four-hour battle that followed, 146 Jews were injured and three killed – one of whom was Bill Bernstein, a young American volunteer crew member.

Once the Royal Navy and Marine troops gained control of the boat, they brought it into Haifa port. The survivors were dragged ashore and transferred to three prison ships for deportation back to Europe.

The second act unfolded far from the eyes of UNSCOP, on 29 July at Port de Bouc on the French Mediterranean coast. The French government had offered the refugees asylum, but all except 21 refused to land, and the French adamantly refused to be party to the forced landing of the Jews on their soil.

The third and final act came six weeks later on the dockside in Hamburg, Germany, where 1,000 heavily armed British troops dragged the younger and more able-bodied of the survivors into a cage erected for them on the dockside, urging them on with steel-tipped truncheons. Women, children and the elderly filed off the boat without resistance. The press was kept at bay, with one journalist arrested for photographing the refugees.

The saga of the *Exodus* ended with internment in the former German army camps at Poppendorf and Amstau, where conditions were described by a British officer as 'the most wretched and abominable accommodation' he had ever seen. Worse yet, these camps were staffed by local Germans, under a small team of British officers. Here the British subdued the refugees with high-pressure hoses. British timing, however, was quite wrong. Instead of impressing UNSCOP with a display of orderly government, they convinced many of its members that the Jews deserved a more humane solution to their desperate struggle for a homeland.

Nor did the battle of the *Exodus* end with incarceration in Germany. Two weeks later, the British delivered an ultimatum to the refugees: either accept resettlement in France or receive the status of German citizens, with rations accordingly reduced – this at a time when Germans were literally dying of malnutrition. The response was an offer from 11,000 concentration camp survivors housed in nearby Bergen-Belsen to pass their precious monthly allocation certificates over to the *Exodus* passengers, thus giving them priority in entering Palestine. Eventually, the barbed wire barriers were removed and the camps came under Jewish administration

The long-drawn-out saga of the *Exodus* brought the unhappy story of the homeless Jew forcibly to the attention of a hitherto indifferent world. A rabbinically-authorised Fast Day for the *Exodus 47* was followed by a national Hamburg Day when the three prison ships reached the mouth of Hamburg's River Elbe: all Jewish work and traffic halted for two hours in Palestine. Two months later, on 29 November, the UN voted to partition Palestine – the crucial vote which led inexorably to the establishment of the state of Israel in May the following year.

The *Exodus 47* epic thus reached far beyond Poppendorf and Amstau, and it still lives on in the Jewish psyche. Its effect on Esther, who lived through the daily drama, was pivotal. She remembered only too clearly the young survivors she had worked with in England, teenagers shattered by memories and nightmares, and she was flooded with shock, disgust and anger at British treatment of the *Exodus 47* survivors. It served to erase her last vestige of trust in the British among whom she had lived most of her life, and to convince her irrevocably that her future lay with the reborn remnants of her people.

Around the dining table in our house in Stamford Hill, we talked endlessly of the ill-fated boat, and there was a lot of 'I told you so' in our conversations. Like Esther, we had been raised to respect, even revere, the British way of life. During the war years, we had relied on our national hero, Winston Churchill: while he was at the helm, there was no danger of Hitler crossing the English Channel and unleashing his terror on our community.

Once the war was over, we Cailingold youngsters, influenced by the socialism of our youth movement, rejoiced at the election of a Labour government – even though our father, a lifelong liberal, saw it as a major tragedy. Anything even approaching socialism was anathema to him; he railed against the evils of communism and its dangerous influence even on the prosaic British Labour Party of those days. Ernest Bevin and his cohorts were no more or less than father had expected.

For Esther in Jerusalem, things must have become clear far earlier than for us still in London. The events of 1947 made it much simpler for her to discard her English ways and identify totally with her adopted country within her first months there. By the summer of 1947, however, we too were no longer comfortable in England and craved anything with the flavour of the Promised Land. A great day for us was when the first 'Jewish' ship, the *SS Kedma,* sailed to Palestine from London, the first time a Jewish flag had been flown on a ship sailing down the River Thames. We all took the day off and flocked to the quayside to catch a glimpse of this wondrous vessel, painted blue and white, which was actually going to touch the treasured shores in a few days' time.

On 20 July, Esther wrote:

> Is there anybody I know coming on the *Kedma*? I was hoping that you would make use of the opportunity to

come on it, and it would have been ideal for Booba and Zada too, as the future trips will all be from Marseilles, which means making the awkward journey through France. Anyway, I hope when Daddy comes back from America he will begin immediately on arrangements for both of you to come out here – and you should bring Booba and Zada with and leave them here.

Auntie Leah is staying with me now. Yesterday, Shabbat, we spent at the Rakovsky's with whom she is very friendly – but a pleasant day was spoilt in the evening by an explosion close by and an alert which made us very late getting home. We had a shock when two policemen came in suddenly, but they only wanted to use the phone. They were very decent fellows, spoke Hebrew and chatted for a while. There were a lot of soldiers and the usual fuss – but, as they reported by phone, they could do nothing and the culprits got away. There have been frequent explosions these last few days and constant sirens, which are meant to stop the traffic. Fortunately they do not impose house curfew any more, except in Netanya [where the search was then going on for the two kidnapped British sergeants].

I had tickets for a bus excursion to the Dead Sea on the second day of a bad *hamsin*. There it is always hot, and people thought that I was mad to go there on such a day but I thoroughly enjoyed it. It must have been well over 100 degrees, but I have acclimatised myself very well and do not mind the heat at all. We stopped at various interesting and historical spots en route, and a guide explained it all, photographs were taken, we stayed a short while in Jericho and then spent an hour bathing in the Dead Sea. You really do float on top, in fact you cannot swim, except on your back, because your legs stick out of the water. It stings terribly in your eyes, but you just lie for a minute with head up to the sun, and it all dries up. It was so hot that the pebbles on the beach were burning, so that one had to go down to the water in sandals.

Events in Palestine in the summer of 1947 seem strangely mixed, with the Jewish community trying to lead some semblance of normal life, despite the efforts of the Arabs – and to a great extent the British – to prevent this. Some 55,000 Jewish refugees were imprisoned in Cyprus, of a total of 70,000 who tried to breach the British blockade and reach Palestine. That same summer saw the kidnap and murder of a 16-year-old Jewish boy by British Major Roy Farran. Tried and acquitted, he was hunted down by the Jewish underground after his return to Britain. A parcel bomb intended for him killed his brother.

Palestine was by now virtually a police state, with one soldier or policeman for every 13 inhabitants. British commander General Barker had issued a secret order to his troops to 'strike the Jew in the place where he feels it: in his pocket'. This all too familiar anti-Semitism was condemned in the House of Commons, but widened still further the chasm between the Jews and the British. In Netanya, 15,000 people were being held in a 'controlled area' (a euphemism for martial law) because of the murder of the British sergeants. In Europe, the death-camp survivors were awaiting their salvation, some of them defying the authorities and attempting the clandestine journey to Palestine.

One brighter note was the release of the 24 youngsters of Birya, who had been imprisoned since May of the year before, for defying the British and returning to re-establish their settlement in the hills near Safad.

Up on Mount Scopus in Jerusalem, the First World Congress of Jewish Studies was held. This was an opportunity for Diaspora Jewish educators to get into Palestine, including the British contingent who travelled on the *Kedma*. Some took the risk of staying on and becoming 'illegal' immigrants.

In Britain, the hanging of the two sergeants caused an upsurge in anti-Semitism, with violent demonstrations by fascist groups. Anti-Jewish riots broke out in London, Liverpool and Glasgow, and synagogues were set alight in the London suburbs of Willesden and Finsbury Park. It was little wonder that Esther constantly urged her family to join her in Palestine. If Jews were to be attacked, they should come home to their own Land, where their chances of defending themselves were infinitely greater.

13 Business as Usual

In the last week of July 1947, we received three letters from Esther, all written from Kibbutz Kfar Etzion – which was to go down in flames some ten months later.

> I have been wanting to visit this kibbutz and the neighbouring ones for a long time, and now that there is curfew in Jerusalem and constant alerts, I thought I would take the opportunity. It is only about 45 minutes bus ride up into the mountains around Jerusalem, and it is really lovely up here, with a glorious view and a cool breeze in the evenings. I am writing this in the kibbutz grounds, and what is most striking is the contrast between the fine modern buildings that they have constructed, in which they accommodate holiday guests, and the kibbutz members sweating away at the building site, hurrying to complete new houses before winter.
>
> In the summer, all the kibbutzniks live in tents. The place is only four years old but is very impressive, with a large glass-fronted hall, erected by a group of Hebrew authors in memory of a South African member who was killed. There are several South Africans here, but they are leaving to form the nucleus of an Anglo-Saxon group at Kibbutz Ein Hanatziv. They want me to join them, and I wish I were free to do so. Maybe sometime in the future. I told them that they could do with some of you from England – conscientious, enthusiastic and Orthodox young people. The kibbutz also has a well-equipped lending library, a reading room which is available to the guests, and

a fine dining hall. Even the nearby kibbutz Massuot Yitzchak, which is barely two years old, has a holiday-home, very beautiful and with a most modern kitchen. The best of all are the surrounding hills, which make a perfect setting for the place.

One of the first things one notices in the country is how everything links up with Biblical and later history. The Kfar Etzion district must have been well-populated in former times. Although it all looks so barren now, there are fascinating caves in which remains have been found (although for good reasons this is not to be made public). Even on our trip to the Dead Sea, through miles of complete desert wilderness, there was always something to be heard about almost every stone. I still have a Sodom apple as a souvenir. It is a large green fruit, empty inside the balloon-like skin, except for some poisonous stuff. This is the only kind of produce from that region, except for the fruit and vegetables of Jericho, and the minerals, particularly potash. There is some farming on a kibbutz that has been set up there in the terrific heat, with salty soil that they have to purify before use.

That same summer, a talent spotted in Esther long ago by her elementary school teacher, Miss Dalton ('Esther's English is so extremely good for her age'), came into use beyond the lengthy and frequent letters. On 6 August she wrote:

On Friday I am going to Be'erot Yitzchak, the first religious kibbutz in the Negev, as I was asked to write an article about the place. This will be the second in a series of articles for a magazine called *Igeret LaGolah* (Letter to the Diaspora), published by the Jewish Agency for immigrants from English-speaking countries. Perhaps you can receive copies in England.

Most of Esther's articles appeared after her death.

Be'erot Yitzchak had been the sole religious kibbutz in the south of the country, close to Gaza, until that summer when

Sa'ad was founded – the first kibbutz established entirely by local Bnei Akiva graduates. In the bitter fighting of the following year, as the Egyptian army marched on Tel Aviv, Sa'ad held out, but Be'erot Yitzchak fell and was destroyed in the fighting. Abandoning its original site, its surviving members moved to the old Templar village of Willhelma, near the airport at Lydda, to rebuild their kibbutz.

Esther starts a letter to her friend Hannah in England by describing her visit to the original Be'erot Yitzchak:

> I have just come back from Shabbat in Be'erot Yitzchak, my first visit to the Negev. This was the first time that I got the impression of size during my visits, because our Land is a neat, compact, little one, but in the Negev you get seemingly vast stretches of open land. The people on the kibbutz are a nice friendly lot and there is one particularly charming American girl.
>
> Tell me how things feel in England now. Why do our Jews have to hang on until they are thrown out of a place? It is much more dignified to leave of your own free will, and now that you have had a clear warning, I hope it has woken people up a bit.

She repeated this remark about the 'clear warning' in letters to our parents. She was referring to the vitriolic anti-Semitism then rampant in Britain, under the seemingly passive eye of the police, and provoking little government reaction. This was all too reminiscent of what we had read about the pogroms in tsarist Russia and elsewhere in eastern Europe. The Kishinev pogroms, described so vividly in Chayim Nachman Bialik's *The City of Slaughter* (virtually required reading in the movement), seemed to be coming to London's Ridley Road, and Esther was bewildered that family and friends, many of whom had escaped from Hitler's Germany, could sit back and watch it happen.

In mid-August, she headed north, this time to gather material for an article on Safad, the city of the Cabbalists. She told our parents:

I have been asked to write some more articles for the magazine issued by the Jewish Agency's Youth Department for abroad, and they are sending me to Safad and Birya. I am writing this now sitting in a bus – after waiting in a long queue. We are waiting in a convoy of buses which will move off together. I think this will quickly blow over, as the Arabs are also antagonistic to the British, and they are not likely to play along with their game, which is strife between Jews and Arabs, which would just prove the British case. I only feel sorry for the old-timers here, who have been through so much already. Aunt Leah, for instance, is taking it very hard. It's a strain on the nerves more than anything else, because when one comes to assess the damage, whether it's the shooting in Jerusalem or the stone-throwing in Tel Aviv, it transpires that the noise is the greatest nuisance. What about your own particular line in riots at the moment? You write nothing of the situation or the atmosphere in the street.

Back in Jerusalem, Esther took up the description of her Galilee trip, with its highlight, visiting the legendary Birya, whose fight had loomed so large in the summer camp programmes of Bnei Akiva in Britain the year before. The battle of Birya had been fought against the British not the Arabs. She wrote:

> went off almost immediately to Birya ... The air there is just exhilarating, but very dry after the dripping heat of Tel Aviv. We had to walk up the hill to reach Birya, which stands as a grey stone fortress on top of one of the hills. I was able to picture how the events which we heard and read about so much last year, actually took place. Then the multitude of young pioneers from all over the country swept up those hills in the teeming rain, with the muddy ground underfoot made more dangerous with endless stones and rocks. The place is actually a little stone fortress, built by the British as part of a string of such installations intended to protect the borders of Palestine from invasion

from the north. The whole compound is surrounded by a barbed wire fence. The watch-tower is not the usual open, simple wooden structure, but also a solid stone building, serving a double purpose.

As I came into the courtyard, the first thing that struck me was the Bnei Akiva emblem, worked in white stones, just the same as we had at last year's camp. But what struck me most was that, although I knew the members were from Palestinian Bnei Akiva, I had expected to see people who were already grown-ups, not these 'babies' who are leading the hard responsible life of men and women. They are no older than Asher and his friends and they are already manning a fortress. They have been here for six months and the prospects are fairly dim. The land all around has been in Jewish hands for 50 years and is now owned by the Jewish National Fund, but in the court case the Arabs won!

I returned home yesterday after travelling most of the day – by bus of course – was I stiff! The journey from Safad down through the hills to the Sea of Galilee and Tiberias is marvellous. There it was very hot, as usual, but Jerusalem is cold in the evening. Thank goodness the curfew has been lifted. It does not look as though I shall have any use of my new dress. I left it at the dressmaker in Bat Yam partly because, with curfew and alerts in Jerusalem, I had no use for it, and partly because I was just in no mood to put on new clothes – I was relieved when the thing was finished and then wanted to have no more to do with it – in fact I have not even seen it with the buttons on. Thank goodness yesterday was the last day of Ramadan and the Moslem holidays – a very tense time. It passed peacefully, so we are hoping it will stay that way the whole year.

It did, in fact, appear there was at last some movement concerning the future of Palestine. UNSCOP's report had stated categorically: 'The Mandate must be cancelled.' The British government was not ready for this, but there was support for it in the British press. The immediate result of the Committee's findings on the ground, however, had been an escalation of violence in Palestine, inspired, as so often, by Muslim clerics during the Ramadan period.

As the long summer vacation of 1947 drew to a close, Esther's letters were increasingly filled with growing impatience with the mandatory authorities, and a total scepticism about their official announcements. Learning that the British media could not be depended on for accurate news, she was beginning to acquire her own sources for reliable information from among the ever-widening circle of family and friends. The fate of the *Exodus 47* passengers, then sadly plying their way back to Europe aboard prison ships, was one example.

She wrote on 21 August:

> It is difficult to get a real picture just from the news reports, and what you hear about things here, I just cannot imagine. They print such shameless lies and distortion. In the Hebrew newspapers we read the details of the hunger strike on the immigrant ships and then I listened to the BBC reporting in sarcastic tones that the whole thing is just propaganda! I have now heard that they have admitted that this was a mistake, but the spokesman says that a correction will not be issued. It just seems that they have abandoned all interest in honesty and decency. Were you ever informed that all those terrorist incidents, every single story reported during the past year, even by the highly reputable *Daily Telegraph*, were false or distorted? There were things I did not know myself at the time about the King David Hotel bombing amongst others. At first I thought it was all local stories and exaggerations, but now I hear and see the deliberate dishonesty of the political powers who deal with this country.
>
> School starts a week from Monday – 1 September. I shall be glad to get back to work even though I know that it will again be very hectic … I met the inspector who monitored my lessons in school last year, and in introducing me to someone, he said that I teach at Evelina and very well too! This was the first complimentary thing he said, as at the time he only mentioned the faults!

While Esther's letters still arrived in London regularly and with much detail, we now know that she was omitting more and more of what was happening. There was heavy firing in Jerusalem on Sunday 31 August, for example, but not a word appeared about the sniping and explosions in her letters home. The sense of excitement and adventure with which she had reacted to the disturbances in her first months in Palestine seems to have evaporated as realisation set in that what was happening on Palestine's streets was far more than a passing adventure. She became much more cautious in her letters, clearly unwilling to alarm our parents by underlining the fact that she was living in a virtual battle zone. Another consideration may have been security: while Palestine's Jewish community saw the Haganah as its official defence force, it was still an illegal, underground organisation and thus a secret. Esther quickly learned that the less she wrote home about the fighting, the healthier it would be for the men and women of the Haganah, and the less she would worry our parents.

Despite the unrest and frequent violence, civilian life in Jerusalem continued with every effort to live up to the Londoners' wartime slogan 'Business as Usual'. With the Jewish shopping area evicted from Jerusalem's town centre the year before so that the British could set up their 'Bevingrad' security zone, a new commercial building went up a short distance away and opened on 1 September 1947. The 'columns building' on Jaffa Road, which was Jerusalem's first version of a shopping mall, still stands today.

Esther wrote home on 1 September, at the end of what seems to have been an exhausting first day back at school, impatient with the way the principal, Mrs Levy, ran the school, and comparing staff meetings with the Mad Hatter's tea party!

> This year I have Class IV, older girls than the last lot, which I enjoy more although they are a difficult lot. However, I hope we shall carry on as well as we started today. I am also teaching them History, and actually have one lesson less than last year.

105

To Hannah in London, she wrote:

> Here school has started again. The teacher from
> Manchester who has just come out seems a very pleasant
> person, and we are getting along well. She is older than I,
> but young enough to be chummy. [This was May Wallfish,
> who later followed Esther into the Haganah.] I am det-
> ermined, for the sake of efficiency and common sense, not
> to work so hard. Only pray for me please to have patience
> and fortitude, and above all, iron nerves! What I haven't
> learnt during these past months and learnt the hard way
> too! But it's life and it's living and I am satisfied.

'School is so rigid and formal, which was acceptable in
England, but here one can achieve much more in a spirit of
friendliness and natural behaviour,' she complained in a family
letter.

> I have started Hebrew lessons again after the summer
> break. Jerusalem is very cool now in the mornings and
> evenings although it is still hot under the daytime sun. The
> general reaction here to the UN plans which have just been
> announced is pretty favourable and the atmosphere is now
> much better. Things have been so uncertain and depressing
> that any kind of concrete suggestion is welcome. It is still
> very difficult to imagine that there will soon really be a
> solution to our problems.

As schoolchildren in Palestine settled back at their desks that
September, the British released seven Arabs who had been
sentenced to life imprisonment for their role in the bloody riots
of 1936. British troops and police made house-to-house searches
throughout Jerusalem, leaving the inevitable damage to
property and goodwill in their wake.

A flurry of letters arrived in late September, as Esther
celebrated the festivals away from the family for the first time.
Rosh Hashanah, the Jewish New Year, fell on 15 September that
year. Esther's eve-of-the-festival letter begins with the

customary fervent prayer that we all be inscribed in the Book of Life for the coming year, and that we should all meet up again soon in our Land. She continues:

> We have only too much to ask of the New Year, and for me at any rate, the asking will be something more real and personal than before. If we may be granted just a little peace, a slight feeling of security, some hope for the future! So far every year for me has brought some greater gift. I have never lacked anything material that you could give me, and have always acquired anything of any real value that I desired. I can say with full satisfaction that every wish of mine has been fulfilled. The past year has seen the achievement of the most important of them, and in the course of that year I have learnt and experienced more in a short time than in all the years that went before. I suppose that would have been so anyway, but so many new steps were taken in one period, and the learning has not all been so easy and pleasant – but for that too, I must be grateful.
>
> Now I can only pray, as we all should, that all those who are bearing the sufferings of our people, should receive any merit or grace that we can earn for them. They must receive Divine blessing and help, and let us hope that their time has at last arrived.

The day after the festival, Esther recounted her first Rosh Hashanah in Jerusalem:

> Dear Mummy and Daddy, Thank you so much for your letters. I hope that you all spent a happy and satisfying festival, no trouble with synagogue seats etc! I thought of you all the time. I took quite a decent place in a little synagogue nearby. The cantor was quite amateur but I had plenty to pray about for myself, so needed no help. As you see, I did not go to Bat Yam after all. I hope they will not be offended, but I phoned to explain that I could not risk getting back to school late in the morning. I was very uncertain about what to do, but I am now glad that I stayed

in Jerusalem. It was a worthwhile experience to be able to go to the *Kotel* (Western Wall) on the eve of the Festival and to spend my first New Year in Jerusalem.

The first fruits for the New Year were a sight for sore eyes. I bought my first pomegranate, which I am still eating, and I had mango (nice, like a pineapple) and stewed quince, not so good. Also something called curra, tastes like a stewed citrus fruit – very good. Today I bought the first clementines of the season, just like small round oranges. I had quite a few presents to buy, which is accepted practice here for festivals. I bought flowers (very expensive), wine and boxes of chocolates. It is an old Jerusalem custom to make a series of blessings over different cooked vegetables on the first night of Rosh Hashanah – a little bit like the start of the *Seder* on Pesach ... I was thinking during the services here during Rosh Hashanah about last year's services at the Bachad House, and the tunes – remember? Love ... Esther

That same week, before Yom Kippur, Esther wrote:

I am glad you like the photo I sent you, although personally, I think it makes me look half-witted or worse. Here the town seems to be resounding with the hammering of people making *succot* – everyone seems to make one in Jerusalem. Don't forget to pray for rain extra hard this year. We need it very badly, and here one really appreciates the significance of the prayer ...

I saw the film *The Magic Bow*, exquisite music of course, but not much else. I have also bought myself a ticket for the new season's subscription concerts costing five pounds, which made quite a hole in my purse, but I hope it will be worthwhile and something to look forward to each month.

What a sense of security and optimism to buy a season ticket for that fateful winter of 1947/48! Sadly, she got little use out of her five-pound season ticket. The 29 November UN decision to partition Palestine heralded Israel's War of Independence and left little time for concert-going.

At the end of the Yom Kippur day of fasting and prayer, the *shofar* (ram's horn) was, as usual, sounded at the Western Wall. The traditional blast that year, however, summoned up a British police baton charge, which left two Jews wounded and nine arrested. Across this holy site, the call of the muezzin rang out five times a day and church bells regularly pealed, but the British considered the *shofar* too provocative to Palestine's Muslims, and had banned it. It was 20 years before its blast next marked the ending of Yom Kippur at the Western Wall.

September ended with some progress on the political front. Dr Herbert Evatt of Australia was elected chairman of the UN's Ad Hoc Committee on Palestine and showed at once that British Commonwealth members would not be kowtowing to Whitehall. British Colonial Secretary Arthur Creech-Jones announced to the UN his government's rejection of UNSCOP's findings, and its decision to abandon the mandate and withdraw its troops and civilian personnel at an early date. *The Manchester Guardian* accused the government of cowardice, after spending two years trying to impose on the Jews a solution acceptable to the Arabs. Ben-Gurion quickly responded that the only answer was the establishment of a Jewish state there and then. The Arabs made their own quick response, bombing Café Rehavia, on the street on which Esther lived.

The scene was set for the final showdown. On one side were those who supported the Jewish cause for humanitarian reasons; on the other, those who supported the Arabs for political reasons. The fate of the Jewish people once again hung in the balance.

14 New Priorities

During the first two weeks of October, progress at the United Nations continued, most of it favourable to the Jewish cause. Abba Hillel Silver, the veteran Zionist leader and Reform rabbi from Cleveland, responded to Britain's stand on Palestine by declaring that, if and when the British withdrew their troops, security would be maintained by Jewish forces. Because Abba Hillel Silver spoke from within America's Jewish community, his words deeply impressed both the Jews of Palestine and those in Diaspora communities who feared a bloodbath with the departure of the British army. Jan Masaryk, the Czech leader and long-time friend of the Jews, announced himself in favour of UNSCOP's recommendation that separate Jewish and Arab states be established in a partitioned Palestine. Other Slav-bloc members soon followed suit, and in mid-October the United States issued a statement in support of both partition and Jewish immigration to Palestine. The Americans also proposed setting up a UN volunteer force to maintain law and order in Palestine during the transition period.

The most dramatic moment in this prolonged, nerve-racking time came with a surprise speech from Mr Tsarapkin, Counsellor at the Soviet Embassy in Washington, who declared that his country supported most of UNSCOP's recommendations. In sharp contrast to later Soviet policy on Zionism and the state of Israel, he talked of the suffering of Europe's Jews, and continued:

> All this explains why the Jews strive to create their own state, and it would not be just to deny the Jewish people

the right to fulfill this desire. The creation of the Jewish state is a wholly mature and urgent problem. One cannot avoid a solution to this problem, no matter what efforts are made to complicate it and drown it in a sea of references to historical events going back to depths of ages and even of millennia.

Stalin's interest was not in fulfilment of biblical prophesies or ancient homelands, but he grabbed this golden opportunity both to undermine British influence in the Middle East and show a world aware of his tyranny that he was, in truth, 'a great humanitarian'.

In Jerusalem, a spate of bombings was wreaking havoc on the city's consular missions, as extremist groups on both sides tried to score points and make their cases heard. Within a few days in early October, the American consulate-general in Mamilla Road (now Agron Street) was hit by a hand-grenade, the Polish consulate-general was wrecked by an Arab-planned explosion, and a third bomb blew up the Swedish consulate in east Jerusalem.

On 16 October, every Arab state barred entry to any Jew of any nationality, establishing a precedent under which a baptism certificate was often required to gain entry to certain Arab states. Egypt reacted to the increasingly successful Jewish campaign at the UN by moving 7,000 troops into the Sinai, ready to march rapidly north should the Jews declare independence. Syria moved its forces south into the Golan Heights to staging areas around Kuneitra. The British, still masters in Palestine and mandated to protect its sovereignty, denied that these troop movements were in any way threatening. Their sole concern was Palestine's eastern border and the only properly trained and disciplined force in the area, the eastern border's Arab Legion. They had, however, a treaty with the eastern border's King Abdullah, promising no action against Palestine from within the borders of his kingdom. Abdullah's Arab Legion, which was to play a crucial role in the War of Independence, was commanded by a British lieutenant-general, Sir John Bagot Glubb, known as Glubb Pasha, and by British officers down to

111

company level. The Legion was the only Arab army that made any real territorial gains in the war ahead, spearheading the final attack on the Etzion Bloc settlements, capturing Jerusalem's Old City and cutting the Jerusalem–Tel Aviv road. These approaching dangers were not, of course, of interest to the British in October 1947. Their concern was preparing for a possible withdrawal from Palestine in the following year.

Most people in Palestine, by then, must have known that war would be an inevitable precursor of statehood. It was only two years since the Jews of Europe had gone passively to their destruction, with few examples of real resistance. Now, in 1947, many of Palestine's Jews were looking towards the coming war with a sense that at last the time had come to stand up and fight.

The legacy of the Holocaust remained, with hundreds of thousands of survivors in many countries trying to piece together the shards of their shattered families. As our family name is unusual, we assumed all Cailingolds were related, and any mention of that name among survivors brought great excitement. Esther wrote to our mother on 13 October:

> Aunt Leah heard our name on a Hebrew broadcast for missing relatives, and I went to the Jewish Agency to enquire. It was a Yaacov Cajlingold in Italy, seeking his two brothers Zeev and Moshe from Lubinets in Poland. The official said he had not thought it was our family, as we are from Warsaw, otherwise he would have contacted Zada in Tel Aviv. I have sent the details to the family in Bat Yam and should Daddy want to get in contact with him it has to be done through the Jewish Agency.

Yaacov eventually reached Israel via internment in Cyprus. He is looking for his brothers to this day. They fled Poland for the Soviet Union as the Germans advanced, changing their name to something that sounded more Russian when they joined the Red Army in June 1941.

This was how Jews had lived right up to our own generation, and it was exactly this that the Zionist movement was determined to change. The Jews of Palestine were at a chrysalis stage: they were elbow-deep in clearing the wreckage of the Holocaust, but they were also well on the way to winning and enjoying freedom in their own land. Esther had come to Palestine at just this moment in the nation's metamorphosis, and she quickly absorbed the mood of the times.

A change entered Esther's persistent campaign to have the family at least visit her. She writes to our mother:

> About you and Daddy coming out just to see me, I think that having waited so long, you might just as well see first how things are going to work out here. I personally was very bucked to read about America's statement at the UN Committee. It remains to be seen whether Britain really is clearing out of here, and whether the newspaper reports of the last couple of days about Syrian and Transjordanian troop movements towards the Palestine frontier are anything other than bluff, British rumours or British instigation. I was impressed too by Ben Gurion's speech to our National Council, and I think he has the right idea about us being ready to take over if and when Britain quits.
>
> As for the Arabs, when they do throw a bomb, they do not do the job properly! There was a terrific explosion last night which, as it transpires, came from the furthest suburbs right over the other side of Jerusalem. It must have been some bomb, but all it did was frighten the Polish Consul's dog! Suddenly today, in the middle of lunch, the sirens sounded for a similar incident at the American Consulate. However, Jerusalem generally is as normal and as lively as ever, so we shall see how things turn out. Meanwhile I think it will be quicker if I come to see you first, as I was planning to do anyway next summer.

It was a summer that Esther didn't live to see.

The UN was meeting at Lake Success, and Moshe Shertok (Sharrett), soon to be Israel's first foreign minister, had his hands full refuting Arab arguments for full Arab sovereignty over historic Palestine. A brilliant, modest and honourable man, he led a small team of gifted orators who, at that time, were probably more valuable to the Jewish cause than an entire armoured division, which the Jews did not, in any case, possess.

A majority of the world's nations accepted Shertok's honest and forthright factual presentation and his vivid description of the ongoing tragedy. Britain finally understood it had no chance of retaining its position in Palestine, and announced it would withdraw by March 1949! The pace of events was to place this target date almost a year after the state of Israel was established.

In Britain, an official report showed anti-Semitism there at an all-time high, mainly because of unsympathetic press coverage of events in Palestine. The newspapers featured frequent and detailed accounts of British soldiers shot at and blown up by Jews, but noted very few attacks on them by Arabs – when it was, of course, the Arabs who had inflicted ongoing casualties on the British since the early days of the mandate. The Palestine situation was exploited to the full by Oswald Mosley and his Union of Fascists, who had emerged intact from the Second World War, despite the wartime imprisonment of its leaders for security reasons. Mosley still enjoyed the support of sections of Britain's aristocracy, such as the Mitfords, as well as of growing numbers of misfits and xenophobes.

This naturally made life continuously unpleasant for Britain's Jewish community, and many decided to emigrate, the majority to Canada and Australia. Fascism in Britain declined only with economic recovery and a return to relative national affluence, but the establishment of the state of Israel was to give Britain's Jewish community a new self-confidence in responding to anti-Semitism.

It was eight months since Esther had moved into her temporary flat at 59 Ramban Street, and time to move on. On 20 October, she wrote:

> I have taken a new room and shall be moving in on Friday. It is just a little further than I am now, again a house out on the hills with an even finer view and more modern. It is a beautifully maintained flat owned by an American acquaintance of mine who works at the Hadassah Hospital. The room is very pleasant, with a balcony, fully and neatly

furnished and with a maid every day so that I am not even supposed to make my own bed! I had hoped for something cheaper, but again I have to pay 10 pounds a month.

Last night I went to register with the new Home Guard here, and we are called to a meeting this Shabbat morning. Jerusalem is full of posters telling people where they can register, and it's the same in other towns. The posters are also in Arabic! I was just asked for all my particulars and given a brief medical exam right away.

Wow! That piece of news caused quite a stir in our London home, and if Esther thought she could just slip it in unnoticed, she was badly mistaken. Our father, in particular, was aghast at the thought of his daughter's involvement in anything military, although we tried hard to reassure him it was only civil defence, much as he had undertaken during the Second World War.

With hindsight, it's clear that these weeks led up to Esther's total commitment to the Haganah, but we had no idea of this at the time. In her letters, she conveyed a sense of continuing normality, and it was only after her death that we learned how deep and active had been her association with the Haganah during the six months prior to her death. Even had our parents guessed, they would have known they could not stop their strong-willed daughter from so great a geographical distance. But from the moment they received that letter of 20 October 1947, they never ceased worrying about her, and to some extent even entered a state of anticipatory grief.

Esther was equally tight-lipped with her friends in London about her Haganah connection. She wrote to Hannah as well, on 20 October:

School is going fairly smoothly and I am getting into the stride of things. I think the girls mostly like me, and, at last, respect me (not in a good sense I am afraid, as in this school we are required to be domineering). The new teacher from Manchester, May Wallfish, is a very pleasant person, who taught at the old Jewish school there. We always spend Friday evenings together in my room as she lives nearby

115

and I buy in the supper. I am moving again soon. I have taken a nice room but I am hesitating about it because of the price.

Later that week, another chatty letter arrived at our London home:

Yesterday I had to go to the Department of Migration to renew my visa. All I got for my pains were two forms, one for Mrs Levy as a bond that she is employing me. Next Friday I shall be busy moving things over and shall probably move in on Saturday night. I think the address is 24 Benjamin Metudella Street, Rehavia, c/o Mrs Epstein. Mrs Lange wants me to come again that weekend with Miss Wallfish, but we have a meeting of the Home Guard in the morning, so I don't think we will manage …

This week I went to see *Of Human Bondage* – quite interesting. Dr Rieder had lent me the book to read. Thanks for the bundle of papers which arrived during the week … There is still talk of our being inoculated against cholera, though we have not yet been given details. It appears that Mrs Levy had to pay 60 pounds bond money as long as I remain in this country! I told her that I had hoped it would all be different by the time I needed a new visa.

The news of Esther's Home Guard enrolment was shocking enough in itself. More shocking still, however, was how natural it seemed to my devout sister to attend Home Guard meetings on a Shabbat morning. This was a total reversal from the Esther who was meticulous about attending synagogue and insisted that women as well as men pray and study religious texts – not the usual practice in Orthodox Jewish families in those days.

On 27 October, there was violence in Tel Aviv, but on this occasion it was internecine – Haganah forces trying to convince the dissident Etzel that the forthcoming battles for independence would be fought by a single army and under a single command. While the breakaway Etzel and Lehi were determined to give the British a very clear message that they were not wanted in Palestine, the majority of Palestine's Jews were deeply concerned that acts of violence would be viewed as a Jewish failure to maintain law and order. This would give the major powers an excuse for denying Jewish statehood and imposing an international force on Palestine – something to be avoided at all costs. The course followed by the country's official leadership and the Haganah was to give priority to the recruitment and training of the maximum number of soldiers, and acquisition of the arms and *matériel* necessary for war.

In London, Foreign Secretary Ernest Bevin was still expressing his hope that the partition of Palestine could be prevented. To him, to most of his Labour Party colleagues and to the Foreign Office civil servants, a Jewish state would be a major catastrophe because the Arabs would see it as a historic betrayal.

In the midst of this internal strife and preparation for war, daily life continued. Esther moved to her new room at 24 Metudella Street. Twenty-five years later, our mother, by now a widow, bought her first apartment in Israel at 2 Metudella Street, just up the road. Esther wrote on 5 November:

It is a very comfortable and pleasant room, not big and facing north unfortunately, which is not so good for the winter. It is kept spotlessly clean and I can use the kitchen as it is kosher. There is another girl who has a room here, an American, and the owner, Mrs Epstein is an American administrative worker at the Hadassah Hospital. She has a son of 15 and has been a widow for many years. The flat is very nice and there is a lovely view as it is the last house again. I am at the same distance as before from the bus stop. I got to know Mrs Epstein through the library work which I do every week at the Hospital ...

We had the first meeting of the Home Guard business. It is mostly to get people, particularly the older ones, organised in local groups. The first lesson will be next week and I do not know what we will be learning about. When is Geoffrey's bar mitzvah exactly? [It was in July 1948, after Esther was killed.] I don't know whether I can get away in time.

A letter written to Hannah that same week is less guarded:

> I am tired, although it is only Saturday evening, as I haven't
> been well again this week – but this is just between the two
> of us … As you see, I have moved again and that too has
> kept me busy. I have a very comfortable room with nice
> people. School really goes much smoother now – I feel I
> have control and position, but the work is still so hard and
> long. The children here sap all one's strength, just being in
> charge of them.

There then occurred the first break in letters since Esther
arrived in Palestine a year previously. It's unclear today whether
this was the fault of the postal service or because life was simply
becoming more intense for Esther.

At the United Nations, Britain was playing the role of injured
party. Sir Alexander Cadogan, British delegate to the
Subcommittee on Partition, announced that his country rejected
the partition plan, but would withdraw from Palestine by 1
August. Further, its troops would not be available for the
American–Soviet proposal for a smooth transition. Rumours
buzzed in the corridors at Lake Success and around Jerusalem
that the British planned to withdraw only from the territory
allocated to the Jewish state, and concentrate their forces in the
Arab areas.

With British troops and civilians attacked and killed on the
streets of Palestine every day by this time, it was easy to
understand Britain's desire to get out of Palestine as soon as
possible. On 13 November alone, four English civilians were
killed in Haifa, and a soldier was killed and 29 people hurt when
hand grenades were thrown into the Café Ritz on Jerusalem's
King George Street. Palestine's Jewish leadership tried hard to
maintain order and curb the growing anger of the Jewish
population. Press reports of Golda Myerson (Meir)'s three-day
visit to the detention camps in Cyprus fuelled that anger: she
told of the dire conditions in which children were incarcerated
there, particularly 2,000 unaccompanied orphans.

After a break of nearly three weeks, a letter arrived from Esther with Hannah's uncle and aunt, who had been visiting family in Palestine. By then she had lost faith in the postal service. Despite the long gap, the letter is quite short:

> With this wretched curfew again there is nothing left of the day, and it is impossible to get through everything one wants to do. On Friday morning I hope to go to the Immigration Department to begin work on your visas now that I know that you want to come. I do not think it should be difficult, although I do not know why Daddy was refused.
>
> Rivka spent Shabbat with me, which was very nice since May Wallfish, who usually has supper with me on Friday nights, could not come because of the curfew. There were a lot of 'fireworks' then, for the second night running – just wild shooting. For people living in one of the dangerous streets, near a police station for instance, it is much worse than it was for us in the air raids [in Second World War London]. Bullets pour in and there is no protection in a small flat, except to use the furniture as a barricade. Homes are often ruined by burst water-mains or fires. It won't be for long I hope. Thank you for the three bundles of newspapers and Auntie for the *Jewish Chronicle*; they will find a wide circulation when I have finished with them. Rivka tells me that Zada wants them to sell the house in Bat Yam and move with him to Tel Aviv, but of course Aunt Leah will not agree.

Esther's first year in Palestine was ending. In celebration of her first anniversary on 28 November, she invited over nine friends,

> just fitting into the room nicely. There were some Americans, somebody from school, and Ida and her fiancé. I prepared cake, sweets, nuts, fruit and also savoury things in the 'native' style – black and green olives, anchovies on salty biscuits and salted almonds. Thank goodness the curfew has gone. At least, even if we did not receive an invitation [to the marriage of Princess Elizabeth and Prince Phillip], we can thank The Wedding for that. Was there

119

much excitement in London? What a pity you could not show off your new hat and coat against the Duchess of Gloucester's red velvet!

Esther wrote again later that week, describing the tremendous tension in the build-up to the historic vote on UN Resolution 181, which would decide the future of both Palestine and the Jewish people:

> We are all very much on edge and expectant, but the final version of our fate keeps being postponed. The main trend of things seems to be pretty clear by now and cannot be altered much by a vote one way or another. Anyway, I don't think people got much sleep last night as we were listening to speeches and commentaries from America. Now there is nothing to do but wait again until Shabbat morning. You are mistaken about the anniversary of my arrival in Palestine – it is tomorrow the 28th. It is certainly a historic time anyway.

The fate of the Jewish people was sealed that weekend, when representatives of the world's nations, meeting in solemn assembly at Flushing Meadow, New York, voted 33 in favour, 13 against and ten abstaining that Palestine would be partitioned into separate Jewish and Arab states.

The Arabs did not take up their option of a state and chose instead the path of war, which led rapidly to their defeat. It took two generations for them to return to a point at which statehood again became a viable option for them, but rivers of blood would be spilled before the Oslo agreements held out renewed hope of a Palestinian state. There were Jews, too, who opposed the decision, either because of religious or secular anti-Zionism, or because they found a truncated state unacceptable. Events of the past 50 years have proved them wrong. The creation of a Jewish state enabled the revival of a people. From the depths of the Holocaust's fear and despair, the Jewish people have risen to levels of achievement and self-confidence unknown for close to 2,000 years. Had statehood been won a decade earlier, there would have been a safe haven for the millions who perished under Nazi tyranny.

PART THREE

15 Partition

The United Nations on Saturday, 29 November 1947 was frenetic. Exactly 30 years since the Balfour Declaration had regarded with favour the establishment of a Jewish homeland, a Jewish state was at last a real possibility. Proposals and counter-proposals whirled – some aiming for reconciliation on Palestine, others for setting up a Palestinian federation, still others for postponing the vote on partition altogether. Fearing that King Abdullah would seize for Transjordan the area of partitioned Palestine designated for an Arab state, the other Arab nations desperately sought alternatives to partition. For the first time in UN history, armed police were brought into the UN building to guard against outbreaks of violence.

The official history of Israel's War of Independence begins on that November Saturday, since the UN decision in favour of partitioning Palestine into Arab and Jewish territories, and thus creating a Jewish state, triggered immediate and widespread violence against the Jews. In Palestine, the Arabs followed long-established custom: they declared a three-day strike and launched a rampage of shooting and pillage. In Jerusalem, the commercial centre and shops and homes along Mamillah Road and Princess Mary Avenue bore the brunt. In Tel Aviv, four Jews and two Arabs were killed in attacks on Jewish buses. In Haifa, a series of assaults drove Jews from Arab-held neighbourhoods.

Back in New York, Jewish Agency representatives were simultaneously negotiating a $135 million loan to resettle Jewish DPs in Palestine, and trying to persuade America to supply arms to the Haganah.

For me, in London, the Sunday following the UN vote was one of the strangest days of my life. As one of a small group of active young Zionists, I reported to an office in the West End of London to begin the process of being sworn into the Haganah. The Haganah (which, with the birth of the state, became the Israel Defence Forces), was then operating secretly in various countries, mainly acquiring arms and operating *Aliyah Bet*, the 'illegal' immigration of Jews into Palestine. In 1947, it began recruiting Jewish war veterans, particularly pilots, tank and artillery experts, to fight for the future state. *Agents provocateurs* had to be weeded out from among them, and I became one of the Haganah volunteers given this job.

Esther wrote to us on the Monday after the UN vote, her words jumping off the page with excitement:

> Dear All, Mazal tov!
>
> Much as I have to write and want to write now, I am just too tired to sit any more, so this is just to let you know that I survived the celebration. I am terribly busy now, more so than ever, but I shall find time to describe the wonderful and interesting state of affairs that accompany something that occurs once in 2,000 years! For now I can only write Shalom and let us all meet soon in the Jewish State.
>
> P.S. Just time for a bit more, we Jews are supposed ... Just sent home suddenly from school – lively in the streets – first day of the Arab strike. We can take it!

I no longer remember how much we read into her words 'I am terribly busy now, more so than ever ... '. We knew nothing about what Esther did that week until half a year later, four days after her death, when her friend Shulamit Kogan (née Velikovsky, daughter of the late Princeton scientist Professor Immanuel Velikovsky) wrote to us:

> Esther voluntarily – as it was at that time – joined the Haganah a few days before the outbreak of this war for a Jewish State. It must have been at the beginning or during the middle of November. It was then that I first met her, as

I was a member of the group of girls which she joined – Orthodox girls in the more active branch of the Haganah, who did not train on Shabbat.

It was a few days later that we were called upon to be constantly ready as the present war broke out. For the first few days, girls were merely called upon to hide arms under their clothes, either for purposes of transfer or while escorting a boy in certain neighbourhoods, where he might have needed to use a weapon. These arms had to be concealed for fear that the boy would be stopped and searched by the British, the arms confiscated and the boy imprisoned for a long term, as happened on many occasions.

Although Esther was completely new in the group, she immediately undertook additional responsibilities such as helping billet volunteers and other matters made necessary by our working together night and day. After a few days, Esther returned to teaching but continued to take her turn of duty. She made everyone feel cared for by doing all sorts of little things that meant so much to us all.

Esther, so constant a correspondent until now, did not write us a full letter until five days after the UN vote and that 4 December letter was written on scraps of paper rather than on the usual air-letter forms, of which she always kept a good supply.

December 4, 1947

Dear Mummy,

Excuse this scrap of paper – I now have a moment to write and no paper! First of all, I want to assure you all to take anything the BBC reports on Palestine with a large pinch of salt. I heard their news broadcast and it gives a terrible impression. Incidents occur in scattered places as you hear, but otherwise things are calm. We are all on the watch, every Jew is ready and careful and we can deal very well for ourselves. School is as normal, although it comes in the Arab curfew area which is up to 12 noon each day. Many children cannot get there, but the strike is due to end

125

today, so the curfew may be lifted, and I hope that by next week things will be quiet enough for me to go to Tel Aviv. We are having a week's holiday, as Monday, the first day of Chanukah, is fixed for the official celebration of Independence. Yesterday afternoon we went round for the official collection of Defence money, a minimum of two pounds from each wage-earner.

Now to the eventful Saturday night: everybody was rather pessimistic after the last adjournment of the vote, but when it came, it was so sudden that, listening to the decision at Flushing Meadow, I counted the votes wrongly – gave them two extra and us one less – and it still came to a two-thirds majority! I shall never forget that counting – like numbering your last breath of life, or your first! Then at 1.30 a.m. I went to bed, having to be up at 6.00 as usual. We are too far out to hear anything, but then the whole town came out in its pyjamas and assembled impromptu at the Jewish Agency where there were some words from Ben Gurion and Golda Myerson. In the morning, we sent the children home after prayers – and really it was the children who celebrated. They rode round and round the town piled high on lorries or on the roofs of buses, even on tanks along with the soldiers. The afternoon was quiet with a small procession of kids from the Histadrut building to the Jewish Agency where everybody assembled to hear a speech from the head of the Labour Council. Someone took me up on to the roof of the Jewish Agency building and I took photographs which I shall send. Then people were asked to go home and spend the evening indoors. There were some free barrels of wine on the streets, but on the whole, people just drank their usual coffee in a restaurant and then went home to drink a *L'Chaim* toast. One could not even buy a flag to wave. There had been no atmosphere of preparation for celebration, and since curfew started immediately, we knew that there would be little opportunity to do so for some time to come.

All the men of the *Mishmar Haam* [Home Guard] are called out on duty; younger ones are collecting money;

others are waiting if needed; everyone is busy. On Tuesday there were some biggish fires, and no engines to deal with them. The police, with their 'exemplary behaviour', do nothing but get in the way of the Jews who are trying to protect themselves. Sixteen boys were arrested yesterday while busy scaring off the Arabs in one of the livelier spots. It could all be subdued so quickly, but then the British would not be able to say 'we told you so!'

Later. They are still arresting our boys right and left – it's a shame. The new ship was a real boost to morale. [174 Jewish refugees were landed from a small boat at the mouth of the Yarkon River, having beaten the British blockade.] Last Shabbat I met some of the English people on the one-year course at somebody's tea. I spoke with Gubby Haffner, and he and others came to my room and we then all went to the pictures. I wanted to talk with Gubby about Asher, but there was no chance all week.

This last part was written just before Shabbat and clearly not from Esther's own home:

Friday. The night passed peacefully enough but there is very little chance of today continuing the same way, so I wish you all a really sincere Shabbat Shalom.

P.S. I am watching how some of our kids – not more than that – have taken over the position of the police and are stopping Etzel from getting past to start trouble, while the police themselves have moved off to watch our people directing pedestrians and traffic. The police look ridiculous!

The letter is written as a series of scribbled notes, on the back of scraps of paper. On the reverse of one of them is a note: 'Dear Miss Cailingold, I beg you to excuse my daughter Daisy Ticho for being absent from school on Thursday 20 Nov. '47. She did not feel well. With kind regards. Yours sincerely, Dr Ticho.'

Daisy (whose mother was a Jerusalem dentist, whose uncle was a celebrated Jerusalem eye specialist, and whose aunt was the landscape artist Anna Ticho) was then 11, and remembers that she and her friends adored Esther. She recalls:

> She seemed to be much younger and cleverer than the
> other teachers, and her lessons were always interesting. In
> her English lessons she taught us funny songs and we
> would make the effort to remember the words. She was
> also very popular with the other teachers and we always
> saw her in the company of staff members on the way to and
> from school.

One day in March 1948, Daisy and her school friends saw
Esther getting into a Haganah vehicle in downtown Jerusalem
and they waved to her excitedly. That was the last time they saw
their teacher alive.

Despite the frantic political activity and the growing violence
on the streets of Palestine, its Jewish population tried hard to
lead normal lives. Stores remained open, children got to school
on time, and the man in the street, both Jewish and Arab, hoped
and prayed it would all blow over soon. One Old City Arab
leader reputedly said: 'Without interference from outside Arab
nations, there will be no trouble in Palestine.' The problem was,
however, that there was massive interference from outside Arab
nations, their forces boosted by British army deserters, British
fascist volunteers and German ex-Nazis.

Meanwhile, Jewish refugees continued making their way to
Palestine. 'In the first week in December, 467 Jewish refugee
children and accompanying adults were allowed into the
country and joined the settlers in Raanana,' reported *The
Palestine Post*. At a Jewish Agency executive meeting in Jerusalem
on 3 December, plans were aired for integrating a million Jews
during the next ten years. This figure was not unrealistic: by the
end of 1957, some 909,000 immigrants had arrived in Israel,
688,000 of them during the first four years of statehood.

The urgency of this pre-state immigration policy was not only
a response to the wretched plight of Holocaust survivors or even
to ensure a viable Jewish population in Palestine. The week
following the UN vote, riots broke out in Aden, where Yemenite
Jews had gathered awaiting their redemption. In one of many

incidents, 75 Jews were massacred when Muslims fell on helpless men, women and children sheltering in a synagogue. A synagogue in Jerusalem's Old City was also attacked by Arabs – but here, it ended differently. A Haganah unit was secretly stationed in the Jewish Quarter to protect its 1,700 inhabitants, despite British efforts to confiscate Jewish arms and arrest Jewish fighters, and there was no massacre of helpless citizens.

The Jewish Quarter was, however, becoming increasingly tense, with the small group of defenders responsible for the welfare of its civilians, as well as their protection from their Arab neighbours. The Quarter was under siege by that time, although food and kerosene were brought in daily under British army escort at 8.00 a.m., 12 noon and 4.00 p.m.

That week following the UN vote, the Va'ad Leumi (National Council) mobilised all men and women aged 17 to 25, under the guise of a census of the Jewish population. The British, for their part, made their first gesture towards the forthcoming change of power by turning over to the Jews responsibility for police activities in Tel Aviv, Petach Tikvah, Ramat Gan and Bnei Brak.

The 600,000 Jews then in Palestine were not entirely alone in their struggle. Increasing numbers of their kinsmen all over the world were trying to help – raising funds, using what political clout they could muster and volunteering to fight for independence. In December 1947 in the US alone, 6,500 people volunteered to fight on the Jewish side. During that same month, 5,000 British, German and American volunteers signed up with the Arabs.

The Jewish world, however, was far from united. In America, Lessing Rosenwald and his anti-Zionist followers were discouraging support for the Zionist cause. In Romania, newly appointed Foreign Minister Anna Pauker banned all Jewish Agency activity at a crucial stage in the repatriation of Holocaust survivors (although, fortunately, a deal later struck with the country's communist regime both protected Romanian Jews and assured their right of emigration). Ms Pauker's brother became a neighbour of ours in Haifa ten years later; a strictly orthodox Jew, he could never live down his sister's reputation, and shuffled through the streets, his head hung in permanent shame.

While Palestine's Jews had been granted political legitimacy by the United Nations, they were almost totally isolated as regards economic and military aid from the world outside. Many Diaspora Jews reached out, but their help was often given in secret, as they aided the Haganah agents in Europe and North America in their efforts to acquire arms, find crews for immigrant ships and recruit trained volunteers for the battle ahead.

Esther at this time was living in a kind of limbo. Her public life was still as a teacher in a very British girls' school; but her secret life, which clearly consumed her more and more, was as a member of an underground army, fighting for freedom alongside the men.

16 First Casualties

From the middle of December 1947, it becomes harder to reconstruct how Esther was spending her time. Her letters are filled with everything except her Haganah life, which we now know was absorbing more and more of her time. On December 9, for example, she wrote:

> I expect you listen very anxiously for the news from here, which you certainly receive in an exaggerated form. Nothing big has happened or is now likely to happen, just occasional firing on a bus, which makes any long or unnecessary journey – such as mine to Tel Aviv – out of the question. Yesterday the connection stopped altogether, while any bus passing through Arab quarters is fitted with iron netting against hand-grenades. Of course, we are still 'on the ready' all the time.
>
> Yesterday, the first day of Chanukah, was fixed as a national celebration, but there was nothing seen of it, except that there was no school and therefore every kid was busy as usual with Jewish National Fund collection boxes. Last night I was invited to eat *latkes*, or *levivot* as they are called, by the Rakovsky family at the home of one of their sons.

What Esther didn't mention was something our parents learned from Shulamit Velikovsky-Kogan's letter, months later. 'On Chanukah, her night off,' wrote Shulamit, Esther 'returned to her base with *latkes* for the girls on duty'.

Esther continued:

> As to your plans for coming here, I hope that by the time they materialise, the situation will be good enough for you to see and do something here. At the moment it is impossible.
>
> I was wondering last Sunday what you were all feeling. How are Booba and Zada feeling? What are Mimi and Asher keeping themselves busy with now? I saw their names mentioned as being on the Movement Council. It looked almost like a family monopoly! Do you get oranges yet? I can quite easily send a case of about 20 pounds. What is the food situation otherwise? Here there have been some shortages these last few days because fresh food could not get in all the time. But as last year, all the pastry-cooks have decorated their windows with wonderful concoctions of all sizes and varieties. Just the same, it is difficult to say with conviction here *Chag Sameach* [Happy Holiday] – but I say it to all of you, hoping that next year it will really be that delightful festival which it can be here, for all of us together. Shalom, Esther.

During the last days of Chanukah 1947, the Haganah fought a pitched battle against Arab gangs in Wadi Rushmieh in Haifa. That same week, a convoy on its way to the Ben Shemen children's village was fired on as it passed an Arab Legion camp at Bet Neballah; 14 of the convoy and its escort were killed and ten injured. In the Jewish Quarter in Jerusalem's Old City, the Haganah garrison fought for six hours to repulse an attack. The road to the Etzion Bloc settlements, which Esther had so enjoyed visiting, was becoming a death-trap; during one attack, on 11 December, ten Haganah convoy escorts died and four were seriously hurt.

Among those ten dead was Zeev Safrai, the brother of Ida Gross's fiance, Chaim. He was the first of Esther's many friends to lose their lives in the war for Israel's independence. Ida was living in Jerusalem by that time, studying to be a teacher. Invited to visit Chaim's parents in the city's Etz Chaim Quarter, she was greeted with the news of Zeev's death. Ida (who now called herself Yehudit) and Chaim married shortly afterwards, and their modest Jerusalem flat became the closest Esther had to a home during her last months, the place she came to during her infrequent free time in the Haganah.

In London, we were growing accustomed to longer intervals between Esther's letters, which we attributed to postal service deficiencies during these disturbed times. Anglo-Jewry was in any case feeling more confident, following the sentencing of a 73-year-old former British army officer to 18 months' imprisonment for planting a bomb at 77 Great Russell Street, the headquarters of the Zionist Federation and, it can now be said, one of the Haganah's logistical centres in Britain.

Arab League countries came up with a simple solution to their 'Jewish problem'. They announced that all Jews within their borders when the Jewish state was established would be declared citizens of that state and thus enemies of the Arabs. This opened the door for a massive rescue of Jews living in Arab countries – which, in fact, continues to this day in Muslim countries, both Arab and non-Arab.

On 16 December, Esther wrote:

> I could not get to Tel Aviv for Shabbat. They had a loss in the family, Rivka's uncle, her father's brother, killed on duty. Unfortunately, almost every day there is something of the kind among families I know, like the business of the Kfar Etzion boys, one of them was the brother of Ida's fiancé. These things, however, are the result of sporadic attacks only, so that otherwise life here is fairly normal, although many children do not come to school as it is in a rather risky locality, and we are at present discussing what to do. Yesterday, we had the school concert, drank cocoa and ate doughnuts as usual – doughnuts are the custom here for Chanukah, I have never eaten so many in my life! Food prices have gone up again. We now pay one shilling and sixpence for a loaf of bread and sixpence for eggs – but they are very good. Mrs Levy informs me that she is giving me 10 pounds as a contribution to my Provident Fund, which has recently been arranged.

Part of the reason that Esther filled her letters with domestic trivia was to produce an impression that her life was continuing along its usual course even when it became obvious she had stopped teaching and was on active service. But another, equally important, explanation of why she wrote so little of what she was really doing was clearly her concern that her letters would be censored. Nevertheless, she wrote openly enough on 19 December, and her letter had the impact of a bombshell in our household.

She wrote:

> I am seriously considering full-time National Service. The position at school at the moment is very uncertain. The parents won't send their children to the school and Mrs Levy refuses to move it temporarily to another place. She says we shall close rather than that. In the meantime, I feel that in any case teaching English to a handful of girls is not an important service that the *Yishuv* at the moment demands.

Her next letter was written four days later. 'I cannot see how you can possibly come here at the moment,' she wrote to our parents, after months of pleading with them to visit.

> Once in Jerusalem it would be alright, although not much fun, especially until you get used to the sounds of shooting, etc. The trouble is getting here, as the journey from Lydda airport is very dangerous. Although the British are so fond of reporting how terrible the state of things is here, when asked to take protective measures, or rather to allow us to make our own arrangements, they say there is no need or it would not help, or something like that. Last night it was announced that they refuse to allow the use of a different airport near Jerusalem. I suppose you have heard of the various incidents to travellers from Lydda, and the same applies to the journey from Haifa.
>
> Last night, to celebrate Christmas I suppose, there was a lot of distant shooting. Otherwise the series of isolated

134

incidents continues, and who knows but cholera [then rampant in Egypt] may yet prevent anything on a bigger scale – literally a heaven-sent plague! As usual, the BBC news is sickening, a poor soldier trying to be helpful, being murdered and hated by both sides. Just lies! They themselves [the British] have committed horrible crimes. They stood and watched the husband of one of our teachers attacked and would not help. They join in plundering; they take arms from Jews and give or sell them to Arabs. Individual officers and men vary a lot of course, but they are not behaving well on the whole, and high-up policy is clearly against us.

The parents of the girls – and, in the top class, the girls themselves, imagine it! – have carried out their strike and we have had only 25 per cent attendance all week. Yesterday one class had one girl. Today, three! I had 10 and 12 instead of the usual 43. Mrs Levy has had a big shock and changed her viewpoint a lot, although she still will not transfer the school. She was confident that within two days the school would be back to 80 per cent attendance. There have been countless meetings – parents together, parents with Mrs Levy, Mrs Levy with directors, both with the Vaad Leumi [National Executive] etc. etc., and still nothing has changed except that she is again shortening hours and is also doing away with the stupid school lunch. Most of the week there was no heating in school and, being so empty, it has been very cold. The rain came at last yesterday, and it really poured after a night of howling wind. It is the first rain of this season, and it seemed to me as if we might not have any again. After a second night of it, today is sunny. Well, I will save the rest for another time, and also send you a copy of the paper in which an article of mine appears. I have others to finish for which I have no time at present. Many Happy Returns for Asher's Bar Mitzvah anniversary. Love, Esther.

The events of that week included a two-day attack by the Arabs on Bat Yam and exchanges of fire in the Old City, in which two Jews and an Arab were killed. A company of British troops was positioned between the two sides in the Old City, but it concerned itself solely with escorting food convoys to the Jewish Quarter, and arresting Haganah members and confiscating their weapons.

Jewish Agency leaders – among them Nahum Goldman, Professor Selig Brodetsky and David Horowitz – met in London with Colonial Secretary Arthur Creech-Jones to urge the removal of the Arab Legion from Palestine and an increase in the number of Jewish immigrants. A question was even asked in parliament, but its answer constituted one of the more bizarre British statements of the time. 'The Arab Legion is to stay in Palestine', it read, 'because of Jewish terror.' In London, an Arab Higher Executive representative said 'how pleased he was that the British were supporting the Arab case, thus helping obliterate the mistakes committed by Britain in the past'.

A major difference of opinion, however, was emerging between London's Colonial and Foreign Offices. The former favoured an earlier ending to the mandate in Palestine, while the Foreign Office dug in its heels, lobbying to postpone evacuation of British troops and civilians, and even to reconsider the terms under which the mandate was to end.

In Palestine, heavy fighting continued throughout the last week of December, with constant sniping in Haifa and continued attacks on convoys. In the month that had passed since the UN vote, 316 people had died in fighting in Palestine. Among them was Hans Beyth, acting director of Youth Aliyah, the organisation established to care for youngsters who had fled Hitler for Palestine without their parents. Beyth was on his way back from Haifa, when his convoy was attacked at Castel just outside Jerusalem.

Esther wrote:

> Every day now brings a big funeral, and we are getting used to somebody known, either through personal acquaintance or national importance, being killed in some tragic way or other. The head of Youth Aliyah, Hans Beyth, was an irreplaceable loss – they say he built up the whole

136

operation and was a wonderful person. He had gone to Haifa to meet a party of children from Cyprus, knowing the dangers of the journey. He insisted on riding in a bus, not in a car of the convoy, and was shot in the head when returning the fire with his own gun, when others took cover.

That same week saw the arrival of 700 immigrants on the *SS 29 November*. The ship was boarded by the Royal Navy, and its passengers immediately shipped off to detention in Cyprus. The 15,300 refugees aboard the *Pan York* and the *Pan Crescent* (renamed *The Independence* and *The Ingathering of Refugees*) also ended up in Cyprus. No resistance was offered when two British cruisers and five destroyers escorted the ships into port. The landing took three days and caused the British to frantically expand their detention camps on the island. This was, however, Jewish Agency policy: to strain British resources, and to ensure that there would be a large number of Jews close by to be taken across to the new state as soon as the mandate ended. It also served as a diversion: while the British focused on Cyprus, the two-masted *SS United Nations* secretly beached some 700 'illegal' immigrants off the coast of Nahariya.

Meanwhile, the carnage continued. Jewish workers at the Haifa oil refineries were attacked by a mob of 2,000 Arabs in reprisal for the deaths of six Arabs in an Etzel bombing of the plant. The toll: 39 Jewish dead. Hospital buses came under fire on their way to Hadassah Hospital on Mount Scopus. Jerusalem mail sacks were stolen twice in three days. Arms confiscated from the Jews were found in the possession of the Arabs. Two former SS officers were found among the Arab dead in fighting in Jerusalem. And two car bombs were detonated by Arabs next to the Evelina school, causing considerable damage. This at last tipped the balance away from the school administration's misplaced stoicism that life must go on, and towards the view of teaching staff that the time was long past for evacuating the building.

Esther's last letter home in 1947 was written on 29 December. It was nearly three weeks until she wrote again, as this was when she received her first out-of-town Haganah assignment. This letter, like the others those past few weeks, was bland.

> Dear Mummy, Today was a record – 40 girls came out of 400. Further meetings and arguments – one does not know whether to pity Mrs Levy or condemn her for being so obstinate. The school will move after all, but for a longish period, so it will take time and meanwhile we shall carry on.

On 13 January 1948, the school gates were locked for the last time, and Evelina moved to Ussishkin Street in Rehavia – a move that turned out to be permanent.

17 Estie from Suba

The year 1948 resonates among the Jewish people as that in which 2,000 years of exile came to an end. The beginning of 1948 found virtual civil war in Palestine, Jews and Arabs eager to establish facts on the ground which would improve their truncated territories on the UN maps. The main action was on the highways, with the Arabs determined to disrupt the movement of Jewish passengers and supplies. Tension was also high in neighbourhoods with large populations of Jews and Arabs living side by side – principally, Tel Aviv/Jaffa, parts of Haifa and, most dangerously, the patchwork city of Jerusalem, holy to three faiths.

In January 1948, the Haganah launched a deadly attack on an Arab terror base in Jerusalem, the Semiramis Hotel; the Etzel lobbed a bomb at the Old City's Jaffa Gate, causing heavy casualties; and a major attack on the Etzion Bloc settlements south of Jerusalem was beaten off. But on the night of 15/16 January, a Palmach unit bringing badly needed supplies to the Etzion Bloc settlements was ambushed, and all 35 of its members were killed and their bodies mutilated. The unit's commander was Danny Mass, son of the Jerusalem publisher Reuven Mass, a colleague of our father. Another of the 35 was Moshe Avigdor Perlstein, a graduate of American Bnei Akiva, who had come to Palestine in 1946 and was among Esther's circle of friends.

It's from Shulamit Velikovsky-Kogan's letter to our parents, written six months later, that we know how Esther spent January 1948:

139

The boys were called upon to enlist as full-time soldiers and we were asked for a few volunteers among the girls. Esther was among the first to volunteer, and soon afterwards gave up her teaching. She was then sent to Suba, a small place a few kilometers west of Jerusalem. She was to cook there for the enlisted boys – it was a place where the kitchen was strictly kosher. She stayed there for several weeks, a much longer time than any of the other non-enlisted girls, who had to be changed every few days. The boys there all admired her. I was not there with her, but as far as I know it was there that she learnt to use a gun, for she cooked in the day-time and insisted on keeping watch at times at night. She is still lovingly remembered by many as 'Estie MiSuba' (Estie from Suba).

It was rather quiet there at the time, and she soon got bored just cooking in a quiet place and asked to be given real training. At that time I left the group, but when next I met her she told me that after a stubborn fight on her part, she had joined the rest of the girls in Jerusalem who received two weeks of training. That must have been around Tu B'Shvat [on 26 January that year]. Afterwards she was sent to Nevei Yaacov, north of Jerusalem, again to act as cook for the Haganah unit stationed there. She never liked that sort of job, and the boys who were there tell that when the settlement was attacked, she took a gun and went out to fight. She did not stay in the kitchen as she could have done and, hard to believe, shot down several of the attackers. She then returned to Jerusalem where she complained that there was nothing essential for girls to do. She tried to make herself useful in any place she could think of.

This was an Esther that none of us knew – neither her family and friends in London, nor her colleagues and students at Evelina.

Esther's focus, however, was neither on Suba nor on Nevei Yaakov but on the Jewish Quarter of Jerusalem's Old City, the centre of Jewish faith and history. The situation in the Jewish

Quarter was deteriorating badly by January 1948. The Arabs had blocked all the gates into the walled city, checking even British troops and vehicles to ensure they were not helping the Jews. Over the New Year holiday, no supplies had been brought in to the Jewish community, and there were severe shortages of milk and kerosene. In the 30 years since the establishment of the British mandate in 1917, the number of Jews living behind the city walls had plunged from 15,000 to 1,700. The narrow streets and alleyways had become too poor, too cramped and too dangerous, and most Old City Jews had taken the first opportunity they could to build their lives elsewhere. They had been largely replaced by Hebron Arabs, with their reputation for violence and hatred of the Jews.

On the night of Thursday, 3 January, a convoy finally reached the Jewish Quarter with six tons of food and supplies – but that same night, the Arabs attacked a residential complex in the Quarter known as the Warsaw Houses, in one of many attempts to gain ground. Access to the Jewish cemetery on the Mount of Olives was barred, and 25 Jewish bodies lay in hospital mortuaries awaiting burial. America's Zionist Emergency Council chairman, Dr Israel Goldstein, castigated the British for letting the Arabs seize control in the Old City and endanger Jewish lives.

That same month, the Jewish Agency executive announced completion of detailed plans for the structure of the Jewish state. It would, it stated, welcome a 15,000-strong international force to ensure implementation of the UN's 29 November decision.

Esther received a letter from our parents in mid-January. Deeply involved with the Haganah, the letter's news was badly timed.

In reply she wrote:

> Thank you very much for your letter, which I received on Wednesday after one week, and which did give me a shock. It is really a desperate step to make the journey here now, so you must be far too worried. I certainly was when I got the letter a day after Daddy was due to arrive, and he had not yet been to see me, nor was he at the hotel. There was

no phone connection with Tel Aviv to find out if you were there, and the BOAC office here is closed entirely. Peltours could only tell me that the plane had arrived but not the list of passengers. I had to wait four hours to contact Lydda. Meanwhile your telegram arrived, dated in Jerusalem, January 6, although I did not get it until the 8th, because the General Post Office is still closed. These details give you some idea of the difficulties of contacts here. You might have arrived and left without seeing me, or my knowing it! School is still closed, but is moving over to the Jerusalem Girls' College, which is taking our building. There are still evacuees in the new place, but I suppose it will all fit in.

I assume that you had been forbidden by the authorities to fly here at the last moment, although I can't imagine that stopping you! Here the weather is glorious, though spoilt by the intermittent firing in Jerusalem. However this week we had two days and nights of downpour that more than made up for the previous lack of rain! Otherwise there is no special news. I do guard duty like everyone else, and I daresay that I may eventually be given some special training as everybody between the ages of 19 and 25 has now been required to register for National Service. I have not heard this week from Tel Aviv – have you? Your contacts with them are much better than mine now.

Otherwise there is no other news, so love and best wishes to all of you, and I hope that next time you will really come and in peaceful, normal times. Shalom, Esther.

Clearly the non-arrival of our father must have been a great relief to Esther, who would have had to account for why she was standing guard in a Jerusalem hillside outpost or taking a weapons-training course, rather than setting off each day for school with a bagful of marked exercise books. It would be another month before she told us she had left the school, using for the time being its temporary closure as a cover for what she was doing.

A source of inspiration to Esther and many of the other women volunteers was probably Golda Meir, pleading the case for the Jewish people in her thick Milwaukee accent. In January 1948, she flew to the United States to raise funds for arms, making an unscheduled appearance at the Council of Jewish Federations' general assembly in Chicago. Some 20,000 men and women had signed up in Palestine's first recruitment drive, she told the assembly, although only 9,000 were then actually mobilised. All these people had to be fed, clothed and housed and, most of all, adequately armed.

She returned to Palestine with some $45 million, two-thirds of which was allocated to defence. 'Someday, when history will be written, it will be said that there was a Jewish woman who got the money which made the State possible,' was Ben-Gurion's tribute – a generous statement which nevertheless must be seen in proper perspective. The total cost of the War of Independence was some $278 million, the balance provided by the 600,000 Jews then living in Palestine and the huge numbers of penniless immigrants who arrived soon after independence.

Perhaps most amazing of all was that a people, which had so long prayed for miracles to save it from disaster, was rapidly transforming three competing bands of volunteer freedom fighters into a modern fighting force, which would defeat an enemy far superior in both numbers and in firepower. A total of 116,000 men and women were recruited into the Israel Defence Forces during the War of Independence, the vast majority of them never before having handled weapons. What the IDF did have, however, was a body of Second World War veterans who had received intensive training as field commanders of different ranks. It was this which enabled the Haganah to establish a complete system of military units in a disciplined hierarchy, reporting to a general command in Tel Aviv.

Esther was enrolled in one such unit, the 61st Moriah Battalion, which had been established as part of the Jerusalem (Etzioni) Brigade on 17 December 1947, under the command of Zalman Marat, code-named Shadmi. By a quirk of fate, her first billet in Jerusalem's Bet HaKerem neighbourhood was very close to where Gubby Haffner, whom she had met at Thaxted, was staying, and they sometimes got together on Shabbat and attended services together. Gubby, who had arrived two months before, was spending mornings at a youth leaders' training course, and afternoons digging fortifications on the hillside where the Yad Vashem Holocaust memorial now stands, above the Arab village of Ein Karem. Esther was already soldiering in Jerusalem, and occasionally putting in an appearance at school.

The Moriah, to which she was seconded, was the first infantry battalion to be established, as the Haganah made its transition from underground force to regular army, and Esther was one of its earliest recruits. But she was by no means alone in her decision to join the struggle for a reborn Jewish state. In addition to hundreds of young Zionists who had already arrived in Palestine from the West as kibbutz pioneers, students, doctors, teachers and so on, some 4,000 more (including some non-Jews) would arrive in the framework of *Machal*, the volunteer fighters from abroad. Their numbers were small, even disappointing, to Palestine's Jewish leadership, but their role was significant: the RAF veterans who came formed the backbone of Israel's embryo airforce; the first commander of Israel's navy was the American volunteer Paul Shulman; Colonel David (Micky) Marcus would certainly have played a central role in the IDF, had he not been tragically felled by friendly fire; 20 of the 30 Jewish airmen who died in the War of Independence were *Machal* volunteers. In all, 118 *Machal* fighters died in that war, and a memorial to them stands near Shaar Hagai on the Jerusalem–Tel Aviv highway. Esther's is among the names engraved on the monument, although she arrived in the country a year before *Machal* recruitment began.

Esther's first letter home in 1948 was written on 20 January. It was not, however, posted until two months later, together with a short update. 'It appears that after all Daddy will not turn up now, although I have been expecting him every moment,' she wrote.

> Particularly at this time, I am very glad because the risks of any short journey out of town are really horrible. Yesterday evening I received news of the murder of three good friends, in two separate incidents. I got the news about them within a few minutes, one after the other, and the

effect was shattering. Although I do not for a moment regret being here in these great and stirring times, and would not dream of leaving, yet you are lucky that you are not here and can be spared the heartbreak. I know now what it means to suffer for this land, and what the settlers who have been here for many years have had to go through every time there was an outbreak of disturbances. To learn of the loss of 35 of our boys who went down fighting pierces to the heart, but when one reads the names and recalls the faces and memories of close friends, life becomes for a moment very bitter. The other girl who lives with us, an American, was wounded in the leg when returning from Maale HaHamisha, a nearby kibbutz, and her boyfriend was killed in shielding her, together with another mutual friend. But there is no alternative – one has to get used to this sort of thing, for it is a part of life here.

Within town, however, everything is alright, apart from sporadic noises from various directions, which is part of the pattern of things. The Old City is in a bad situation, but has held out for a couple of months now. Food supplies to there are difficult, while every day Arabs hold up trains and remove loads of food and various provisions while the [British] military look on – unabashed by the fact that they are in full view of onlookers.

What would Asher like me to send him from here for his overdue birthday present? When am I going to get some photographs of you? I have no more news for the moment from here. Lots of love to Zada, Booba and all. Yours ... Esther.

March 24: I have just found this letter, so not to waste money, and to save writing again today, I am sending it to you in case you need a sign that I am still very much in existence on Wednesday, March 24! I started really special work last night.

A week after the first instalment of that letter, on 28 January, she wrote again. There was heavy fighting at the time, particularly around the Castel, in the desperate struggle to keep open the Jerusalem–Tel Aviv highway. Arab gangs countrywide were threatening civilian lives. Esther herself had fought by then at Suba, and taken special weapons-training. Considering all this, her 28 January letter is a masterpiece of obfuscation:

Things are fairly quiet, here. There have been a few sirens sounded lately in Jerusalem, but nothing much. The weather is delightful and spring-like most of the time, although the midday sun is much hotter than any English spring. Today I sent a letter to Tel Aviv through a friend who is travelling there. The ordinary channels of post are impossible – a fortnight for a letter from Kfar Etzion, so close to Jerusalem. They have to wait for convoys. From there they have been attacked again two days running, the second time with two losses. About the heavy loss that they suffered, they write me that all those casualties would never have been caused, had the [British] military, 10 minutes away, not waited an hour before coming to the aid of the convoy.

Have you taken any photos? I am very anxious to see you all again, at least in pictures. How did Asher celebrate his birthday? You do not write whether you would like me to send oranges or grapefruit. How is the food situation at this time? And the weather? How is everybody keeping? Isn't Daddy going to America after all? Has Asher heard any more about his call-up? I am writing this with the pen Daddy gave me, as my Biro has dried up, and refills have not yet arrived from Tel Aviv. Has the roof been repaired yet? I had a letter this week from Hannah, she writes how satisfied her uncle was with his visit here. Did you get a dress eventually for the Epstein wedding? When will it be held? Did Auntie attend theirs in Manchester?

The school is in rather tight quarters in its new building, as it is also still occupied by evacuees from the time when I was turned out of my first room so that one class is even held out of doors. Mrs Levy was very loath to suffer any makeshift arrangements, not befitting the dignity of the school, but was forced to do so in the end.

146

Well there is not any real news, as you see, so I send you all best wishes and love – Booba, Zada and all, and hope to hear from you soon that you are all well.

Her letter is, in fact, a classic 'soldier's letter home'. Unable to write about the battles or hardship, Esther filled the page with queries about the weather, food and social events. My own letters home from the Six-Day War battleground sound much the same.

Reading between the lines, however, the letter is not uninformative. Esther referred to the British, more and more, as 'the authorities' or 'the military', clearly finding it easier to focus on their role rather than their nationality in the Palestine context. It's also clear that she was corresponding with someone on Kibbutz Kfar Etzion, which she had so enjoyed visiting a few weeks earlier. We never learned who her correspondent was, although we later heard she was in deep despair over the fall of the kibbutz and the heroic death of its defenders on the eve of Israel's independence.

The long-seething tension between the Jews and the British in Palestine was beginning to boil by early 1948. It surprised no one when 2,000 former British officers volunteered to fight alongside the Arabs, or when the Union of British Fascists contributed a growing contingent to the various armed bands that attacked Jews all over the country. Anti-Semitism among British troops was manifest. One common practice was to release arrested Haganah men in areas controlled by Arab bands, to be ruthlessly murdered. Late in January, three boys and a 15-year-old girl, all members of Lehi (the Stern Group), were sentenced to life imprisonment for possessing arms. The British then announced they would hold to the *status quo* on immigration until the end of the mandate, despite pleas from Palestine's Jewish leadership that they permit more than the quota of 1,500 desperate refugees to enter the country each month.

Not all non-Jews, of course, supported the Arabs. Several British soldiers, and even a few officers, joined the ranks of Israel's fledgling army, some even bringing their equipment with them.

Manoeuvring and skirmishes continued. The Jewish Agency managed to purchase 21 two-seater planes, parked at a small Tel Aviv airfield as surplus, despite a last-minute British bid to cancel the deal. In London, the Joint Palestine Appeal raised the astonishing sum of £530,000 in a single month, an important boost to funding the struggle for Jewish independence. The battles around the Castel continued, with the strategic outpost changing hands several times. A band of 750 armed Arabs crossed the Jordan River to join the fight against the Jews. The British denied an American Zionist accusation that their response to the Arab blockade of the Old City was passive, and counterclaimed that the Jews were trying to smuggle in 'unauthorised persons' and that Jewish terrorists were responsible for the troubles.

Probably anticipating that she would have little time to write during the busy times ahead, Esther sent home a series of letters in late January, written within a few days of each other. She even wrote a second letter on 28 January in her efforts to reassure the family in England that all was well.

It seems for me, too, that long periods pass before I hear from you, although I do try to write regularly. You do not seem to have received all my letters, where I tell you about school and other new details, nor did you ever acknowledge the last lot of photographs I sent, including some of the 'Declaration of Independence' Day.

I am not in need of any money at the moment, as I have very few expenses. I intended leaving my room as it is so expensive, but Mrs Epstein wants me to stay on, and we shall make some fresh arrangement. I do not even have to pay bus fares, as the school is now in Rehavia, not Princess Mary Avenue, which is a 'hot spot' and closed up. [She was by now no longer teaching at the school.]

Your remarks about the size of the classes in school and the interest or influence of the 'British authorities' are, I am afraid, not to the point. The first is a fact, and the second is non-existent – now more so than ever. Where did you ever hear of the Government taking an interest in Jewish

148

education? When they published a report on education here, they criticised our schools for being too independent – have we any option? We pay the taxes and the Arabs get the schools, so we manage as best we can on very high school fees, and naturally do as we like.

I was very pleased to get a letter at last from Rivka, which took exactly a month to reach me. I send messages to the family in Tel Aviv whenever I can, though I do not hear from them. She wrote that they were all staying in Tel Aviv but hoped to return to Bat Yam if they get their armoured bus, which is now being made. Daddy, you need not regret having avoided the five-hour journey from Tel Aviv in something worse than a cattle truck – stuffy, cramped and dim, squatting on low benches. I hope your journey to America will be a much more profitable one. Thank Asher for his letter, why didn't Mimi write?

This is a letter written in the classic twilight zone between two regimes. Our parents still had faith in British governance and fair play, asking their questions about British involvement in the size of the classes in a Jewish school in Jerusalem. Esther's pulse, however, demonstrably beat with that of Jewish Palestine. Having emerged from the terrible Holocaust years, and with hundreds of thousands of homeless refugees to worry about, Palestine's Jews were not prepared to passively accept British perfidy. Their position was that no one was going to stop the UN resolution being implemented – and, if that meant war, every effort would be expended to make the Jewish state as strategically secure as humanly possible, and this was surely Esther's mood as she made her decision to dedicate herself to the struggle for independence.

18 Chaos in the Holy Land

February 1948 arrived literally with a bang. At 11.00 p.m. on the night of 1 February, Jerusalem rocked with the bombing of *The Palestine Post* building. It was followed by a yet more devastating attack later that month on Ben Yehuda Street, and in March by a third, at the Jewish Agency building.

Responsibility for the bombings was claimed by Abdul Khader el-Husseini, leader of the Arab irregulars then in the area (and uncle to Faisal Husseini, a senior figure in today's Palestinian Authority). Rumours of British involvement in the attacks were never proven. *The Palestine Post* staff rose to the challenge, producing a newspaper for the following morning, in dramatic illustration of the Israeli 'yihye beseder' (it'll be OK) response to adversity.

The only English-language newspaper in the country, *The Palestine Post* was read, if not equally esteemed, by British, Arabs and Jews alike. In terms of international news, however, the bombing of the *Post* building was overshadowed by the funeral of India's beloved Mahatma Ghandi, the man who had almost single-handedly convinced the mighty British Empire that India had no desire to be governed by a foreign power and a conflicting culture.

Esther wrote to our parents the next day. Her letter's emotional impact on our household was almost equal to that of the bombing. She wrote:

> I am in full-time service now, and fairly busy, though I beg you not to worry. The state of things here is not nearly as bad as you seem to think and there is no personal danger

except for unlucky chances of fortune which are anyway impossible to avoid in life. There is nothing like the constant and concentrated danger of the [Second World War] London bombing.

I was much reminded of this today, when I was in town and saw the wreckage from the explosions in *The Palestine Post* building, which you will have heard of. One of our teachers, Mrs Aaronson lives next door to the *Post* building. Her husband is stuck in Tel Aviv, and she and her two children were in a bad state. I went there to help her pack some things and tidy up her flat. I waited with her until it was boarded up – no doors or windows. There were still some fires burning in the morning, and general disorder, but *The Palestine Post* appeared nevertheless, smaller and printed elsewhere. One heard the explosions a long way out of town, and it was a miracle that casualties and damage were no worse.

Well, I acted on my decision to leave school. Mrs Levy was surprisingly decent and understanding, although apparently the committee members were not pleased. They left it to her discretion, and she refunded me all the fare money I've been paying off for the journey here. I thought I might get half back, and was quite overwhelmed.

Despite Esther's assurance that 'things are not nearly as bad as you think', the country was visibly preparing for war, with conditions in the Old City, in particular, becoming intolerable. That week there was heavy shooting across the Tel Aviv–Jaffa border, and a convoy came under concentrated fire in the narrow Bab el Wad pass on the Jerusalem ascent. Syrian gangs were infiltrating from the north, and attacking Jewish road traffic. This was happening even though British troops and police were still very much present, and still officially responsible for defending Palestine's borders and ensuring the safety of its inhabitants.

But law and order had, in fact, broken down. Food supplies, schooling and postal and telephone services were all at the mercy of marauding gangs, with British attention focused on preventing the immigration of Jews and turned away from protecting the civilian population. The UN General Assembly had recommended that a port be made available for Jewish immigration from 1 February. Not only did 1 February see no available port, but on that day the Royal Navy intercepted a refugee ship, *The 35 Heroes of Kfar Etzion*, and deported its 280 passengers to Cyprus.

Remarkably, despite this situation of near anarchy, the Jewish community was successfully organising itself to take control immediately the British left. In most areas of what was to become the Jewish state, preparations had been made for the military to ensure the safety of the local population, and then be replaced by civilian authority. Although a war was fought simultaneously on several fronts, there was no hiatus.

One notable exception to this state of preparedness was the Jewish Quarter in the Old City of Jerusalem. The tiny Jewish garrison stationed there was responsible for both the safety and welfare of 1,700 civilians. With reinforcements unable to penetrate the double British and Arab siege lines, the garrison could only be bolstered by subterfuge. The British admitted teachers, for example, to the Jewish Quarter to work with children. These teachers, of course, immediately took their place among the Haganah fighters. Esther, impatient that women fighters were assigned away from danger, leaped at the opportunity that her teacher's status afforded her: it would get her into the Old City, where she felt she could make a real contribution.

Esther filled a letter dated 5 February to our parents with innocuous news and a series of mundane questions – behind which she could conceal what she was really doing. Her letters until then had always been neatly written, the air-letter forms she wrote on crammed to the last millimetre. This one had large unfilled spaces, the ink was smudged and she seems to have used three different pens:

> Dear Mummy and Daddy, I am taking this opportunity to start a letter, and hope to be able to finish it today. I am very well, apart from a bit of a cold, though even that I have not

had for a long time. We have been having quite a bit of rain lately, which of course is a very good thing, though a bit uncomfortable on *shmira* [guard duty]. However it makes the security situation at night also much better, since apparently the Arabs do not like going out in the rain any more than we do! What sort of winter are you having? As cold as the last? How is the food situation? Here the usual bountiful supplies to Jerusalem are a bit cut down, as supplies of eggs, milk etc. from the kibbutzim are sometimes rather erratic. There is also registration for kerosene – the staple cooking fuel here.

Prices are also still higher – but none of this affects me. We are quite royally fed and clad – you should see me. Sometime I shall show you photographs. We alone get meat, there still being none on sale for the public. I am much better off, less strung-up with work and responsibility than when I was at school. Physical conditions are sometimes a bit rougher, but that makes for fitness. I go into school when I have the chance, and I think that Mrs Levy is privately a bit pleased at releasing a member of her staff for National Service, and certainly all the others on the staff are thrilled.

I want to send this off now so with all my love and best wishes and do not worry, Yours, Esther.

We get a more accurate picture of what Esther was doing at that time from her commander, Dina Schur, who wrote a long letter to our parents after the War of Independence. She wrote:

I came to know Esther on a February day in Bet Hakerem, the lovely suburb of Jerusalem. Snow had fallen during the night for the only time this year. Esther and I had some mutual friends in a house nearby and so we went there together. The snowflakes settled in her dark curls and on her khaki uniform. She was the first girl among us to wear one. At that time our unit had just returned from Motza near Jerusalem, where it had guarded the area. The few girls attached to it, and among them Esther, had

153

undertaken to take care of the physical welfare of our soldiers, and cooked and cleaned with fervour, though with little professional knowledge. At that period, only very few girls had joined the embryo army full-time. Esther was among those for she had left her work at school in order to become a soldier of Israel.

When she returned to town, the whole unit went through an additional two weeks of training. They went out into the surrounding green valleys in order to learn about field movement, and also received further lessons in the use of rifles, Sten guns and small arms. Esther always enjoyed these lessons very much, and she was especially good at them. The days were pleasant and tranquil. The war as we came to know it later on, had not yet started in full force and was limited to some incidents which did not concern our unit as we were in training. The girls lived in a nice small house and there were pleasant evenings when we listened to the wireless or attended a film show put on specially for us in a nearby school. Each Friday evening after supper there was a festive gathering attended by all, which included some artistic programme, music and folk dancing. Shabbat afternoon and evening we were all off duty and free to enjoy ourselves.

After a fortnight, the girls ended their training and returned to their various civilian occupations, while the boys carried on with their training for another month. Only a very few girls stayed behind. At first they accompanied a small detachment to Nevei Yaacov, a nearby settlement [now a Jerusalem suburb], where the guards needed to be replaced. There again the girls cooked and tried to make the strenuous life of our guards as comfortable as possible. The days and nights were wet and cold, the ground soggy, the guard duty long and arduous. The girls did all they could to cheer up our warriors.

There was a sudden heavy attack on the settlement and all the males rushed to their positions with their weapons. The girls were ordered to stay in their houses, but this was not good enough for Esther. I was told by one of the boys that she joined them in their outpost and fired back as well as any of them. After some hours the attack was repelled.

During the first part of February, there were continued skirmishes on several fronts, although, as Dina pointed out, the real war had not yet begun. The Arabs were making determined efforts to swing world opinion against a Jewish state: among other ploys, they spread a rumour that the Soviets were planning to send 1,500,000 Jewish communists to Palestine to gain a foothold in the Middle East! This and similar propaganda met with considerable success in the West, and soon US Secretary of State George Marshall was urging his country to abandon its support for a Jewish state and adopt instead a 'temporary trusteeship' in Palestine.

On 10 February, the Arabs launched a heavy attack on Jerusalem's Yemin Moshe Quarter, a key link in the lines of communication between the Old City and the new. The Haganah hung grimly on to their positions on the slopes facing the ancient walls. On that day, the British allowed three convoys of food and civilian supplies through to the beleaguered Old City garrison. By then, the Haganah was expert at smuggling in small quantities of military *matériel* in false-bottomed fuel tanks fitted to the trucks, and in this way the defenders maintained a reasonable degree of firepower. And also on that day, the mandate established a 300-man Jerusalem police force, half Jewish and half Arab.

With hindsight, it's clear that Esther's next letter was written when she was training in the hills and valleys around Jerusalem, learning to handle weapons and acquiring basic military skills:

> The almond blossom was out for Tu B'Shvat (Arbour Day), and now there are bright red anemones and other wild flowers. The wadis are brilliantly green from the rain, but soon it will be hot and the hills brown and parched again. Now when the weather is fine it is sheer joy to be out of town.
>
> I was in town yesterday and got your letter of January 29. I do not understand why you do not get mine – I write

twice a week and will try and make it more often, but I
sometimes have to give the letters to someone else to post.
Also one lot of letters to and from England was stolen by
Arabs.

I do wish you would not worry, because there is really
nothing dreadful going on. Please thank Mimi for her letter,
which I was very glad to have. I also received one from
Hannah and some newspapers. It is very encouraging to
hear of your activities and money collecting, although we
wish it could be in more concrete form. When you ask me
what I would like you to send me, and what I need, I only
wish I could reply frankly!

If Esther had sent a true wish list, she no doubt would have
asked for a large supply of automatic weapons and a squadron
of tanks. Haganah training in those days was often carried out
with broomsticks for guns, and recruits shouting 'Pow! Pow!' as
they charged an imagined enemy.

It was probably around this time that Esther managed to
write two more articles for the Jewish Agency publication, *Igeret
LaGolah*. Both were published after her death in the magazine's
June and July issues, and both are based on her Haganah
experiences.

The first, 'With Only One Casualty', is about her posting at
the isolated settlement of Nevei Yaacov. It tells the sad story of
Gusik the puppy, mascot of the unit, chased out of the bunker
for fear his yapping would give away their position. When the
firing ends, Gusik is found lying in the road, a bullet through his
tiny body.

The second article, which Esther called 'An Army Marches On
Its Stomach', was reprinted in several British and North
American newspapers and magazines. It describes a young
woman making the round of Haganah positions on a Friday
evening during the siege of Jerusalem, distributing meal tickets
to the men on duty. It's probably based on her first experiences
as a Haganah volunteer during the closing weeks of 1947, and
she describes the incredible sight of at least one Shabbat candle
alight in each of those darkened outposts.

156

By mid-February 1948, the Holy Land had descended into chaos. In Haifa, a unit of the British-officered Transjordan Legion stationed at a camp in Ahuza on Mount Carmel opened fire on Jewish pedestrians, killing and wounding many. After constant sniping causing Jewish casualties, the Haganah blew up an Arab HQ in Jerusalem's Old City. Jewish and British wounded alike were treated at the Jewish Quarter's Misgav Ladach Hospital. Although it was not a Hadassah facility, a Hadassah medical and surgical team were staffing Misgav LaDach, and did so with distinction until the Old City fell.

The British were now chiefly concerned with safely withdrawing their troops and civilian personnel, and were still unwilling to comply with UN recommendations or Jewish demands for increased immigration and greater autonomy in defence. They did, however, urgently inform the Five-Nation UN Commission on Partition that Palestine had been invaded by armed Arab bands from neighbouring countries.

Mid-February also saw the arrival in Palestine of 28 members of a special United Jewish Appeal (UJA) mission from the USA. They toured the country, often at great personal risk (they were fired on in Wadi Rushmieh, an Arab suburb of Haifa), and assessed the resources that the soon-to-be-born Jewish state would need in order to absorb large numbers of Holocaust survivors and other refugees. Their conclusion: $25 million, an enormous and unprecedented sum, which they pledged to raise. The UJA could provide only non-military aid. There was, however, no shortage of other, less official sources, anxious to fund the war – including a growing network of emissaries charged with buying arms, leasing immigration ships and recruiting volunteers for the Jewish army.

While the UJA mission was in Palestine, the Haganah carried out a daring and vital operation in the north of the country, blowing up strategic bridges linking Palestine and its neighbours, thus impeding the movement of enemy troops and armed bands.

In the midst of all this, on Friday, 13 February, Esther's friend Ida Gross from Heathland Road in London married Chaim Safrai, whom she had met on Kibbutz Sdei Eliyahu, soon after arriving in Palestine. Esther missed the marriage ceremony, but saw the couple a few days later. The wedding was celebrated in Jerusalem, so Chaim and Ida (Yehudit) were spared a ten-hour battle fought later that week to repel a heavy Arab attack on their kibbutz, Sdei Eliyahu, and the other two religious Bet Shean valley settlements – Tirat Zvi and Ein Hanatziv. The Arabs used automatic weapons and three-inch mortars, but nonetheless suffered a heavy defeat and severe casualties. The Haganah carried out a reprisal raid the following day in the nearby Arab town of Beit Shean. A classic strike-and-withdraw operation, they sustained no casualties.

There is a gap of over two weeks before Esther's next letter on 22 February, but earlier letters may have been sent but not arrived:

> I am writing this in Ida's flat, and very nice it is too. Last week I got an urgent message from her saying that she was marrying on the Friday, and would I try to be there. I should certainly have done so, only I got the letter several days after the event, it having gone through various channels to reach me. I was very disappointed, and so was she, especially as I happened to be in town.
>
> I now have three days' leave and have met Ida's new husband. I slept overnight in their flat and shall do so until I return. Even then, I shall be near them in a very nice suburb of Jerusalem where I shall be taking part in two or three weeks of further training. I called on friends this Shabbat and spent Friday night with the group out here from England for a year's study – Gubby Haffner and the rest. They too are in the same district, so it is all very convenient. We stay in 'pensions' as they are called here – or posh boarding houses with lovely gardens, scenery, woods etc. The weather is pleasant, though still quite cool for here.
>
> Something I would like you to send me if possible, and it is worth risking by post, is one of our knapsacks.

Knapsacks, as they were known in those days, had been an essential part of our family's equipment since the dark days leading up to the Second World War. We had marched off to our evacuation trains, our possessions on our backs in knapsacks, ready to foil Hitler in his plan to wipe out London's civilian population. In subsequent years, those same packs had been put to good use in many a youth movement outing and summer camp. Now one of them was being summoned to further duty, this time in the service of what we then emotionally referred to as 'the first Jewish army in 2,000 years'.

19 Frenetic Activity

Just after 6.00 a.m. on Sunday, 22 February, there came another cruel blow: the centre of central Jerualem's popular shopping and café area was torn apart as a massive bomb detonated in Ben Yehuda Street. Six British deserters had been handsomely bribed by the Arab irregulars' leader Abdel Khader el Husseini to bring an armoured car and three trucks, packed with explosives, from Latrun into the centre of Jewish Jerusalem. By thus demonstrating to the world that chaos reigned in the Holy Land, Husseini hoped to reverse the UN decision on Palestine. The British deserters, fuelled by anti-Semitic propaganda and tired of British army discipline, deluded themselves that they would become generals in the victorious Arab army.

This outrage took the lives of 44 innocent people and wounded more than 130. There were further injuries and deaths caused by heavy firing in Jerusalem's streets following the bombing. Among the dead were Jewish bus passengers, fired on by passing British armoured cars. Contrary to contemporary street opinion, there is no evidence of official British complicity, but the Jewish Agency nonetheless attacked the mandate in a lengthy memorandum to the UN Security Council, accusing the British of obstructing the UN Palestine Commission and failing to maintain law and order in the Holy Land.

Two days later, Esther wrote her own account:

> We received a most terrible blow, the centre of town wrecked, damage even as far as the outskirts, and so many of our precious souls killed. I was staying with Ida in a suburb, and we just heard the explosion, though in the

160

afternoon, when I was in town, a road-mine broke her windows. Worst was the feeling of frustration, nothing one could do, so many people already on the spot, working day and night. One could just keep out of the way. I gave a blood donation like everybody else. What with the battles that ensued and the general sense of shock, the atmosphere is taut and, from sheer depression, exhausting. A doctor told me that the first donors who rushed to give blood all had high blood pressure and fast pulse!

But our spirit is not affected. We are turning out soldiers all the time. Today our group of girls has begun a refresher course of basic training. If there was any doubt, at least as far as we are concerned, about the attitude of our 'rulers', it has now been made bitterly clear to us. Although we know that we have to pass through a period of sacrifices and hardship before we achieve our independence, yet such a beastly and heartless act is difficult to believe possible. Of course your Government cannot accept its own responsibility, but do not for goodness sake write to me again that you think it was the Arabs! I don't know what they tell you but we here saw it, heard it, know the facts, difficult as they are for you to swallow. Two of the girls at school lost parents, though they themselves escaped. One, among many others, had left home after *The Palestine Post* affair, and gone into one of the hostels that was wrecked in this latest bombing.

Esther's anger with the land of her birth leaps off the page – as does her determination not to sit idly by as a silent witness to the injustices perpetrated on her people. It's clear that she wanted to contribute her utmost and to do so where the fighting was thickest. Finishing a letter to her friend Hannah in London around the same time, she writes:

There is really no need to worry, things are fairly normal except that occasionally we suffer a loss, which we feel very deeply, when some incident occurs. Anyway, these are stirring times for us, and I am proud to be here, very.

161

Esther's friends in Palestine remember her very much the way she comes across in her letters – a young woman with a ready sense of humour, who retained her calm in the most difficult of circumstances. The only times this control slipped was when people close to her died. Yehudit (Ida) remembers that after a good friend fell in one of the battles over the road to Jerusalem, Esther could not speak for several days. Her reaction to the tragedy of the 35 young men killed bringing supplies to Kfar Etzion was similar. By the time Esther joined the Haganah, she had a huge network of friends among Jerusalem's younger set and in nearby Kfar Etzion. All too many of them were numbered among the 6,000 men and women who gave their lives in the War of Independence.

February ended with the arrival in Jerusalem of a food convoy, that had fought a pitched battle against attacking Arab gangs along three kilometres of the highway. The convoy had lost three drivers to enemy fire, and 16 of the Haganah escort were wounded. David Ben-Gurion arrived in the city for consultations with the local Haganah leadership, who were responsible for formulating plans to protect the civilian population and secure the city as the seat of the future government of the new state. That same week saw a supply convoy reach the besieged fighters and civilians in Jerusalem's Old City. Yet another attempt at a truce was made, but the exchange of fire in the ancient city's narrow streets continued unabated.

On the morning of Monday, 1 March 1948, a British troop train from Cairo was blown up by the underground Lehi group as it passed through Rehovot, killing 28 soldiers. That same day, 23 Jews were killed in incidents, which included sniping on Yemin Moshe by Arabs and British troops 'looking for a bit of target practice'. In the north of the country there was a temporary respite, as a result of a freak snowfall.

The mandatory government issued a report, accusing the Jewish Agency of inciting violence in Palestine, resulting in 1,378 deaths within three months – among them, 546 Jews. Since the 29 November UN decision on partition, 5,000 armed Arabs were reported to have entered Palestine, and vast Syrian convoys were observed moving towards the border. The Arabs attacked Bat Yam – which grandfather Naftali had wisely abandoned in December 1947, following the UN partition vote, for the comparative safety of Uncle Reuven's Tel Aviv home. And in Jerusalem's Old City, Arab snipers continued making life intolerable.

On the diplomatic front, the United States proposed setting up a five-power forum on the future of Palestine – a suggestion strongly opposed by the unique alliance of Britain and the USSR. In the aftermath of the Ben Yehuda Street bombing, Oswald Mosley's British Union of Fascists proudly claimed responsibility for killing and wounding scores of Jews in Jerusalem. One can only imagine Esther's reaction.

The British authorities announced that all incoming parcel mail would be halted from 1 April. What was to become of the haversack I had sent Esther? Then, on 10 April, it was announced that all postal services in Jerusalem were to be curtailed. With 11 weeks to independence, this breakdown in British administration resulted in Palestine's Jewish community taking over the reins of government and issuing decrees, particularly in matters of defence. There had already been an 85 per cent response in Jerusalem to the call-up of young people for military service, despite the lack of any legal enforcement. One of Esther's tasks at this time was tracking down deserters – a job she detested and from which she managed to get herself transferred very quickly.

In Tel Aviv, the situation was somewhat different; at least a third of 18- to 25-year-olds had not reported for service, and newspapers called out to 'those of you languishing in the cafés of Tel Aviv, while your contemporaries in other parts of the country are risking their lives to defend our homeland, sign up now for military service!'

We know from Dina Schur what Esther was doing at this time:

> It was the beginning of March and there came orders that the girls would not be allowed any more to participate actively in the fighting, and they were all to be transferred

to the ATS [women's section], which would be formed soon. Esther was terribly affronted. She argued that girls could take their turn as guards in outposts as well as any boy, and sometimes even better, thus taking their full share of responsibility and freeing males for the actual fighting. But despite her objections, the orders were not reversed, and still worse, the transfer to the ATS operated very slowly so that our girls remained for the time being without work altogether.

Esther refused to enjoy this time of comparative leisure. She had joined up to help actively in the fight of her people for their State, and she wanted to fulfill active duty each minute as long as the fight lasted. She looked around for work and found it. The underground broadcasting station of the Haganah needed English broadcasters. As soon as she heard about it, she volunteered, and gone were her free evenings. Every day she was on duty on time, cancelling all her social appointments, visits to the cinema etc.

Esther was a feminist before there was feminism. Not only had she received a very liberal education at both high school and at university, she had also been born in the land of Emmeline Pankhurst and the other courageous women who had chained themselves to the gates of parliament in their fight for universal suffrage. In addition to that, she couldn't bear wasting time. Her family remembers her poring over books, reading by candlelight, while we crouched in our basement-shelter during the worst of the London bombing. She was always busy with something. Even during vacation from school and university, she had a full schedule of Hebrew-language and Bible classes, concerts to attend, helping out at Thaxted farm, volunteering with child Holocaust survivors and, inevitably, the book she just had to finish reading on the bus or train.

Esther's frenetic activity during March and April, much of it self-motivated, is thus very much in character. She worked with the wounded, broadcast from the Haganah's secret radio station and did intelligence work, as well as her temporary assignment with the military police to hunt for deserters. Yet this was still not enough, and it was at this point she began her quest to join the beleaguered fighters in the Old City. Contrary to popular myth, Israeli women rarely served in combat positions, even in the early days. So even in the context of 1948, Esther's decision to fight in the Old City was highly unusual. It was only possible, in fact, because the British allowed her through as a non-combatant.

On the evening of Saturday, 6 March, Esther wrote:

> I hope that you have the impression already that I did a good thing in leaving school – I certainly feel it. As for a job in Tel Aviv, that will come afterwards. In a few days I shall be back in town for a stretch – Bet Hakerem actually, which should be pleasant. Everybody in town is angry about the matter of the four boys taken and murdered. [They were kidnapped by British soldiers, resulting in a reprisal operation by the Etzel, with the hanging of four British sergeants.] There is already a new order in connection with this incident, and they will not get a chance to do it again.

A few days later, probably in response to a worried letter from our parents, Esther wrote again, in the same light-hearted tone. She wrote, however, half in pen and half in pencil, with many ink blots staining the page – most unusual for tidy, orderly Esther. She was probably resting the paper on her knees, in a break in between some field exercise:

> Dear All, Nothing much to write except all is well, and I hope so with you too. I always seem to be in luck – when I am in Jerusalem it is quiet and as soon as I leave it becomes lively. On the whole, however, life is much more interesting than at school, and less strenuous. Among other things that I have learnt, believe it or not, is to cook! At times, with a small group, I have done the cooking instead of other duties, and have really made progress. I have catered fully – and under difficult field conditions – for up to 15 people – *cholent* and *lokshen kugel* and *borsht* and *tzimmes* for Shabbat, in addition to various dishes that are eaten here,

meat and fish – all on a little primus (kerosene) stove. We live and learn – through bitter experience only!

I bought myself a watch last week, a practical one, anti-water, because of the sand here in the summer, and luminous. It cost 8 pounds at a reduction. In case I do not have time to add more before I send this. Love and best wishes, Esther.

Esther volunteered to take over the cooking on several Haganah assignments, it seems, because she didn't trust others to maintain a kosher kitchen.

Realising our parents were not going to be reassured by her sparse letters, she must have asked her friend Ida (Yehudit) to write and tell them that all was well:

Dear Mrs Cailingold, I thought I would just write you a few words in assurance. I received a letter from you for Esther this week. Unfortunately, on going to the base, I found that she had already left on the same day. She had stayed with us on Friday evening and returned again on Shabbat. She looks really well and quite 'the thing' in uniform. It always amuses me to see her dressed up so, knowing her innate objection to all uniforms. Actually, Esther was in no danger from those explosions. Most of these incidents take place in the centre of town and she was posted far out in the outskirts.

Seeing Esther in uniform, and other acquaintances from England also doing their 'bit', gives me a real sense of pride, but it also makes me feel that I should be doing more. However, I am hoping to return to the kibbutz within a month to take up my duties in work and protecting the place, which should give me back my self-confidence.

Weather conditions here are not much better than they were in England. Last week we lost three windows and Chaim managed to insert one new pane, but the others have been replaced by strong oiled paper. However, the wind and rain and the general house structures make one long for the large fires at which we used to warm ourselves in England. On Shabbat we took out all the blankets and lay on the beds cuddled up and warm. Later on, even with the wind blowing, we set out for a brisk walk in the beautiful sunshine and it was a real pleasure, particularly since the British have been warned to keep off the roads of the Jewish zones!

It is wonderful to be here in such times and this gives us tremendous encouragement to believe that we will eventually build up a Jewish People in a Jewish State. Small things make everyday life feel really special. Leaving the bus in the evening you say *Shalom* and the driver answers *Uveracha* (and blessings to you). When one thinks of the meaning of these words and then one remembers what is happening in this country, one realises how meaningful and beautiful are these words of greeting.

Our lectures are continuing as best as conditions allow, with homework and guard duty taking up all free time. There is a very strong feeling, even stronger than in London during the War, that one must make the effort to overcome difficulties and to be strong. People willingly take up their duties and carry them out well and in a good spirit, despite the fact that life here for the ordinary citizen is, in any case, hard and dangerous enough.

I hope you are all well. Please give my regards to your parents. I can assure you that Esther is well and looking bonny (nicer than saying she is putting on weight again), and is certainly doing a good job. Shalom, Yehudit.

20 Proud to be Here

March 1948 was a month of upheaval not only in Palestine and the Middle East, but in other parts of the world, too, where the Cold War was growing warmer by the day. Even in Britain, flushed by its victory over the Nazis, paranoia prevailed. Clement Attlee's Labour government issued a Security Order, banning the appointment of communists to all sensitive civil service jobs; fascists were included under the ban, almost as an afterthought. That same month, Britain warned Argentina against challenging British rule in the Falkland Islands – a warning heeded for the next 34 years. In Prague, a dear friend of the Jews met his death with the suicide/murder of Czech Foreign Minister Jan Masaryk, shortly after the communists seized power – but not before Czechoslovakia had played a crucial role in supplying arms and even aircraft to Israel's fledgling army; the Czech-made German army rifles issued to Israel's infantry units all had their Nazi insignia carefully removed.

Thursday, 11 March saw the third Jerusalem bomb outrage: a murderous explosion at the heart of Jewish sovereignty – Jewish Agency headquarters on King George Street. An Arab drove a US consular car, American flag flying, into the Agency compound at 9.40 a.m. Five minutes later, the car blew up, killing 13 people and injuring over 50. One victim was Leib Yaffe, head of Keren Hayesod, one of the Agency's fund-raising arms. For many years afterwards, the front of that landmark building was scarred by barbed wire and blast-proof walls – a traditional 'locking of the stable door after the horse has bolted'. Even today, with the entrance restored to its former glory, the compound is kept car-bomb proof in the reality of modern Israel.

The week of 14 March opened with fierce fighting in Jerusalem where Jewish neighbourhoods bordered on those of the Arab ones. It was the day of the sniper, and increasing sectors of the city became no-go areas for all but the bravest souls. The British, who had a company of 145 Scottish infantry-men in the Old City, as well as 43 policemen 'guarding' the Jewish Quarter, issued a policy statement on the situation there: 'When the Arabs and the Jews fire at each other, we leave them to it.' Much depended on the officer in charge; some would turn a blind eye to Haganah efforts to bring in supplies, particularly if there was a cash-gift involved; others could be quite vicious, arresting Jewish fighters at will and confiscating their weapons.

On 14 March, Esther was back in Jerusalem and, having collected her mail, wrote:

> Most of the time now, I am at some small settlement where it is quiet and away from the terrible events and depressing atmosphere of Jerusalem. The whole idea, you see, is to reinforce the villages and all Jewish-held points with additional manpower. Things are not nearly as exciting as you seem to think. I assure you it is often very dull, especially with the dirty weather we are still having.
>
> It seems that Ida wrote to you – everybody says my uniform suits me. For the haphazard people's army that we still are here, I have acquired for myself a comparatively smart attire, bit by bit. As you say Mimi, I have not had time to finish my second article, although it has been almost ready for a long time. I go to Ida's place when I am on leave as it is near our headquarters. I shall certainly miss her when they finally return to the kibbutz – they are so hospitable.

At 9.00 p.m. the following evening, heavy snow began falling in Jerusalem, most unusual for the time of year. Next morning, the city was covered by a thick white blanket, and an unbelievable silence, empty of gunfire. Esther used the time to write what was to be her last letter to her friend Hannah in London:

My Dear Hannah, I owe you a letter for such a long time that I hardly know where to begin. First of all, although my parents do not seem to believe me, I am very well and glad not to be at school, although again life is not nearly as exciting as you all seem to think. As I constantly write, you get a very prejudiced view of things from the BBC and your newspapers, including *The Jewish Chronicle*. First of all, we are just a defence organisation (talking about my own present activities in general), although in the process of turning into a still very new army. So that there are really comparatively few daring exploits or grand heroics. In fact, as I constantly write to my mother, stationed in some quiet outpost, one is far better off as far as danger goes than being at home in town where one never knows when your dear countrymen will suddenly decide to blow us all up in our beds. Apart from which, the economic life of the civilian becomes increasingly difficult – food shortages, no kerosene for cooking or heating, barricaded streets, general depression when family and friends are killed – do you know what that feels like, when even a slight acquaintance is killed? Not that there is ever depression about our general situation or the final outcome, although sometimes it is really not healthy to think about that too much. We are, quite illogically, convinced that 'yihye beseder' – it'll be alright – that is the 'password', a sort of psychological bolster to the spirits, and the accepted closing words for any discussion about present conditions here.

One thing that I am getting out of all this, at the very least, is that I am speaking Hebrew all the time at last, to make up for all the time when I had no chance to practice it – Hebrew at its most colloquial too! I see a lot of Ida again as she is living quite near my headquarters, so I often go there to sleep and when I am on leave. She seems very happy and they make a fine pair. I also see Gubby Haffner if you remember him from the Thaxted Farm, as well as the

170

others from England who are on a course here, also nearby. It seems you too have had bad weather. We have just had snow! Lots of love, Esther.

Although Esther wrote over and over again to her family and friends that her 'life is not nearly as exciting' as it appears, excitement does seem to be the very thing she craved. In her last letter (quoted in Collins and Lapierre's *O Jerusalem* and in Sir Martin Gilbert's and Herbert Krosny's documentary film *Birth of a Nation*), Esther writes, 'But I did find the excitement I have always needed and have enjoyed it.' Her thirst for adventure was concealed by 'her tranquil appearance, her calm and soft voice, and her gentle smile', as Gubby Haffner remembers, even as she was planning to extricate herself from Brigade HQ and join the fighters in the Old City.

Esther's next letter is dated 18 March, and bears yet another return address, this time c/o May Wallfish, 34, Alfasi Street, Rehavia, Jerusalem:

This week I got my post at last – two letters from you of three weeks back, as well as newspapers, telegram and magazines. Great news – we had real snow this week! Just one day of it but great excitement. What does Daddy write from America? I am glad you did not tell Booba and Zada about what I am doing, because they would only worry needlessly, but I had hoped that you would understand. However it is plain from letters, newspapers etc. that it is difficult for you there to understand the situation over here. The fact that you still ask me to come back is revealing. You must think that I am the exception in answering the call to duty. I hope though that you will feel more at ease if I tell you that we are gradually, though with difficulty, turning into a regular army, with defined duties and everything else that goes with it. Today I was asked if I would like to work on the psychological warfare side, using English, and tomorrow I have to see a well known journalist now working with us. I shall let you know what comes of it – something interesting I hope.

I am giving you now the address of the Manchester girl who came out after me to teach at the school, as all the other addresses are not permanent. I did not take the room in Jaffa Road – it was not vacant – nor any other so far. Not that it was anywhere near the scene of the tragedy anyway. As a matter of fact, windows were broken by that blast even far out in the suburbs, so you see, you never can tell. As I wrote before, being stationed in some quiet outpost, fed, clothed, paid and with all provided, I am much better off than in town and over-working at school.

May Wallfish, 'the Manchester girl who came out after me to teach at the school', lived in a rented room next door to Gershon Agron, the founder-editor of *The Jerusalem* (then *Palestine*) *Post*. Her absence from school was not 'due to a severe facial skin ailment,' as Esther wrote, but because she was monitoring British police and army radio channels for Haganah intelligence in Jerusalem. On certain evenings, she would go through the garden and enter Agron's house through the back door to pick up from him information he had gleaned from the British officers and civilian officials he entertained in his home, with the help of a regular supply of good Scotch. Esther had joined the intelligence team and found it convenient to stay with May Wallfish. She was also vetting would-be volunteers to the Jewish cause from among the ranks of the British troops.

Not in combat at this time, Esther made great efforts to write home regularly. Her letter of late March vents her anger at political developments – with the US as her focus. US Secretary of State George Marshall had come up with another of his plans: this time it was to forsake the UN decision on partitioning Palestine into two independent states for a trusteeship over the disputed territory. His proposal was backed by President Truman, who believed that once the British left on 15 May, law and order would break down and chaos would reign in Palestine.

Palestine's Jewish leadership reacted swiftly. Chaim Weizmann, soon to be elected as president of the state of Israel, was in New York at the time. He responded angrily to Truman's betrayal and accused the Americans of inciting the Arabs by bowing to their violence. The leaders of Mapai, the Zionist movement's major political party, called for the immediate formation of a Jewish government. Abba Hillel Silver, a leading American Zionist, spoke out against this 'shocking reversal', and headlines such as 'BETRAYAL!' and 'BLACK FRIDAY!' appeared in Jewish newspapers in many countries. Ben-Gurion, Mapai's leading personality and Israel's future prime minister, declared in inimitable style that a Jewish state already existed!

Esther wrote:

Daddy now has the satisfaction of knowing that his own verdict of America, putting the blame on her rather than on England, is fully justified. Of all the blows, physical and moral, that we have had to suffer, this at first seemed to be the most terrible. Yet so determined and unalterable is the will of everybody here to see this thing through, that in the course of the day, any bad mood straightened itself out, and plans and work went ahead as they always do in difficult times.

The only change I discern is in the increased determination of everyone here. Just as the *Yishuv* celebrated the UN declaration of support for our independence with comparative restraint – and, at that time, I marvelled that much greater fuss was not made on such a momentous occasion – so now that everything seems to be reversed once more, I marvel that people do not seem to feel it more deeply. You would be surprised to know that, despite all that is said about Jews to the contrary, how unemotional and unexcitable they are here. The reason is that people are just too busy with the challenges of their everyday life as individuals and with the business of running their own community. They just cannot afford to risk everything by letting themselves lose control in the heat of the moment. What has been laboriously built up here, automatically carries on and grows and develops of itself. Nothing that foreign powers care to decide among themselves can make the slightest difference to this natural process.

Jewish independence is a fact which nothing now can alter, and we know that whether others care to hinder us or to help us in our difficulties, we will in any case overcome them eventually anyway. The popular reaction is that we are better off without the grudging help of others and that we can look after ourselves quite well, thank you! It is not as though we have not already tasted the bitterness of the process. We already know full well the price we have to pay. The *Yishuv* has always had to suffer for its existence and we didn't need this latest reminder of what suffering feels like.

I am proud to be here now, more than ever, and only hope that however small and remote a duty I may receive, I will get the satisfaction of feeling that I am working with all the others for a just cause.

21 *Macadam the Scot*

To our surprise Esther wrote again the next day, 22 March:

> Dear Mummy, I hope you are satisfied with the frequency of my letters, although I cannot promise that it will last. I am just now at a transitory stage, with my plans for the future not yet decided. I am reflecting on where my duties lie and my own personal satisfaction in fulfilling them, before I enter our version of the ATS [Women's Corps] into which we are now being organised. I considered Daddy's suggestion of going to Tel Aviv and getting a job there, but I really feel that I would be doing nothing but pampering myself by this, and in our present critical situation this is not the rule of action. I am very tempted to do now what I had always wanted to do on finishing my contract with the school, and that is to enter a kibbutz, perhaps to go with Ida when she and her husband return to Sdei Eliyahu. There I would be both useful and would find my satisfaction. What do you think of my idea?
>
> On the other hand, I must admit that I am very loathe to leave Jerusalem for a place so far away. I have become very attached to this city, and tomorrow I am beginning work on a special assignment, something that I was once supposed to do, but this time in a very different context, although in the same language. I have also started doing some writing for it. Today I sent in two pieces and am awaiting reaction.
>
> I am writing this at Ida's place, where I sleep each night. Yesterday I met Daddy's friend, Mr Perachodnik, who was

slightly hurt in the Ben Yehuda affair. He is quite better now but one sees changes in him as in many others now. On the other hand, everybody comments that I seem to thrive in my new conditions. Luxurious boarding-house life, no worries, no tummy troubles, since I have no chance to think of them!

The letter included a note to Mimi and myself:

Thanks for your recent letters. Have you heard anything, Asher, of *aliyah* opportunities? I hardly have any use of my clothes now, which is a great saving. Our 'uniform' is khaki, and not uniform at all, because it is made up of all the outfits of the Australian, English, American and New Zealand armies, so nobody looks quite the same. I have a battle-dress (boy's), rather too large for me; the trousers I swapped with a girl, who had been in the ATS, for her husband's three-quarter boots; socks, military or my own, according to need; a scarf which can be turned into a cap when needed; an enormously big pullover; ditto vest, which I wear over my clothes like a sweater (great material!); and beautiful white woollen mittens, a present! We shall soon be completely fitted out, with skirts instead of trousers for outdoor use.

We found out about the 'special assignment', on which she was to begin work the next day, from author and broadcaster Harry Levin in a letter that he sent our parents four months later. He wrote:

I knew Esther for only a short time, but sufficiently long to enable me to appreciate her fine qualities. I was in charge of the Haganah English Broadcasting Service in Jerusalem, and she worked for me for a time as a continuity announcer. Although she was already doing full-time service in the Haganah, she offered to add this task to her other duties; and after having her voice tested, I found her suited to this purpose. She came on the air every second evening and her function was to open the station, to introduce the news before the news-announcer came on, introduce the feature talk or commentary after the news, and finally to close down. She liked this work enormously, and would have been glad to come on every night had there been need of it. She did it well and there were many favourable comments on her work. Her identity was not at that stage known as the service was, until May 15, still underground.

She lived a good distance from the place where we transmitted. Sometimes she had to walk back home owing to the acute shortage of transport, but she never commented on this, and certainly never complained.

When her pressure to go to the Old City led finally to her transfer, I asked her to write one or two short feature stories about her experiences there for broadcasting, which she gladly agreed to do.

In point of fact, some time elapsed before a convoy was able to get through to the Old City, and although I had made arrangements at once to replace her, I was glad to continue using her services until the evening before she finally left.

About a week after she arrived in the Old City I had a cheerful note from her mentioning that she had not yet had time to write the features but would do so as soon as time permitted. She asked me to have broadcast on the Hebrew service her greetings to her relatives in Tel Aviv, which I did. She also asked to be remembered to her colleagues in our Service, all of whom were pleased to hear of her when I handed on her message.

On one occasion during the latter stages of the siege of the Old City, I was one of a group of correspondents who accompanied a Haganah unit which tried to break through Zion Gate to relieve the Jewish Quarter. I did not expect to be able to see her myself, but hoped to be able to pass on to someone a note and a bar of chocolate for her that I had managed to obtain. In the event, we were unable to break through.

I found Esther to be a very sweet, sincere person, and most charming. We did not have the opportunity of lengthy conversations, but when we did speak of things other than our work, she showed herself to be a girl of ideals and of courage.

Harry Levin's book *Jerusalem Embattled*, published in London in 1950 by Victor Gollancz, mentions Esther several times. He describes her as 'quiet and unassuming; looks as if she has plenty of character' (p. 34). Later, on 29 April, he writes:

We are looking for another continuity announcer. Esther C. is finally getting transferred to the Old City, will get in on a food convoy. I know she has been trying to smuggle herself in for weeks. Says she feels that is where she can do most good. Perhaps she is right. That calm faith of hers and sense of duty may be needed more in the Old City in the hard days ahead than anywhere else. Shall be sorry to lose her (p. 108).

Among the very few of Esther's possessions which remain are some of the typed notes she used for her underground radio broadcasts during late March and April 1948. Some are marked with her own pencilled notes and corrections. Addressing a target audience of British troops and civilians, one such bulletin reads:

YEMIN MOSHE: Troops of the Arab Legion were involved in an unprovoked attack on the Yemin Moshe quarter of Jerusalem this afternoon. A convoy passing along the Bethlehem road, opened small-arms and artillery fire at Yemin Moshe, but caused no damage or casualties. The Jewish defenders of the Quarter held their fire.

Last night, Arab gangs aided by a British army searchlight which illuminated the area, directed heavy mortar fire at Yemin Moshe. The snipers attacking Yemin Moshe kept up heavy fire until the early hours of this morning, but none of the inhabitants or the Haganah guards were hurt.

Friday, 26 March should have been joyful for Jerusalemites. It was Shushan Purim, the day on which Jews in walled cities celebrate the 2,400-year-old victory of Mordechai and the Jews over the wicked Haman and his cohorts in Shushan, capital of the Persian King Ahasuerus. Usually a day of carnival, that year Jews were instead busy defending their besieged city. Gubby Haffner (today Yehuda Avner and Mimi's husband) saw Esther for the last time that day. They met at Café Atara, in Ben Yehuda Street, at a time when it was an act of defiance to patronise the cafés that stayed open in areas which had suffered terrorist bombings. Two months earlier, days after arriving in Palestine, Gubby had had a most unusual encounter. Outside the King David Hotel – a symbol of Jewish defiance, since the Etzel had blown up the wing housing the secretariat of the Palestine government in July 1946 – he had run into a kilted Scotsman, seated at the wheel of a bright red MG sports coupé. More amazing still, the flamboyant Scotsman was fulsome in his praise of the 'brave laddies' who had blown up the building and roundly cursed the 'Sassenachs' who had got what they deserved. The Scot introduced himself as Macadam, and offered Gubby a ride, pumping him all the way about how he might volunteer to fight for the Jews. Gubby promised to try and find out for him.

So here they were, two months later, Gubby turning up to meet Esther, who arrived with a shoebox under her arm, a suitcase in her hand, and, surprisingly enough, with Macadam in tow. He had volunteered for the Haganah, handing over his red MG (for which he could no longer obtain petrol, in any case) and citing Gubby as a character reference. Esther, by then, no doubt, proficient in sorting out the genuine friends among her former countrymen from the *provocateurs*, solved the problem of Macadam in the first minutes by instructing Gubby to take the Scot into his group, digging trenches in the hills above Ein Karem. The three then settled down to chat. In those dark days, all a café could offer its civilian clientele was a cup of ersatz tea or coffee and maybe a dry biscuit. Gubby remembers being really hungry most of the time, and was therefore ecstatic when Esther opened the shoebox to reveal egg sandwiches and vegetable cutlets, 'liberated' from the canteen at the Schneller base where she was stationed.

They were tucking into the goodies when two British soldiers entered the café and began mocking Esther, who was dressed in what looked like British army uniform. Macadam was enraged and, threatening to beat them up, chased them out of the café and all the way down Ben Yehuda Street.

When they stopped laughing, Esther and Gubby talked more seriously. Why, Gubby wanted to know, was Esther carrying a suitcase? She told him it went with her everywhere. She was trying to get into the Old City, and reported regularly to the British checkpoint, in the hope of getting one of the randomly assigned places on a supply convoy to the Jewish Quarter. She already had a permit to go in as a teacher. She was urgently hoping, she told Gubby, to get into the Old City in time to celebrate Passover there.

Shortly afterwards, a Haganah car came to take her back to Schneller. Gubby recalls sitting in the café, paralysed by the thought of Esther scheming to get herself into the most dangerous place of all. From the King David Hotel to the Old City walls was already a no-go area. Three days after the 29 November UN decision on partition, an Arab mob had run riot here – the area where David's Village and the Hilton Hotel now stand – and it had been unsafe for Jews on the streets ever since. Arab snipers lined the tower of the YMCA building, and the Musrara and Jaffa Gate areas were death-traps. Gubby shuddered at the thought of Esther going beyond this danger zone.

During that last week of March, there was heavy fighting in the north and on the Jerusalem front, as the Haganah battled to keep open the lines of communication between areas of Jewish settlement. They managed to get a convoy through to the isolated Negev settlements after a two-week battle, and to destroy an Arab convoy of arms and men heading for Haifa. In those two battles, three of the 12 Medals of Heroism awarded for acts of valour in the War of Independence were earned.

Tragically counterbalancing those victories, however, were three catastrophic attacks on Jewish convoys. On 27/28 March,

30 supply trucks got through to Kfar Etzion but, on their return journey, they were ambushed near Nebi Daniel by thousands of Arab irregulars. In the ensuing battle, 12 convoy escorts were killed and scores wounded. British troops entered the fray at this point to confiscate all weapons and all convoy vehicles, including the precious armoured cars, as the price for safe passage of the survivors back to Jerusalem. On 28 March, a convoy en route from Nahariyah to the isolated settlement Yehiam was attacked and destroyed, with the loss of 42 lives among its Haganah escorts. And on 31 March, a Jerusalem-bound convoy was attacked at Hulda, resulting in 17 more Jewish dead.

Heavy fighting continued in the vital Bab el Wad defile. A Palmach battalion was seconded to attack the Arab positions commanding this bottleneck on the Jerusalem road, with orders to hold the Arab sniper posts until the convoy safely passed. Later, the Arab villages above Bab el Wad (now known by its Hebrew name of Sha'ar Haggai) were occupied by Palmach troops and soldiers from Esther's Moriah Battalion, and passage to Jerusalem was at last unobstructed.

The Jewish Agency, now meeting as the future government of the Jewish state, formally decided to comply with the 29 November UN resolution on partition and reject the American trusteeship proposal out of hand. Danish and Norwegian troops were put on alert at UN request for possible policing duties in Jerusalem. British troops continued to harass the tiny Jewish garrison in the Old City; they blew up two strategic Jewish buildings, fired mortar shells at Haganah positions, and, in a 29 March clash, three Jews and one British soldier were killed. The desperate battles to keep the southern flank of the city open continued unabated, with the isolated Etzion settlements under constant attack from hordes of armed Arabs from nearby towns and villages.

Through the turmoil, Esther tried to keep up her letters home. On 28 March, she wrote:

> A few days ago I sent you a letter written in a sad mood [the letter never reached us]. Now again, I must warn you

that today I feel the deepest despair that has occurred here. It is a terrible day. The battle of Kfar Etzion has gone on for more than 24 hours – if only something good will come of it, we shall feel better. We have news of 12 of our people killed and 100 Arabs, but they are 20 times our number.

Monday, March 29: Well, thank goodness yesterday is over. It was a terrible day, tense and anxious. There was a bread shortage and it looks as though there are strong possibilities we may suffer something like Europe did during the War. Despite abundant rain, we may not have water, if the pumping stations remain in Arab hands, as do the electricity power plants. Each year, the Mandatory Government promised to bring in the necessary machinery for adequate supplies, but never did so. There are no vegetables, potatoes are a luxury, no fish, no meat for a long time now, even the standbys of sausage, *lokshen* [pasta], beans are short. Imagine being short of oranges and olives here!

At last they brought everybody back from the Kfar Etzion convoy, including the 12 dead. I was at the Jewish Agency building when they arrived there and helped to hand round water and cigarettes. They transferred the wounded by lamplight from army ambulances to our own Magen David Adom vehicles. Fortunately, there were very few seriously wounded. The 12 were killed when they reversed their vehicle to keep off the attackers with their fire until the rest had entrenched themselves in the empty houses of an Arab village. They were preparing to rejoin the main body, and three managed to do so, when they were blown up in their armoured car. This could have been a great victory for us and a great example of courage, and believe me, for all our mistakes and lack of knowledge in the art of warfare, there is nothing like the real heroism of every one of our boys in battle. Sadly all this has cost us very dearly, because the British confiscated all their weapons and refused even to evacuate the wounded until they had searched even those on stretchers. Worst of all, just as we were feeling a little relieved at the return of the convoy, we heard of 42 Jewish bodies found in the north. It is still not clear what happened. All this is after the convoy attacks of last week when I lost many friends. On Purim and on Shabbat, I visited others who were wounded and are in hospital. This will probably be a part of my regular duties soon, as I shall probably receive a job in the Welfare branch.

Yet the very worst news is from abroad. It is like 1939 all over again – Denmark cancels army leave and stops pulling down air-raid shelters. All the talk of there not being a war is a sure sign! So, after all, I wish that you were all here, where we could be together and at home and still have happy times when the weather is fine, and feel like independent human beings, decent and normal in our own right. Well, I do not suppose that things are nearly as black as they have seemed to be in the last few days.

On the last day of March 1948, Esther wrote again:

Every time I write, I wonder whether this will be the last letter I shall be able to send. Let's hope that some arrangement will be made for mail to get through and if not, you will have to periodically send me pre-paid telegrams. Anyway, don't worry about me. If you want to worry then think of our poor boys who are being killed off, the cream of the lot, the brilliant students, the leaders, and others who have been here so short a time after surviving the horrors of Europe. Or think of those who are still alive but mutilated in the prime of their youth and health, which is much worse. Think of them if you must, but please remember that I am well looked after, no standing in line for kerosene, bread, milk or anything else that you can think of, or standing in long queues on wet days. Yes it is raining again and cold after a one day *hamsin*. The only thing there is no queue for is the cinema and we even get free tickets for that. There is no more news, so will close with love to you all and best wishes.

PART FOUR

22 B.G. Knows Best

By April 1948, Mandatory Palestine was in its death throes, with both Arabs and breakaway Jewish groups spreading terror virtually unchecked. The underground Lehi group blew up a train between Zichron-Yaacov and Benyamina, killing 40 Arabs and injuring over 60. Nearby, in Pardess Chana, the Etzel attacked the 'Camp 80' British base, slaying its commander and five soldiers, and taking rifles, Sten and Bren guns and Piat anti-tank rifles. Meeting in Tel Aviv, the 77 members of the Zionist General Council urgently called for the establishment of a central Zionist authority to absorb and control these two groups.

By the end of the first week in April, Jewish forces in the north were reporting victories at Mishmar HaEmek and in the Galilee Panhandle, but the Jerusalem front remained the scene of bitter pitched battles – at Bab el Wad on the Jerusalem highway, in the Suba quarries and on the strategic Castel hill. On 8 April, the charismatic Arab commander, Abdel Khader el Husseini, was killed on the slopes of the Castel, and thousands of his followers flocked to his funeral – leaving the stronghold to the Haganah and ending the prolonged, bloody struggle for this vital hill. At Maaleh HaHamisha, Haganah Piper Cub planes supplied the besieged HQ of the Palmach's Harel Brigade, under the command of Yitzchak Rabin. In the Old City, British troops proved as much the adversary as the Arabs. They damaged the famous Hurva Synagogue in a sustained bombardment, announced that Haganah and Etzel forces were 'a menace to peace', and confiscated weapons from Jewish fighters at every opportunity.

Casualties among Jewish fighting groups between December and March numbered 851 dead and 1,781 injured. Amid the turmoil, the Anglo-Jewish Association optimistically placed an advertisement in *The Palestine Post* of 8 April, announcing registration for 'A New Evelina de Rothschild School to open on Ussishkin Street, Jerusalem, on 1 September 1948.'

In Flushing Meadows, New York, the UN Security Council voted unanimously for a cease-fire in Palestine, while on the streets of New York, 60,000 Jewish war veterans marched to protest America's reversal on partition. The American counterproposal was a 57-nation trusteeship over Palestine, 'until Jews and Arabs agree on a form of Government'. David Ben-Gurion accepted the cease-fire proposal but dismissed the trusteeship out of hand.

Ben-Gurion was not by nature a military man. He had risen to corporal in the Jewish Legion in the First World War, but lost his stripes for sleeping on guard. His public career was divided into three equal parts: for 15 years he headed the Histadrut Trade Union Executive; for 15 years, he headed the Jewish Agency; and for 15 years he was Israel's prime minister and defence minister. His interest in security began in 1939, with the promulgation of the British White Paper, which limited immigration of Jews to Palestine and acquisition of land for settlement. With disaster approaching for European Jews, it was clear to him that Jewish independence in Palestine would be won only by force of arms. He therefore began intensively reading up on defence. In 1940, he went to London, where he spent part of the Blitz. Winston Churchill fascinated him, and served him as a role model – a leader who successfully combined the jobs of prime minister and defence minister, without high military rank.

In 1946, Ben-Gurion was given the Jewish Agency Executive's defence portfolio. He set up a seminar for the study of security issues, and cut himself off from all other duties for several weeks, immersing himself totally in military material. Thereafter, he frequently demonstrated his total belief in his own judgement of security matters. For three months in 1952, for example, he abandoned all other duties in order to visit every unit in the IDF, and then went on to write Israel's Defence Doctrine, which is still used today.

Ben-Gurion's tendency to 'know best', however, brought him into constant conflict, first with the Haganah High Command and later with the IDF General Staff. His appointment of David Shaltiel to command the Etzioni Brigade in February 1948 raised many a Haganah eyebrow. The position was highly sensitive: Etzioni's commander was also military commander of Jerusalem, with responsibility for the area stretching from Bab el Wad in the west to the Etzion Bloc in the south. Shaltiel's earlier battle experience had been as a French Foreign Legion sergeant in Algeria in the late 1920s, and he had never commanded more than a squad in the field. His tenure as Jerusalem commander was fraught with controversy, not least with the Palmach Harel Brigade, which was heavily involved in the Jerusalem area fighting. The Palmach leaders never accepted Shaltiel's authority as overall regional commander, and constantly criticised his judgement. His own field unit commanders became increasingly disillusioned; at total odds with Haganah (and later IDF) doctrine, he never visited troops in the field. Heavily preoccupied with discipline and insignia, his 21 May 'Top Secret and Immediate' order to all commanders, from squad leaders upward, declared that any soldier who retreated, refused an order to advance or refused to dig fortifications was to be shot! This was one week after the establishment of the state – and there's no record of this order ever being carried out or, in fact, ever being taken seriously.

In late May, Ben-Gurion appointed American volunteer Colonel David Marcus (known by his *nom-de-guerre*, Micky Stone) Jerusalem commander, over Shaltiel's head, giving him the rank of *aluf* and thus making him the first to hold general officer rank in Israel's armed forces. On 11 June, the eve of the first cease-fire, Micky Marcus was shot and killed by one of his own sentries, when he failed to recall the Hebrew password. Shaltiel was again briefly in charge, but was replaced within the month by Moshe Dayan, to a huge sigh of relief from the officers and men of the Jerusalem command.

Under weak, inexperienced and uncoordinated leadership, Jerusalem in April 1948 was under virtual siege and facing starvation, while battles raged in and around the city. None of Esther's letters from the first part of April survive (if she, in fact, wrote any), and it's from her friends that we know how she spent that time.

Dina Schur wrote:

By the end of March, we were transferred to the Schneller Camp, our new military headquarters. Only too soon, our boys were sent to take and hold the Castel near Jerusalem. Daily, our wounded started to come in. My task, as welfare officer of the Company, was to await them and take care of them. There were many and it was hard to find time to visit them all daily so as to look after their needs, as I had other duties to attend. Esther at once perceived the situation and offered to help. Daily she made the rounds of the hospitals, bringing with her small gifts – cigarettes, sweets, illustrated magazines, but chiefly and most important, a smiling face. She would take an interest in every one of them. Of course, I learned soon enough that she did not reserve her sympathy for the wounded of our Company alone, but made a habit of visiting and getting to know all the soldiers lying in hospital in various parts of town. The rest of the time she spent in Camp and she shared with us her free hours, always trying to make things easier and more comfortable for us. Whenever we went to the dining hall with her, we were sure to find her managing to procure a clean table and second helpings.

She was always around with her camera and made many of us happy by presenting us with snapshots in warrior-like poses. Whenever I was with her, I was always astonished to discover how many people knew and liked her. It was hard to keep moving as people were always coming up to greet her from all sides. Everyone wanted to exchange a few words with her and she always knew the name of the person addressing her and all about him or her, inquiring about their welfare and their family.

190

All the time we served together, Esther remained deeply religious and kept all the rules of our faith. She never ate anywhere without making sure that it was *kasher*, and in Bet Hakerem she lived on cold meals for some weeks as the pension where we were staying was not up to the level of *kashrut* that she required. She was very upset to discover there was no place where girls could pray in the new synagogue in our Camp. She used to go there each Shabbat with her prayerbook and take part in the prayers while standing outside.

We tried to get her into the Welfare Branch of our growing army, but she had heard about the possibility of going to the Old City where girls were needed. In a matter of days, she succeeded in getting her transfer application approved, and in being released from her broadcasting duties and from our Company. There remained some obstacles, as being a British subject it was hard to get a permit from the British Security authorities which was then still necessary, but she managed to surmount that obstacle too.

All was ready and there remained only the problem of being taken along by one of the British convoys, which were then the only link with the Old City. They used to select people quite at random, leaving the others behind. Few tried to join a convoy for a second or third time. Not so Esther, who used to turn up at the starting point with her packages, wait for several hours, be refused and try again as soon as the next convoy was due to depart. I do not know how many times we said goodbye to each other, only to meet again.

During that period, I was wounded severely and remained unconscious for the most part of two weeks. I remember once waking up and seeing Esther sitting watch beside me, but she would not let me try to speak. It was the last time I beheld her dear face. When I finally woke up, I was told that she had visited me daily, taking over while my nurse went for her lunch. She came to see me up to the last day when the convoy finally took her along, which was

191

just after the end of Pesach. Even then she left only after arranging for another girl to take her place. She sent me a letter from behind the Old City walls, and also greetings over the radio. She seemed to be happy with the burden of her new job as liaison for one of the sectors of the Jewish Quarter defence lines.

Esther spent April in a besieged and bombarded Jerusalem, literally running between her tasks in different parts of town – always making sure to present herself at the British convoy assembly point several times a week, hoping to be allowed through to the Old City. Five letters from her, written mostly in pencil between 11 and 26 April, reached our London home.
She wrote:

I now have two separate jobs, Intelligence and Broadcasting and apart from that I have my duties with the wounded, who are brought in all too often now. Nearly all my unit went out in battle two weeks ago and we spent a very worried period thinking that most of them were lost. In the end there were not as many as we had feared, though I needn't tell you again that it's not a happy feeling to lose one's friends, wonderful boys, full of life and goodness. It's difficult to grasp that someone I knew well is no longer with us even though one is getting used to these sensations.

I suppose the past week's news has worried you more than ever and yesterday sounded like a minor air raid with the outer suburbs being shelled. In camp, however, we feel comparatively little of water and food shortages.

You obviously do not understand the position here if you even suggest that I go to Tel Aviv. You see the road is impassable, there are battles raging in the whole of that area, and no means of transport except a very high priority plane on a roundabout route. You cannot imagine the thrill when a food convoy finally gets through after a period of total siege. Perhaps the position will change soon if we can hold onto our gains and if the British do not interfere.

It was at this time that something occurred in Jerusalem that shook Jew and non-Jew alike, and is used as anti-Zionist propaganda until this day. On Friday, 9 April, Etzel and Lehi fighters attacked the Arab village of Deir Yassin on Jerusalem's western outskirts, a place used as a training ground for Abdel Khader's irregulars and a base for attacks on nearby Jewish neighbourhoods and settlements.

Without passing judgement on the operation's success or failure or on its alleged atrocities (HQ Etzioni Brigade reported in full to Ben-Gurion and the Haganah High Command in Tel Aviv, describing the operation as 'pointless and horrific'), suffice it to say that the Arabs used the Deir Yassin attack to excuse terrible brutality in the weeks to come. 'Revenge' for Deir Yassin included the bloody attack on a convoy of doctors, nurses and medical supplies to Hadassah Hospital four days later and the attempted lynching of Jewish prisoners in the Old City, in late May. The mutilated bodies of the 35 young Palmachniks slain on their way to Kfar Etzion three months earlier, however, were evidence enough of Arab savagery, without excuses such as Deir Yassin.

> We had the horrible attack on the Hadassah convoy going up to the Hospital, where we lost some of our greatest doctors and professors, as well as nurses, workers and patients. My Mrs Epstein had a narrow escape, as she should have been on the convoy but for a chance change of plan. I don't think the BBC bothered to inform you it was a hospital convoy that was attacked – great white ambulances with the Red Magen David emblem very plainly displayed. Yet when we attack a strategically dangerous Arab village, we are accused of unscrupulous behaviour.

On Tuesday, 13 April, Jerusalemites thrilled to the arrival of a 175-truck convoy of urgently needed food and supplies. Operation Nachshon, designed to gain control of the vital route to the coast, was beginning to succeed, and this was the first convoy in many months to have escaped attack. Further good news came from south of Jerusalem, with the repelling of a large Arab force at Kfar Etzion.

Jews abroad were also under attack. Jewish Agency offices in Argentina were bombed, and street clashes between fascists and Jewish groups had become a regular occurrence in England. Britain's Zionist youth movements were intensively recruiting volunteers and acquiring arms for the struggle in Palestine.

On 14 April, Esther wrote, again in a mixed scribble of pen and pencil:

> First the good news! Great excitement yesterday when a big supply convoy got through – cattle, eggs, poultry, dried and tinned goods, cigarettes etc. The kindergarten kids stood along the roads and cheered, and there were crowds who turned out to greet the escort guards. Oh, and potatoes which we haven't seen for some weeks. People have been going back to nature with the children picking wild plants after school, before the heat dries up all the greenery. Just like in wartime Britain, we have *Woman's Corner* on the radio, telling us how to improvise with the meagre supplies.
>
> Matzos are being distributed here now. We received a big package per person, the same as last year, which is enough. This week, pastries were baked again, plain ones with dark flour, but it shows that we are not doing too badly. As Ida wrote home, their quarter was shelled on Shabbat. I usually stay with them for Shabbat but just that day I couldn't be with them.

Two days later she wrote again, after receiving a package from London which I recall wrapping and sending off with great excitement to my big sister, the soldier in Jerusalem:

> Much to my surprise and that of everyone else, the haversack arrived in fine form and I am finding it useful already! It took just four weeks to get here.
>
> I shall have to start writing 'last letters' especially to all the people to whom I have never written because soon there will be no communications, not even by phone or

telegraph, even via America, unless something is done at the last moment. I know we shall be thinking of one another, especially during the *Seder* – let's hope for a *Seder* all together next year, but of course 'Next Year in *Our* Jerusalem!'

23 *Hunger in Jerusalem*

Esther's flippancy about 'last letters', in anticipation of the breakdown in postal services, has great poignancy. Only five more of her letters were to reach the family in London, the last of them after her death. The tone in which she wrote home remained cheerful and optimistic, in the chatty style that our parents expected from their clever daughter, blessed with a creative pen and a ready sense of humour. Her Haganah colleagues, too, testify that she always had a bright smile and a cheerful word, and could be relied on to boost morale, whatever the circumstances.

None of us sensed her despair and anger as more and more of the young men she knew were maimed and killed. She never even hinted to us of a special attachment to any one person, but we learned later that she was especially close to one of the Kfar Etzion commanders, and, later, to a young man who was killed in the Old City.

By mid-April, Esther was burning to be in action. She was one of very few young women to take part in the actual fighting in Israel's War of Independence, even within the Old City garrison, where most of the women served as nurses, cooks or in supply roles. Of the 1,200 members in Palmach's Harel Brigade, for example, 400 were women but only five were in combat. Esther was thus very much an exception to the rule that the real fighting was for the men.

She wrote to us on 18 April:

> I must say that I am very sober about our chances and prospects in general, but that's just part of the general

tendency here not to get over-hopeful in case of disappointment. It's so easy to get excited in other ways though, even to an unhealthy extent. One example is when the British stood by and let over 80 hospital and university staff be murdered – patients and professors, travelling in an ambulance convoy practically undefended by our people. Some of them were horribly burnt alive – the details are terrible. Yet public opinion is furious only against ourselves, because we should have known what to expect of the British and we had no right to have taken notice of their 'warnings' about us not keeping to some non-existent convoy 'rules' and daring to make our own arrangements to defend ourselves. Then when we sent out relief forces, the British would not let them through.

Outside Jerusalem, Jewish forces were winning key victories. On 19 April, the ancient walled city of Tiberias became an all-Jewish town. Three days later, the Haganah secured Haifa, with the British retaining control only of the vital port, through which to evacuate their troops three weeks later. Six days after that, Jewish forces penetrated the Arab lines at Jaffa. The Arabs surrendered two weeks later after heavy resistance.

In those chaotic days, it was often difficult to distinguish enemies from neutrals among the three groupings of British, Jews and Arabs – the last comprising both locally organised gangs and elements of armies infiltrating from neighbouring countries. Adding to the confusion was the Transjordan Arab Legion, under Lieutenant-General Sir John Bagot Glubb (known to his troops as Glubb Pasha), who later wrote, 'The Arab Legion in Palestine was operating as an allied army with the British army.'

That spring, Glubb had served as interpreter at a private meeting in London between Transjordan Prime Minister Taufiq Pasha and British Foreign Secretary Ernest Bevin. Under discussion was a Transjordan proposal to send the Arab Legion across the Jordan River immediately the British left, 'to occupy that part of Palestine awarded to the Arabs which was contiguous with the frontier of Transjordan', so that the area should fall neither to the Jews nor to the Mufti, who had cooperated with Hitler in the Second World War. Bevin's reply, as recorded by Glubb, was, 'It seems the obvious thing to do.'

Tacit British approval was thus given for entry into the fray of a fully trained and equipped, British-officered, division-sized Arab army. Fighting primarily on the Jerusalem front (at Latrun, Kfar Etzion and in the Old City), its role was pivotal and it scored the major Arab victories of the War of Independence. Glubb later complained that he had only 4,500 troops and was not allocated extra ammunition for the campaign. What he didn't mention are his armoured cars and artillery which shelled Jerusalem from Nebi Samuel throughout the siege. Arab Legion heavy mortars were firing on Jewish neighbourhoods as early as the third week in April. Among their direct hits – a school and a hospital.

On 21 April, the Jewish Agency demanded withdrawal of the Arab Legion from Palestine. On 22 April, 30 busloads of Arab Legion troops arrived in Jerusalem to back up the Arab gangs. On 26 April, the Arab League decided that Glubb Pasha's Arab Legion would spearhead the attack on Palestine and that no other Arab country need send regular troops. The only other major military force to take part in the invasion was, in fact, that of Egypt – which threatened Jerusalem and got to within 20 miles of Tel Aviv.

On the political front, Australia's prime minister backed the Jewish cause, rejecting America's trusteeship proposal and insisting that the UN decision on partition be enforced. Meanwhile, Britain's House of Lords passed a bill setting 15 May as the last day of Britain's 29-year-old mandate in Palestine. Transjordan's King Abdullah declared war on Zionism and vowed to defend the honour of the Arab people. The mayors of Hebron, Gaza and Beersheba responded by proclaiming Abdullah king of southern Palestine.

On the evening of Friday, 23 April, Jews around the world sat down to the *Seder* ceremony. In Jerusalem, the traditional description of *matza* as the 'bread of affliction' took on new meaning. There was little else to eat: Jerusalemites were drawing water from long-unused artesian wells and carefully collecting weeds from odd patches of earth to cook as vegetables for empty plates.

That weekend's news was not encouraging. In response to the deadly attack on the Hadassah convoy, the Haganah had driven the Arab gangs out of the vital Sheikh Jarrah district, which linked west Jerusalem with the hospital and university enclave on Mount Scopus. But on 25 April, the British army intervened, taking Sheikh Jarrah and killing two Haganah fighters in the process. That same day, the British evacuated the country's sole international airport at Lydda, and allowed it to pass into Arab hands.

The official founding of *Chen*, the women's branch of the Haganah and later of the IDF, also took place on 25 April. All women from the age of 18 were to serve, and henceforth would do so within *Chen*. For Esther and the handful of other young women in combat units, this had no practical meaning, and they continued serving in partisan fashion. The Haganah conducted its first open parade in Jerusalem that day, in joint celebration of Passover and the signing of a pact with the dissident Etzel. In the Old City, a shaky truce was in place: Jewish and Arab representatives at Lake Success had agreed on a temporary cease-fire there, allowing the Jews to celebrate Passover, and granting the weary Jewish Quarter fighters a brief respite.

Esther spent the *Seder* with friends of our father, and her 26 April letter describing it was the last she wrote before entering the Old City – or the last that reached our home in London:

> I don't know if there's much point in writing now, since Lydda Airport was occupied yesterday, but maybe something will be arranged. Well, Seder I spent with Mr Freund. There was quite a crowd, and everything was repeated five times by different heads of families. Although there was not much singing, it took about four hours and we finished at midnight. We had quite a good meal too – chopped fish, soup, meat and potatoes. For nearly everybody, except those of us in the army, this was the first good meal they had eaten for some time, probably for about three months, and what with fish and meat, many had tummy-ache!

Not that many people have been actually hungry, except the very poor, who always suffer more. But it really has been a great problem and there is the feeling of uncertainty about tomorrow's meals. There are ration books but no fixed portions for any defined period, just whatever manages to get through is equally shared out, and everybody ekes out with any stock of canned goods that they manage to acquire. Then there are problems like no fuel to cook with, if you have anything to cook, or no water to wash the vegetables with, if you have any vegetables. The uncertainty of it all, as well as the atmosphere and conditions, makes the food shortage and general situation much different from what it was in England during the war.

For a couple of nights when we were blowing up nearby villages, or during our attack on Sheikh Jarrah to clear the road to the university, the town could not sleep at all, although I am ashamed to admit that nothing disturbs me these days! I sleep through it all – and you know what I used to be like! But now I eat well, sleep well, and have given up worrying. Even more so than during the London air raids, the feeling is that if it's coming your way anyway, there is nothing that one can do.

The last day of April 1948 coincided with the end of the Passover festival. By then, there was real fear that starvation would bring the Jewish population to its knees. Jerusalem's Haganah commanders urgently radioed Tel Aviv HQ to send more supplies, especially food. Dov Joseph, the Canadian-born Jewish Agency leader whom Ben-Gurion had placed in charge of Jerusalem's supplies, sent Ben-Gurion a 'shopping list' of the minimum quantities of food needed to sustain Jerusalem's 110,000 residents for four weeks. His list included 750,000 eggs and over 4,000 tons of other food items.

24 Into the Old City

Saturday, 1 May, the day after Passover, saw Jerusalem's suburbs finally freed from Arab attack. In the north, too, the Haganah was succeeding, defeating pockets of Arab resistance and taking eastern Galilee, including the long-disputed settlement of Birya.

As the British got ready to leave, the Schneller base in Jerusalem, HQ of the Haganah's 6th Brigade, was in a bustle of preparation to fight for control of the city. Among the Haganah men and women in their makeshift uniforms were 20 teachers, with permits to enter the Old City – ostensibly to work with the children in the closing term of the school year. They were the last group to get into the Jewish Quarter, and the only reinforcements the garrison received, apart from the reservists who came in with the Palmach assault on the night of 18/19 May.

Esther, of course, was among these 20, and one of very few who had undergone military training and had field experience. She was, by then, a well-known figure around HQ, as she ran between her intelligence, welfare and radio work. A note to her survives in IDF archives, instructing her to take last-minute orders before going into the Old City, from the Moriah Battalion's operations officer, Yehoshafat Harkavi.

A regular Jewish army already existed inside the Old City, even though the British still treated its soldiers as criminals and outlaws, to be arrested even on suspicion of carrying arms. Daily Orders No. 82, issued by the Old City's Haganah commander on Sunday, 2 May, for example, mentions training in house-to-house fighting to take place that day; removal of YM from his outpost for disobeying orders (for which he was later fined 20 *mils*); and new appointments, including Rika Menashe (Meidav) as HQ secretary.

201

As long ago as 1932, the Haganah had designated the Old City Area A in its defence plan for Jerusalem and set up look-out posts facing the Temple Mount. Avraham Halperin was the first commander of the Jewish Quarter. At his instigation, a huge arms dump was built under the Yochanan Ben Zakkai Synagogue, proving an invaluable hiding place both for military equipment smuggled in over the years, and for soldiers and citizens when the mob attacked. Boosting of Haganah forces, as well as the small and poorly armed groups of Etzel and Lehi fighters, began with the UN decision on partition in November 1947. In mid-December, the British sent in a company of the Highland Light Infantry to surround the Jewish Quarter as a barrier between Jew and Arab. They also accompanied the convoys of non-military supplies and personnel, but refused to relieve the Arab siege.

With the appointment of David Shaltiel as Jerusalem area commander late in January 1948, came Ben-Gurion's order that the Old City not be abandoned at any cost. Shaltiel considered this policy mistaken, seeing no point in wasting valuable resources on an area without intrinsic strategic value. On 20 January, Avraham Halperin returned to the Jewish Quarter as military governor, with the rank of a Haganah company commander. With a budget of 5,000 Palestinian pounds, his job was to ensure the smooth running of civilian affairs and, through an Armenian middleman, to buy weapons looted by Arabs from British stores. He was extremely successful, gaining the confidence and cooperation of all Jewish sectors – including Mordechai Weingarten, official *mukhtar* of the Quarter, who usually saw himself independent of the Zionist authorities.

On 3 March, the British struck a cruel blow when they expelled Halperin from the Old City. He was replaced by a young and inexperienced platoon leader named Moshe Rousnak, who spent the weeks until the Old City fell pleading with Battalion HQ to send a more senior officer. He had got through the British blockade into the Old City three months earlier, on 14 December, posing as a doctor at the wheel of an ambulance, although he knew no medicine. Although he was a graduate of Haganah courses for squad commanders and platoon leaders, the Haganah hierarchy nonetheless treated Rousnak with suspicion, since he had known right-wing sympathies and was a former member of Lehi.

Rousnak may have been inexperienced, but he was a good organiser and disciplinarian. While under Halperin's command, he had set up a reserve food store which kept his fighting force supplied through the long weeks of siege. He did not, however, receive the necessary back-up. He argued bitterly with his superiors about the Jewish Quarter battle orders: unaltered since being drawn up in the 1930s, at the time of the Arab riots, they were purely defensive, with the Haganah's role being to protect the civilians and hold out until the arrival of British troops! No officer at battalion or brigade level visited the Old City during his command, he charged, and he recalled no occasion when he received tactical instructions relevant either to his position or to battle conditions.

The major problems of the Jewish Quarter defenders were supplies, arms and manpower. For supplies, they were largely dependent on the British escorting the food and supply convoys. For arms, any and all ways were used. Palms were greased. False compartments in the fuel tanks of convoy vehicles were built and filled – to such a degree that kerosene for fuel and cooking was almost non-existent in the Old City. Rabbi Weingarten's daughter, Masha, once brought in an entire Lewis machine gun, dismantled in her suitcase. Homemade grenades were formed from nails and explosives stuffed into Players cigarette cans that had been discarded by British Tommies.

The shortage of manpower proved the most serious problem of all. The number of Jewish fighters inside the Old City never exceeded 150, including Esther and a number of other teachers who came in with her on that last convoy at the beginning of May. The term Old City 'fighters' included 15-year-old Yosef Tanje, who was sent to the Gadna Youth contingent in the Old City, and 16-year-old Yehudit Jouran, who came home to spend Passover with her parents in the Jewish Quarter and found herself recruited into the Haganah garrison. Her school first-aid training was put to use in the field hospital, but she also took her place on the barricades when the fighting became desperate, and physically barred the advance of Arab irregulars to cover the evacuation of the wounded in the last battle. She remembers Esther as like an older sister to her. She admired her skill with weapons and the way she moved between outposts under fire.

A 5 May Haganah report refers to 140 men, women and teenagers in the Old City garrison. An 11 May weapons report lists two two-inch mortars with 93 shells, one Bren and one Lewis gun with 2,000 rounds, 17 Sten guns and five Finnish sub-machine guns with 18,800 rounds, 16 British rifles with 3,500 rounds, 38 pistols and revolvers with about 1,500 bullets and 430 hand grenades. This in the face not only of the Arab irregulars, but also the Arab Legion with its armoured cars, six-pounder artillery and three-inch mortars.

Rousnak's desperate appeals for reinforcements are thus understandable. He asks that *yeshiva* students who had left the Jewish Quarter be returned to defend it, and that Jewish police serving in the Old City desert to join his forces. One such policeman who had already signed up with him was Achia Hashiloni, a Haganah man since 1936. He continued to report for police work each day, and then went off to command 20 fighters manning outposts, and to create a solid defence line against Arab attack by building escape routes over the roofs of the houses, and stone barricades behind every door.

In west Jerusalem, victories were being scored by the beginning of May, but in the Old City, Haganah troops were grappling with the British refusal to allow in food convoys. The 2 May convoy that should have brought in food and 20 teachers was cancelled because of two rifles stolen from the police station. On Friday, 7 May, two rifles were handed over to the British and the convoy finally assembled in the courtyard of the Jewish Agency building. British troops then swept vehicles with mine detectors, but a considerable quantity of weapons and ammunition still slipped past – including the Lewis gun in Masha Weingarten's suitcase.

Most of the male passengers were left behind for lack of room on the overloaded trucks. Esther and the other female teachers were taken aboard, as was Shaar-Yashuv Cohen, a *yeshiva* student volunteer (and today Chief Rabbi of Haifa). He was the son of a leading figure in Orthodox Jewry, an ascetic, who spent his days in prayer, fasting and in the study of the holy scripts, but who saw it as a privilege that his son defend the area most holy to the Jewish people. Appointed cultural officer in the Old City garrison, Shaar-Yashuv Cohen took up arms in the final battle, suffered several bullet wounds and, despite a shattered leg which has left him with a permanent limp, was taken to Transjordan by the Arab Legion as a prisoner of war.

The convoy made its way along King George Street, turned left into Mamilla Road (today, Agron Road), and stopped by the US consulate to be checked through the British army barrier which separated Jewish and Arab Jerusalem. Guarded by British armoured cars, the convoy then made its slow way down into the Hinnom Valley and up the Armenian Patriarch Road to the Zion Gate.

Esther and the other teachers reported at once to Haganah HQ in the Old City, meeting their commander, Moshe Rousnak for the first time. Teaching was out of the question by then, since it was far too dangerous to group children together in classrooms. Several youngsters had already been hurt when an Arab shell hit a schoolroom. Esther, with her military experience, was appointed liaison for the western fortifications sectors, responsible for the needs of all its outposts, from arms and ammunition to food and drink. This involved her moving constantly between her sector outposts along the rooftop routes recently laid out under Hashiloni. One young fighter remembers her coming to his outpost and finding he had left his food in the open to become covered in dust and flies. She reprimanded him sternly, declaring herself unready to risk her life to bring him food if this was his response. Nonetheless, she returned shortly afterwards with a fresh supply.

Her fellow fighters also remember her as particularly caring of the young Gadna cadets, who acted as runners between outposts, and remember how she constantly sought to protect them from unnecessary exposure to fire.

Among the Old City defenders was Adina Argaman. 'I met Esther in the dining-hall the day she arrived, which was just after Pesach,' she remembers.

She seemed a little lost, at first. She came to the Old City to replace one of the girls who had spent a long time there during the siege, entering in the guise of a teacher (she had, in fact, been an English teacher at the Evelina de Rothschild School), although she had no intention of working in that role. I helped her get organised and introduced her to the members of the garrison staff. One of the girls working in the club-room knew her from west Jerusalem and she brought her that evening to the communal meal held each Shabbat by the teachers, which was her introduction to our social group, where she quickly became very popular. She was appointed to the role of sector liaison and when the fighting began, she took care of all the outposts in her sector, bringing food and ammunition to the defenders. She moved around from one outpost to the other, encouraging our people and inquiring about their needs. She had a special kind of tranquility, dodging the shells and bullets with no sign of fear.

Esther wrote to us on 9 May, her letter franked *Old City Under Siege*. She sent it via Ida (who handed over this and her other letters to our father, two months later), and gave us no indication she was in the Old City:

Well, things are more or less at a standstill at the moment, although everybody is sceptical I think of truce talks, as this at best would not be worth much to us. We have had our victories, though I personally am not so thrilled about Haifa. These large-scale evacuations [of Arabs] have surely an ominous significance, and I was much more pleased to hear that the Arabs are returning to Haifa. There was even special permission to bake bread for them during Pesach.

She then describes in detail her *Seder* with the Freunds, clearly forgetting she had already written about this, and continues:

I am very well indeed, except for an awful cold which I got from my typhus injection the other day. The weather is rather strange – we had rain again today in the middle of May! I wonder if you will believe me when I say that I am quite happy and very well, with jolly company and no personal worries, two things which are far more important than anything else. I am still hoping that some time in the summer I may get over to see you all somehow, if only for a week or two. Who knows?

The British departure from Palestine was just six days away. With it would come the major onslaught on the Jewish Quarter, leading to one of the few Arab victories in the whole 20 months of Israel's War of Independence.

25 A State is Born

The night of 10/11 May 1948, the start of the Hebrew month of Iyar, was moonless. Hunched under cover of darkness and the thick cloak of an Arab woman, Golda Myerson (Meir) crossed into Transjordan at Shuneh in the Jordan Valley, to try and convince King Abdullah to stay out of a war against the Jews. The King agreed, on condition that the Jews give up the idea of a Jewish state, which Golda refused.

The results of that secret meeting were costly to Jews and Arabs alike. The West Bank of the Jordan and Jerusalem's Old City were occupied by the Arab Legion for the next 19 years; and Abdullah's contacts with the Jews led to his assassination at the hands of an Arab extremist on the steps of the El Aksa Mosque three years later. The Arab world's refusal to accept partition led directly to what the Arabs called their *Naqba* (catastrophe), and has been the source of ongoing strife in the Middle East to this day.

On the same night that Golda made her secret visit to Jordan, Safed fell to Jewish forces, who routed local Arab gangs reinforced by Iraqi and Syrian troops, and the Haganah cleared the last stretch of highway between Bab el Wad and Jerusalem. Jerusalem's waterlines and pumps were blown up by Arabs in a parting gesture, and the city was without water for several days. Its arms situation also remained critical. Shaltiel sent an urgent message to the Haganah's Chief of Operations in Tel Aviv, Yigael Yadin:

> Having been informed that the planes are busy elsewhere and they cannot bring us arms and shells, eight sacks

British Tommies guard the approaches to 'Evelina'.

The new Haganah volunteer.

Learning to use a Sten gun.

With a group of Haganah volunteers (far right).

Esther (on right) 'playing soldiers'.

In Motza, outside Jerusalem.

The Company cook – 'Estie MiSuba'.

Esther in a lighter moment.

Sniper practice outside Jerusalem.

Old City fighters.

The eve of battle in the Old City.

Esther in the Old City of Jerusalem, May 1948.

With Sten gun ready inside the Old City.

Esther's father at the dedication of the Esther Cailingold memorial forest, planted at Kibbutz Lavi, 1953.

Esther's brother and sister, Asher and Mimi at the memorial to Jerusalem's fallen heroes.

arrived by air-mail today, containing a large number of packages with cooking-oil, coffee, cakes, salami and eggs. The oil was spilt, the eggs smashed and the aerial photographs and operational documents you sent us arrived covered in oil and eggs. You are surely aware of our arms situation and that we do not have a single 3-inch mortar shell or hand grenade.

Shaltiel had to wait another four days before Yadin could inform him that a supply of three-inch shells would be dropped by air at dawn on 14 May.

The Old City fighters were preparing themselves as best they could for the battle ahead. Their appeals for help reached Shaltiel's HQ on a daily and sometimes an hourly basis, much as Shaltiel was bombarding Yadin with his own requests. Along with his continual reminders to Brigade HQ of the desperate shortage of arms and ammunition, were Moshe Rousnak's insistent pleas that he be replaced by a more experienced and senior officer.

On 12 May, with things still relatively calm in the Old City, Esther sat down to write what was to be her last pre-battle letter home, again with no indication as to where she was and again sending it via Ida:

This week I think we can count some real victories, and things do look rather more promising, though whether Abdullah really means not to interfere, and whether their side is really so disorganised, or just the sort of thing we used to hear about Germany during the war, remains to be seen. We are all waiting for the 15th, hopefully, as well as expectantly, of what it will bring. Jerusalem has been most uncommonly quiet most of the week, so there is really no news. I am still bothered by a bad cold after my injection, but I suppose it is all worthwhile since there is typhus in the Arab part of the Old City. There is a water stoppage again, electricity is cut three times a day and there is no kerosene oil. Some people are cooking what food there is on wood fires, but we manage. I am going to have the rest of the white material you sent me made into blouses. I had two last summer and they are very serviceable. Lots of love to all the family, and best wishes. I am so uncertain as to whether you will get this, that there does not seem point in writing any more, so, Shalom ... Esther.

Her conscious effort to retain a sense of normality for her family, when all around her was descending into chaos, is wonderfully illustrated by her thoughts of white material for blouses.

At 5.30 p.m. on 13 May, the brave saga of the Etzion Bloc settlements reached its tragic end with a message from Yigal Yadin to Shaltiel. It ordered him to negotiate the evacuation of the Etzion Bloc with the British. If this was impossible, he was to inform the Bloc's defenders, in the name of the Haganah High Command, that they were free to raise the white flag to save lives. If possible, all arms and military equipment were to be destroyed.

The next day, Etzioni Brigade units, following departing British troops, took over the security zones in central Jerusalem (including Bevingrad), with little Arab resistance, in Operation Kilshon. In the Old City, however, a drama was being enacted between Jewish forces and the departing British. On the morning of Thursday, 13 May, the major in command of the Old City's Suffolk Regiment troops informed Rabbi Weingarten, as liaison with the Jews, that he would be withdrawing his men that day. Rousnak immediately began readying his forces to take over British positions, breaking open his hidden arms cache and issuing weapons openly for the first time. At 2.00 p.m., a British officer issued two rifles to Hashiloni and another Jewish policeman, as if it were simply another day. At 6.00 p.m., the British major announced that the withdrawal would begin in 15 minutes and, in a rare gesture of support, handed Rabbi Weingarten a Sten gun and magazine, as well as the key to Zion Gate, where the convoys had entered the Jewish Quarter during the long weeks of siege.

The Arabs seem to have been unaware of the details of the British departure, but seeing movement from Haganah lines, they opened fire, and then complained to the UN's Consular

Committee that the Jews had broken the 11-day-old Old City cease-fire.

Meanwhile, Rousnak's people were hurriedly occupying the 'Cross' outpost atop the Greek Orthodox church in the Armenian Quarter, as well as two positions on the city's southern wall, one on the Zion Gate tower and another on the 'Green Shutters' building. At midnight, the Armenians came to Weingarten and demanded that the Haganah withdraw from the Greek church roof and the city walls outposts, as this threatened their sovereignty. After all-night negotiations, Brigade HQ acceded in return for an Armenian promise of neutrality. This was to prove to be a grave mistake for the Jews. The Armenian Quarter was immediately invaded by Arab irregulars, who set up sniper posts on the monastery roof and occupied the Cross position which Rousnak's men had ceded to the Armenians. The Armenian Quarter later became a major staging area for the Arab Legion attack.

Amid the confusion of that day, a 23-year-old British Tommy, one Albert Brittain, fell asleep in an abandoned building, having imbibed a drop too much from a bottle of stolen liquor. He woke some hours later to find his colleagues gone and himself surrounded by Jewish soldiers who had taken over his position. Pressed into service as a sentry, Private Brittain laid claim to being the only English soldier to desert to the Jews on the Old City front. He tended to wander about during the quieter periods, and Adina Argaman recalls Esther warning Haganah commanders not to trust him. After the surrender of the Jewish Quarter two weeks later, he was held overnight with Jewish prisoners. Later, threatened by a group of his countrymen who had deserted from the British army to join the Arab side, he had to be protected by the Arab Legion officers.

Early on 14 May, heavy fire was being directed at the Jewish Quarter from Arab lines. That afternoon, Arab Legion tanks and armoured vehicles were seen approaching from the direction of Jericho. Later that evening, Lehi's Jerusalem commander proposed to Shaltiel that an attack be launched against the Old City. Shaltiel rejected the idea, claiming there were enough fighters in the Jewish Quarter to ensure its safety!

At the time the British withdrew, Arab forces in Jerusalem were weak and consisted largely of poorly trained and undisciplined irregulars. Hopes were high, therefore, that the Arabs would agree to a general cease-fire in the capital, heeding UN and Christian pleas to protect the holy places. Throughout 14 and 15 May, cease-fire coordinator Chaim Herzog (later head of Military Intelligence and President of the State of Israel), waited for his Arab counterpart in the French consulate behind the King David Hotel. He waited, however, in vain and the firing continued.

The Arabs were playing for time, knowing that King Abdullah had ordered Glubb Pasha to save Jerusalem as the jewel for his crown. Anxious to prevent Syria, Lebanon, Iraq and especially Egypt grabbing Palestine for themselves, Abdullah sent his Legion across the Jordan at the Allenby Bridge on the morning of 15 May.

Over to the west in Tel Aviv, the first all-Hebrew city, a different type of drama was being enacted. The top political leadership and a small number of invited guests were receiving secret invitations via motorcycle dispatch riders to attend the signing of the Declaration of Independence of the new Jewish state. The name of the state was still not decided, with Judea and Ivria both real possibilities. At exactly 4.00 p.m. on Friday, 14 May, David Ben-Gurion mounted the rostrum at the Tel Aviv Museum, read out the historic Declaration and invited the provisional government council members to sign the document. The ceremony ended with the singing of *Hatikvah*, the Jewish national anthem. By ten minutes to five, the hall was empty, as people rushed home for Shabbat. That evening, Egyptian planes flew over Tel Aviv, dropping bombs on the most unmilitary and unprotected targets they could find. Two days later, the first Israel Air Force fighters went into action and shot two Egyptian planes out of the Tel Aviv skies.

In the Old City, a modest flag-raising ceremony marked the declaration of the state, with the standing at attention and saluting not quite up to the standard of the recently departed British troops. By now, the situation in the Old City was desperate. Attempts to break through to the fighters from the

Jaffa Gate had failed. The area outside Zion Gate, through which supplies had entered under the British, was now heavily entrenched with Arab soldiers, some of them led by British officers.

On the evening of Saturday, 15 May, Moshe Rousnak reported to HQ over his 'Zabar' radio that his forces were being bombarded with two-inch mortars and heavy machine-guns. He requested a steady barrage of three-inch mortar shells onto five coordinates. Minutes later, he reported a bombardment of incendiary shells. Shaltiel turned down his request, however, because 'in the light of current negotiations, it is not politically expedient to shell the Arab positions from outside the walls and the Old City garrison should return the fire using its own resources'. At 10.30 p.m., Rousnak warned of an imminent Arab attack, for which he strengthened his defences by sending to the perimeter outposts his reserve troops, who included teachers and others with little or no real military training. Despite his complaints that he was neither sufficiently senior nor experienced to command the Old City garrison, Rousnak was proving himself a competent officer.

The attack came at 9.10 a.m. on the morning of 16 May. Within 40 minutes, the Arabs claimed that the Jewish Quarter was about to surrender and declared their intention to put all Jewish inhabitants 'against the wall' to teach the Jews a lesson. Thus began a two-week battle, the longest single battle in the War of Independence and probably in all Israel's history. During those two weeks, outgunned and outnumbered by Arab Legion troops as well as local irregulars, a handful of men and women managed to stave off continued attacks and continual shelling, and protect the lives of almost all the 1,700 civilians crouched in the cellars of the Quarter's ruined buildings.

Another of many desperate messages to Moriah HQ came over the 'Zabar' radio at 4.10 p.m. on that day: 'House after house blown up. Can't hold out one more minute. At least tell us how to surrender.' At 6.00 p.m., Rousnak requested that the Misgav LaDach Hospital be transferred to the Red Cross; next day, the Red Cross flag flew over the Hospital compound, and non-combatant women and children were taken there. The

Arabs, however, continued to fire on the Hospital until it was evacuated on the last day of battle.

The house-to-house fighting of Sunday, 16 May, probably saw some of the greatest IDF bravery in all its wars. On that day, the Arabs attacked the Street of the Jews, which was the main artery of the besieged Jewish Quarter, as well as the dividing line between the two Haganah defence sectors. Two of the teachers were wounded. One, Immanuel Meidav, had moved forward to mine the no-man's-land area in front of the Turgeman position and prevent the Arab advance. A scout leader, Immanuel had come to the Old City as a youth worker, but was also one of the few fully-trained Haganah commanders there, and very popular with the Old City fighters, particularly the youngsters. He took four of these youngsters with him on his mission, leaving a 16-year-old to provide covering fire. Assembling two land mines and two explosive devices, he just managed to call out that the fuse was too short when there was an almighty explosion. Blinded and limbless, Immanuel Meidav lingered semi-conscious in Misgav Ladach for three days, occasionally mumbling phrases from Bible lectures he had given at the University in happier times. By his side was his girlfriend Rika Menashe, who later married Immanuel's brother.

At 3.00 p.m. that day, Esther's section commander, Motke Pinkas, ordered Shlomo Cohen to return to an abandoned outpost on the Old City wall to retrieve the grenades and ammunition left behind in the retreat. Shlomo took with him two of the teachers, Chaim Katzburg and Esther Cailingold. These two moved ahead, with Shlomo covering the rear. Within minutes they were spotted and fired on by the Arabs. Chaim ran back to Shlomo and told him Esther needed cover-fire, as she was lying wounded in a trench. She bound up her wound with a handkerchief, while Shlomo crawled forward under fire. He was soon hit, as well, and the two of them lay where they were, one pistol between them, their retreat cut off by Arab snipers.

Some 15 minutes later, with a lull in the fire directed at them from the 'Cross' atop the Greek church (abandoned by the Haganah at the insistence of the Armenians), they crawled to a small gap in the wall protecting them, and then dashed across the few metres separating them from safety in their own lines. Esther made her own way to Misgav LaDach hospital, stayed long enough to have the wound in her side dressed, and then returned to her post, refusing doctor's orders to rest, and accepting only a cigarette to calm her nerves.

Harry Levin writes in *Jerusalem Embattled*:

> May 17 – The Old City is in the fourth day of its agony. The crackling and roaring echo throughout the town. All we can do is hope that the Haganah break through in time … Thought today of Esther C., wondering how she is faring in that Gehennum. Her wish is fulfilled; to help defend the Old City. Last week I had a scribbled note from her (a British soldier must have smuggled it out) saying how happy she was to be there.

Adina Argaman makes the point that none of the Old City women fighters lost their nerve or suffered battle shock. Both before and after she was hurt, Esther ran between endangered outposts bringing ammunition and food, urging the young men there to stay and fight when all seemed lost.

26 The Zion Gate Tragedy

Chaos reigned on the Jerusalem front in the days after the state of Israel was born. Desperate signals from Rousnak's Old City command post barraged Shaltiel, and were duly passed up the fledgling IDF's command ladder. At noon on 16 May, Shaltiel cabled Yigal Yadin in Tel Aviv: 'OC [Old City] under attack. Short of 3-inch shells, so can't help them.' This was followed by a 2.45 p.m. message sent to Yadin and Yitzhak Rabin at Palmach Brigade HQ at Maaleh HaHamishah:

> OC position worsening, cries of despair received. Must act today to save lives. Situation most serious. Requesting four platoons not two as you suggested, even if this means delaying opening the road.

Shaltiel had decided to send four platoons into the Old City. They were to go in that night through Jaffa Gate, capture the western sector and join up with the Jewish Quarter defenders. The plan was to create a corridor through which either to reinforce the garrison or evacuate the enclave – but the operation was unfortunately bungled. The Jewish Quarter defenders knew nothing about it; the four platoons were taken to the wrong gate and pinned down by fire from the Old City walls as they made their way to the right one. And, in any case, the Arabs had so heavily reinforced the Jaffa Gate position that nothing short of an armoured regiment and heavy artillery could have broken through.

The operation was called off at dawn, Monday, 17 May. Shaltiel pleaded again for Palmach reinforcements, and Rabin ordered Yosef Tabenkin, OC of the Harel's 4th Battalion, to assemble a force to fight for the Old City. With two assault companies of reduced size and a heavy-weapons unit readied, Rabin and his Palmach officers held a planning meeting with Shaltiel. Their proposal was to strike in force at Notre Dame and the Rockefeller Museum, so as to create a wedge between Jerusalem and Ramallah and relieve Arab pressure on the Old City. Shaltiel wanted a diversionary Palmach attack at the Zion Gate. Rabin, certain it would fail, agreed with reluctance. Uzi Narkiss was given field command of the Palmach troops.

At 10.45 that Monday morning, Shaltiel sent a dramatic message to Rousnak:

> We are very near you. At right moment we will attack the Gate, also possibly from other directions. We will inform you. Spare your ammunition. No other way to rescue except house-to-house battle. We are holding and pounding the enemy on all fronts. Be strong, eyes of the world are on you. See you soon.

At 3.05 p.m. that day, Rousnak's 'Zabar' radio picked up further encouragement from Brigade HQ: 'Battalion will attack in one hour.' At 5.30 p.m., 'Hold out a little longer and we will rescue you.' At 8.05 p.m., 'We will enter from the south at nightfall.'

At 6.00 p.m., Narkiss led his Palmachniks into the Yemin Moshe Synagogue, across the valley from the Old City walls, where they rested while their officers scouted the area. Shaltiel's battalion, which was to enter through the Jaffa Gate, was again pinned down by fire and suffering casualties.

That night, 17/18 May, Narkiss threw his two units against Mount Zion, backing them with three two-inch mortars, a *Davidka* (the Haganah's improvised mortar that created more noise than damage), a two-pounder anti-tank gun and several light and medium machine-guns. They captured the mount, secured their position, took prisoners (two British officers among them) and captured a large cache of weapons. The 120-man Palmach force had lost one dead and ten wounded. Even though the Jaffa Gate assault had failed, the Palmach took up attack positions at Zion Gate. Cries for help from behind the walls continued crackling over the radio, including one which said: 'If reinforcements not here in 20 minutes, all is lost!'

During those dramatic hours, a furious spate of politicking was underway, aiming to preserve the holy places and prevent bloodshed. The momentum of military activity, however, was such that neither negotiations nor strongly worded resolutions would halt it.

The Palmach's capture of Mount Zion panicked the Arabs, who pleaded for Arab Legion intervention. King Abdullah spoke personally to the Legion's area battalion commander, Colonel Abdullah el Tal, and at dawn on Tuesday, 18 May, Tal seconded a company to the Old City, entering the Lions' Gate (through which Israeli paratroopers would storm 19 years later to reunite Jerusalem).

Light years away in London, Britain's Jewish community was celebrating Israel's birth. During the critical hours when Uzi Narkiss's Palmach force prepared for the assault on the Old City, London Jews were meeting at the Shacklewell Lane Synagogue in Stoke Newington, where Rabbi Israel Brodie, then Senior Chaplain to Jewish soldiers in the British army and soon to be appointed Chief Rabbi of the British Commonwealth, gave a stirring address. A special prayer was followed by Bible passages read aloud in Hebrew and English by members of Bnei Akiva. While Esther was dodging across rooftops between her Old City sector's outposts, her brother and sister, Asher and Mimi, were among those reading Torah verses in that emotional London ceremony.

Throughout that Tuesday, Shaltiel and the Palmach disputed tactics. Shaltiel wanted the Palmach to go into the Jewish Quarter and hold it until the whole of the Old City could be taken. Narkiss and his officers wanted to take the Zion Gate and create a corridor through the Armenian Quarter, which Etzioni Brigade infantry could use to enter and occupy the area. Narkiss and his deputy David (Dado) Elazar stated very clearly: 'We do not undertake static roles.'

Meanwhile, at Brigade HQ in the Schneller base, 87 men were assembling under a seasoned Moriah Battalion Company commander named Mordechai Gazit. Most were only recently recruited, and had little or no training. A considerable proportion were old or ill. They were, they were told, on temporary assignment to relieve the fatigued Palmach fighters on Mount Zion.

Gazit and his men reached Yemin Moshe at 3.00 p.m. that Tuesday afternoon. At 6.00, Gazit met Narkiss and his officers, who told him of a change in orders: Gazit must now lead his men into the Old City behind the Palmach attack force, and take over the Jewish Quarter.

The confusion and failed coordination of that day were tragic. Gazit claimed not to have been told that the attack was postponed until 3.00 a.m. on 19 May, and he waited through the night with his increasingly nerve-racked men. Rousnak claims he could have unlocked the Zion Gate as soon as the Palmach captured Mount Zion, using the key that the British officer had given to Weingarten. At 3.30 a.m., however, the gate was blown open by a Palmach sapper, and unit commander Uri Ben Ari led in 24 fighters (two of them women), under heavy fire from Arabs atop the city wall. Entering the Old City, they made a historic, if short-lived, link-up with the besieged garrison.

A small force of Old City fighters led by Motke Pinkas, Esther among them, greeted the Palmachniks at the gate with jugs of warm milk in a moment of pure joy. Here at last were the promised reinforcements – a well-armed Palmach assault group, which was surely the spearhead of a larger fighting force! Over the Palmach radio transmitter, Narkiss ordered Pinkas to tell the Arabs through his loudspeaker that they were surrounded and should leave the Old City through the Lions' Gate. This was a popular tactic of the Jewish forces, but it didn't work this time because Abdullah el Tal was already moving his Legionaires into battle positions through that same gate.

Mordechai Gazit, meanwhile, was leading his men forward in the footsteps of the Palmachniks, laden with ammunition and medical supplies, including urgently needed plasma for Misgav LaDach's operating room. Behind him, at Yemin Moshe, he left

20 military policemen, useless as reinforcements because they had no weapons. Among Gazit's group was Chaim Safrai, newly married to Esther's friend Ida from London. Chaim was one of the few among them who knew how to handle a gun, but he was unfortunately ravaged by malaria and unfit for combat. Posted to the Porat Yosef outpost, he watched Esther with awe as she scurried between positions, carrying vital supplies and ammunition.

Six Palmachniks were sent into the Armenian Quarter to scout for the capture of the planned corridor. They returned to report that this was impossible with the forces available, and the Palmach's main Old City battle plan was aborted.

Moshe Rousnak, meanwhile, told chief medical officer Dr Laufer to prepare the wounded for evacuation. His colleague, British-born physician Dr Reiss, was instructed to identify the dead as they were taken to the new city through Zion Gate. Civilians, too, began making their way towards Zion Gate in the hope of evacuation.

Orders to begin evacuating the dead and wounded to Mount Zion were given at 5.30 a.m. when it was suddenly discovered that the Palmach force had already withdrawn, without waiting to be relieved. Narkiss, it seems, believed that his small group of fighters were too battle-weary to continue. In any case, he was not prepared to have them used as a static occupation force. He radioed Rabin at Harel HQ that replacements had not arrived, but was told to withdraw nonetheless. He informed Shaltiel that the Palmach were leaving the Old City: Shaltiel forbade him to withdraw and Narkiss demanded a replacement force. A shouting match ensued through the early hours of 19 May. It ended with Narkiss ordering Dado to withdraw his troops through Zion Gate. Gazit and his men were ordered to stay in the Old City, while the 20 policemen he had left behind were to hold Mount Zion together with a small Palmach group. The remainder of Narkiss's force returned to their base at Kiryat Anavim. They left several rifles and light machine-guns for the force on Mount Zion, but none in the Old City.

At 3.45 a.m. on Wednesday, 19 May, the Arab Legion fell on the Sheikh Jarrah corridor with 300 men backed by artillery and a further 400 men joined the battle some hours later. Two days later, a fresh regiment brought in from Nablus relieved them. That Wednesday morning, Glubb Pasha visited his Old City troops, reporting later to King Abdullah that the holy sites were safe.

At 6.15 a.m., came the first of a series of despairing messages from Rousnak: 'Leave Palmach in Old City to capture School and Church in Armenian Quarter and link up with Western Wall as soon as possible.' At 6.22: 'Artillery fire on Misgav LaDach and Batei Machaseh.' At 7.00: 'If you don't at least double the reinforcements and arms and don't leave the Palmach for at least one more day, situation will deteriorate. Send in additional Palmach commander immediately.' At 8.00, Shaltiel to GHQ: 'Palmach is leaving. Situation desperate. We will lose contact with Old City. Under constant attack and have no spare forces. We cannot replace Palmach Company.'

A dangerous situation was meanwhile developing at the Zion Gate. The Palmach withdrew, leaving it abandoned and unguarded. At 10.00 a.m., two Jewish civilians walked through the Gate undisturbed, with food for their relatives in the Old City. They were not to make the return journey. By noon, Arab troops were on the walls and in control of the Gate.

Rousnak, relieved to be replaced by Gazit, decided to sleep, leaving the new commander to disperse his reluctant troops and tour positions with his deputy, Avraham Orenstein. Within hours, at noon that Wednesday, 19 May, Gazit was hit by sniper fire and badly injured. He was taken to the hospital where, weakened by earlier wounds, he was confined to a stretcher until the surrender of the Old City. Rousnak was back as commander after a few short hours of much-needed sleep. The arms and ammunition that Gazit's men had brought in helped the garrison hold out for a further nine days. Six of Gazit's group fell in the subsequent battle and many more were wounded.

Confusion and misinformation continued swirling through that Wednesday. Shaltiel was reporting the planned evacuation of the wounded long after Arab Legion troops had taken up battle positions along the entire length of the wall. At 7.30 that evening, Ben-Gurion still believed the Legion had got no further than Sheikh Jarrah, and Yigal Alon reported to the General Staff: 'We have reinforced the Old City and saved 1,700 people.' Next day, Thursday, 20 May, Etzioni Brigade HQ sent a special communiqué: 'To all the brave fighters, blessings from Chief Rabbi Herzog for saving the Old City.'

By all accounts, there were sufficient Jewish troops to have taken the Armenian Quarter. Had the Palmach Company, the Old City garrison, Gazit's troops and the 20 military policemen at Yemin Moshe been coordinated, and had the enemy been distracted by a serious diversionary action at Jaffa Gate, a quick victory could well have been won. The distrust between Yitzchak Rabin and his Palmachniks on the one hand and Shaltiel and his Etzioni Brigade on the other introduced complications that resulted in a tragic series of lost opportunities. The failure to hold Zion Gate joined the surrender of the 'Cross' position on the Armenian Quarter's Greek church as the two fatal mistakes which lost the Jewish Quarter.

27 Mortally Wounded

A major attack on the Jewish Quarter was unleashed by Abdullah el Tal's Arab Legion battalion at 7.00 a.m. on Thursday, 20 May. One of their key gains was the imposing Nissan Bek Synagogue, which was not only a popular place of worship but a vital strategic outpost. At 8.20 that morning, Rousnak reported to Etzioni over 'Zabar' radio:

> The Arabs have captured Nissan Bek and are shelling the Misgav LaDach Hospital. We have no forces to remove them. Our people are in shock, the civilians are rebelling. Send reinforcements immediately.

Five minutes later came the reply: 'Hold on! Reinforcements will reach you in good time. Hold on and be brave.' The rest of that day saw a constant back-and-forth between Rousnak's command post and Etzioni HQ in the new city, with the tenor of messages growing ever more panic-stricken. Frantic pleas were made for mortar fire to be directed on various coordinates. At one point Rousnak reported that his sapper, Yaacov Zak, had been killed, but 20 minutes later reversed that message. Zak was alive and well.

Achiah Hashiloni recalls the terrible bombardment that began on the night of 20 May, following the Palmach withdrawal. Legion artillery began shelling the Jewish Quarter with two-pounder guns from the Mount of Olives. By then, the Arabs had abandoned frontal assault and were advancing by blowing up house after house. After midnight, Achiah went below ground to sleep. He was desperately tired and wanted to preserve ammunition which was in very short supply. He woke up on the Friday morning to find Motke Pinkas had joined him, since his sector had been lost to the Arab advance. Pinkas brought him a welcome present of some food and a clean pair of socks, before going off to a new assignment. They next met 10 days later, in a Transjordan prisoner-of-war camp.

Together with Motke Pinkas in the small hours of that Friday morning was Esther, his assistant and logistics coordinator, who from then on remained in Hashiloni's sector. Rika Menashe (Meidav), by then assigned to a combat position, remembers seeing Esther that night making the rounds of outposts and bunkers:

> She moved around from one post to another as if she was taking a stroll, but there was a gleam in her eyes, fire and brimstone. She helped the fighters at each outpost but didn't stay long in any one place. I shouted to her to be careful, not to move about on the rooftops as there was constant shooting. But Esther was as if possessed and didn't listen to anyone.

Adina Argaman recalls Esther encouraging young fighters who had abandoned their posts in shock after particularly heavy enemy fire, and leading them back to their firing positions.

Friday, 21 May saw further escalation in the Arab attack. Jewish reinforcements could not get through, and none of the several attempts to link up with the Jewish Quarter garrison succeeded. Explosives laid close to the Zion Gate resulted in no more than minor scratches on the massive ancient stones. Three attacks by Etzioni troops failed, while dozens of stretcher-bearers waited in vain to evacuate the wounded. At Ben-Gurion's personal intervention, the Palmach sent in three companies of assault troops, to no avail. Ammunition was parachuted to the embattled garrison several times, but the containers always fell into Arab hands.

That Friday, Hadassah Hospital on Mount Scopus ceased functioning, destroyed by Arab Legion artillery. Brigade Intelligence reported at 1.10 p.m. that the Arabs would win the battle for the Old City within the next half hour. Tal radioed Glubb at 1.30 p.m.:

The Jews have failed in their attempts to save their civilians in the Old City and have suffered heavy casualties. The big synagogue has been captured after it was cleared of Jewish criminals. Appropriate action is being to taken to conclude the plan to close the chain on the enemy.

That night and the following day, the Old City defenders – including the strictly orthodox among them, such as Shaar-Yashuv Cohen and Esther – invoked the Jewish law that the sanctity of life overrules the laws guarding the holy Sabbath. They were there to save the lives of 1,700 men, women and children, as well as to win the site most holy to the Jewish people. The carrying of arms and preparation of food, proscribed on the Sabbath, were on that day holy tasks.

Saturday, 22 May was a day of desperation for the Jews. The Old City was falling and the isolated kibbutz of Ramat Rahel, south of Jerusalem, was besieged by an Egyptian mechanised force. In the suburb of Talpiot, banished Old City commander Avraham Halperin was directing three-inch mortar fire on Legion positions, hoping to relieve the pressure on his colleagues behind the walls.

In the Jewish Quarter, hundreds of frightened, hungry civilians crouched in synagogue cellars, as Arab Legion shells rained down on the tiny enclave. The Arabs were conducting psychological warfare learned from the Jews, broadcasting calls for surrender through loudspeakers, day and night. Their message was that the Jews of the new city had long since been defeated, and the Old City Jews should no longer allow 'Haganah criminals' to endanger their lives.

Sanitary conditions in the Jewish Quarter were becoming intolerable, compounded by the prohibition against burial of the dead within the Old City walls. On Friday, 21 May, Rabbi Orenstein and several civilian helpers finally buried 23 people in a makeshift grave in the middle of the Quarter. Three days later, another 11 victims were added to the mass grave, including Orenstein and his wife, killed by a direct hit during the shelling.

The morning of Sunday, 23 May found Esther sobbing inconsolably in the command post courtyard. Another close friend, Zvi Greenberger, had fallen in battle. He had arrived in the Old City with Mordechai Gazit, one of the few young and skilled fighters in the group. By next day, he was in hospital with shrapnel in his eye, but when he heard his fellow Bren-gunner had been killed, he rushed back to his post. Early that Sunday, he volunteered to take the Bren gun to a position about to fall, and held off the Legion troops with steady and constant fire. Fatally wounded in the head by machine-gun fire, his body was added to the mass Old City grave.

Later that day, Esther found two sheets of plain white paper and a sharpened pencil, and sat down to write her last letter in an underground command post, writing clearly and in good North London Collegiate School style. The letter complete, Esther folded it and hurried to give it to Chavah Leurer, one of several Old City teachers whom the Haganah had asked to stay on in the Jewish Quarter and help out wherever needed. Esther found her broadcasting Rousnak's messages to Brigade HQ over 'Zabar' radio, and added her letter to Chavah's growing collection, too many of which were sadly handed on to next of kin after the surrender of the Old City. When she got to the new city, Chavah gave Esther's letter to Harry Levin, who kept it until our father came to Jerusalem in July. Levin recalls both father and himself weeping as they read it.

Shells continued falling on the Jewish Quarter all that Sunday, destroying building after building, and easing the work of the Arab demolition squads, placing their deadly charges under Jewish houses. In three weeks of fighting, some 10,000 shells fell on Jewish Jerusalem; in the Old City, the shelling played a key role in sapping the will of the defenders in their steadily shrinking enclave. There were now six Arab Legion companies in Jerusalem, with 900 infantry, three armoured squadrons and eight artillery batteries.

The entire Jerusalem front was in trouble: bitter battles were being fought to the west around Shaar Hagai and the Latrun fortress, with the main highway to the coast cut off once again. To the south, the Etzion Bloc had fallen, and the fate of Ramat

Rachel still hung in the balance. The vital Sheikh Jarrah corridor to Mount Scopus was occupied by the Legion, and the heights to the east of the city were also under Arab control.

Shaltiel was becoming more frantic and angry by the minute. At 9.25 a.m. on Sunday, 23 May, he signalled Yadin at GHQ:

> I received your superfluous message regarding conscription of civilians for building fortifications and military duties. This I did long before your request and, at that time, against the wishes of community leaders. Since your message is in reaction to the advice of Yitzhak Rabin, please ask him to concern himself with carrying out his operations more efficiently and with better organisation, rather than interfering in matters about which he knows nothing. My request to you is to send me the arms and ammunition I have been demanding constantly these past two months.

At 1.00 p.m. the following day, Monday 24 May, the Haganah High Command announced a UN Security Council cease-fire for 9.00 p.m., and all brigades were to honour it unless fired on. Two hours later, Shaltiel was again pleading for ammunition: 'After 11 days of constant battle, we are about to run out of ammunition of all types. Am prepared to fight without food but cannot do so without ammunition.' Half an hour after that, a further angry message reached Yadin: 'My urgent request is that you remove Harel (Palmach Brigade) from Jerusalem and replace them with 400 fresh troops equipped with sufficient arms and ammunition.' Yadin replied that Harel in Jerusalem had been ordered to coordinate with Etzioni, and he promised that a new overall area commander would shortly be appointed (Colonel David 'Micky Stone' Marcus), and that heavy weapons would reach Jerusalem as soon as the road was open. Later, he promised to parachute flame-throwers and anti-tank guns for the Old City.

The 24 May cease-fire failed within the hour, with an Arab artillery bombardment of the Jewish Quarter. Neither Glubb nor Tal was giving up the chance of presenting Abdullah with a great and symbolic victory.

At 10.00 p.m. that Monday night, Rousnak sent another message: 'We have done everything we can. The next battle will be for the lives of 1,700 souls.' Two hours later he added: 'Stop playing with the lives of 1,700 people.'

The defenders were near despair, with further casualties among their diminishing ranks. Rousnak reported that all his commanders were dead or injured, that his men were abandoning their posts and that ammunition was almost exhausted. Later he added that the civilians were demanding a surrender. He pleaded for more support fire from beyond the walls, for more parachute drops of ammunition and for another attempt to break through and link up with his force. Four more attempts were made to supply him with arms and ammunition from the air. All containers fell into enemy hands.

All through Tuesday, 24 May, the pleas for help came over the air from Rousnak, warning that the garrison could not withstand a frontal attack. By 6.35 p.m., the radio operator was semi-hysterical: 'Shell immediately and accurately, at least three shells on coordinate 85, range 100 metres.' Half an hour later, the radio crackled a further message: the Arabs were breaking through and support fire was needed from outside the walls. Later that evening, Rousnak informed his superiors that Jewish civilians were trying to physically remove his troops from their posts.

Further attempts to parachute in ammunition were made early on Wednesday, 26 May, again to no avail. The prevailing winds were giving the Arabs a steady supply of fresh ammunition. Towards midday, the Legion brought into the battle an armoured vehicle which began pumping deadly fire onto Israeli positions. With no anti-tank weapon, Rousnak had no response to this new threat.

Unable to move freely and without ammunition or supplies to deliver, Esther had joined Achiah Hashiloni's outpost, where he and his force were holding off the enemy with accurate fire. A vital protective bastion in Hashiloni's lines was the Alaloof building, which guarded the approach to the enclave housing the command post, the hospital and buildings where civilians were sheltering. That afternoon, Hashiloni heard strange knocking noises from under the Alaloof. Fearing the worst, he moved forward, taking Esther and one other fighter with him. He remembers Esther running ahead and getting to the building six strides ahead of him. There was a tremendous explosion as the door blew outward and all three were smothered in debris and flying nails. Hashiloni's scarred face, hands and legs still testify to that deadly charge. Managing to free himself from the wreckage, he shouted 'Go and see what's happened to Esther!'

At that point he lost consciousness. Risking their own lives, other fighters rushed forward to dig Esther out of the rubble. She had deep wounds across her side and chest and a shattered spine. Gently laying her on a torn-off door, they carried her to the Misgav LaDach Hospital, where Dr Laufer and Dr Reiss tried to make her comfortable. Their orders were that she should not be moved, as this could endanger her life.

So Esther lay there, racked with pain, trying not to disturb those lying on adjacent stretchers. Her fellow fighters came by to comfort her, telling her she would come through this one as she had when wounded the week before.

The next day, Thursday, 27 May, Rousnak reported to HQ that Arab Legion troops were everywhere and that the famous Hurva Synagogue, centrepiece of the Jewish Quarter, had been blown up. His latest casualty figures were five dead and 22 seriously wounded, leaving him with 40 active fighters. The remainder of that day saw shelling of the enclave, the advance of armoured vehicles into the Jewish Quarter and the steady demolition of its shrinking perimeters. Calls for help and support fire went largely unanswered.

28 The Last Letter

Through the early hours of Friday, 28 May, news reached Rousnak's command post of a planned counterattack from Mount Zion to link up with the Jewish Quarter garrison. Rousnak was even asked for the exact location of his defence lines to avoid any 'friendly-fire' errors. Hope, however, was short-lived. At 4.50 on Friday morning, he was informed that three attempts to break through had failed and the troops were returning to base. A message from Etzioni HQ at 6.25 a.m. urged:

> Hold on for one more day. We will make every effort to break through at nightfall. We will arrive with a strong force to save you. Prepare yourselves – and don't give up.

It was too late. The Jews could no longer defend their enclave without risking a massacre of its entire Jewish population. Rousnak's HQ had been debating surrender since the Alaloof building was blown up on the Wednesday, two days before. The Misgav LaDach Hospital, under constant Arab mortar and machine-gun fire despite the large red cross on the building, was abandoned early Thursday: Dr Laufer and Dr Reiss came to Adina Argaman in the small hours of Thursday morning, ordering her to clear and clean two rooms and a large balcony in the Batei Machaseh building where she slept. She rounded up three other young women and they worked till dawn to ready a makeshift hospital. With first light on Thursday, the wounded arrived, some limping, others, like Esther, gently carried in on stretchers. The destruction of the Hurva Synagogue later that day was the final straw for the Quarter's demoralised civilians – and, in fact, for many of the fighters in the bunkers.

At 8.55 on Friday morning, a message came from Shaltiel forbidding the Old City garrison to allow any negotiation attempts by the civilians. 'We will attack tonight and you must act only in accordance with my instructions,' was the message. A group of rabbis, attempting to approach Arab lines with a white flag, was stopped by Jewish fighters. One of them, Rabbi Chazan, said later: 'All I wanted was to avoid the loss of brave young lives and to prevent destruction and devastation.'

At 12.55 p.m. on Friday afternoon, Jewish troops on Mount Zion saw a delegation with a white flag, and at 1.20, Rousnak reported he was negotiating a cease-fire in order to remove the dead. Shaltiel permitted a cease-fire solely for that purpose but, he said, on no account was a surrender to be negotiated. Rousnak should play for time while a force large enough to break through was gathered.

All that Friday, delegations went back and forth between Jewish and Arab lines. The Arabs held three of the rabbis hostage at one point, and negotiations were halted until their release. Around midday, civilians began emerging from their hiding places, moving towards Arab lines and talking to Legion soldiers. The Jewish Quarter defence lines simply collapsed at that point, and there was nothing Rousnak and his fighters could do to regain their defensive position.

At 2.00 p.m., a delegation comprising Rousnak, Nissan Zeldas, David Eisen, Rabbi Weingarten and his daughter Yehudit sat down with Abdullah el Tal and signed a surrender agreement. At 2.05 Shaltiel received a message from the Old City, urging him to send in Red Cross and UN representatives to prevent a massacre.

At 5.00 p.m. on that last day, shortly before the start of the Sabbath, Rousnak radioed his last dramatic message:

> We have surrendered and negotiated the total evacuation of all inhabitants. Tell Mount Zion to prepare to receive us. Tell the hospital to prepare to receive wounded. Not yet clear if they will take prisoners. Probably will take the

fighters, may agree to an exchange on the spot. The radio is now being destroyed!

The Arabs were ecstatic. King Abdullah came in person to the Old City and knelt for Friday prayers at the Mosque of Omar. The place most holy to three world religions was in Arab hands. Amman Radio informed the world of the Arab victory, asserting that King Abdullah's presence in the Old City and his prayers at the Mosque had given his brave fighters courage to overcome the enemy. Three years later, Abdullah was assassinated on the very spot where he had prayed for an Arab victory.

At 7.40 that Friday evening, the Belgian consul informed his French colleague in west Jerusalem that the Jews had surrendered and that a consular representative should be sent to the Old City to observe and help supervise the situation. The terms of surrender required that:

- The Jewish garrison hand over all arms, ammunition and military equipment.
- All Jews capable of bearing arms be taken prisoner (it was verbally agreed that the prisoners would be taken to Amman under Red Cross and UN supervision).
- All women, children and wounded fighters be transferred to the Jewish area outside the Old City, under supervision of a UN representative.
- The entire Jewish Quarter had been captured by Arab Legion forces.
- Arab Legion officers be responsible for the safety and well-being of all civilians, prisoners and the wounded, until they reach their agreed destinations.

UN representative Dr Pablo de Azcarate urged evacuation of the wounded before the civilians, but he was not heeded for fear the mob would massacre the civilian population. By 8.30 on Friday evening, the first 50 elderly people, women and children had reached Mount Zion. By 10 o'clock, their number had reached 700. The evacuation continued through the night, with Jewish Quarter civilians reaching safety, and housed in ab-

andoned Arab homes in west Jerusalem's Katamon neighbourhood.

The Arab Legion conducted themselves honourably. In one
instance, at least, Legionnaires opened fire on local Arabs to
protect the injured and the POWs. When an Arab soldier tried
to snatch a watch from a young women evacuee, a Legion
officer fired his pistol at the soldier's feet, explaining, 'We must
maintain our high standards of discipline so that the Jews will
accept us when we conquer West Jerusalem.' Bloodthirsty cries
of 'itbach al Yahud' (kill the Jews!) and 'Deir Yassin'
accompanied the evacuation through that evening and the
following day, when the prisoners were led away to a Jordanian
POW camp. Without doubt, the Old City Arabs would have
fallen on the Jewish evacuees and torn them apart, but for the
Arab Legion officers.

Night fell on the Old City as that terrible Friday drew to an
end. The wounded lay huddled in the Batei Machaseh building.
Doctors, nurses and orderlies did what they could to make their
patients comfortable and keep their wounds clean, but they had
few drugs or painkillers left, and, with no electricity for the
refrigerator, the plasma was useless. The medical team had done
a heroic job under appalling conditions, managing to save most
of the severely wounded. Dr Laufer, head of the Old City's
Hadassah team, had ensured the highest standards of surgical
and medical practice throughout the siege. He had made it clear
to Rousnak that the medical team could continue to care for the
wounded and there was no need for surrender on their behalf.

Even during the transfer to the temporary hospital in Batei
Machaseh, medical standards were maintained. Ora, the head
nurse, even insisted that Adina and the other women helping
out in the hospital sweep the floors before Arab Legion officers
came in to supervise the evacuation. 'It wouldn't be right to
show them a dirty and disorderly hospital. We must maintain
our high standards up to the last minute,' she said, herself
taking a broom to sweep the kitchen floor.

Chaim Safrai, who had been wounded at 11.00 that morning,
was lying on the floor in Batei Machaseh. He remembered that
Esther had two candles, and managed to stretch out her hand to

kindle the Sabbath lights, with the appropriate prayer. Shulamit Velikovsky, by Esther's side, wrote to our parents about those last hours, four days after Esther's death:

> She was completely conscious and kept an interest in what was happening. On Friday evening, she asked for a *siddur* [prayer book] and we prayed *Kabbalat Shabbat* together with love and particular appreciation for certain passages. I stayed with her and we continued talking for several hours after concluding our prayers. At that time, she did not know of her impending death.

All Friday evening, the Old City Arabs looted and burned the Jewish Quarter, prevented from entering the Batei Machaseh only by a heavy iron gate. Arab Legion officers, accompanied by two trained nurses (both of them, Rabbi Weingarten's daughters) and a Red Cross representative, came to facilitate the evacuation. The Legionnaires took over the Armenian school close to the Zion Gate as their HQ, allocating the top-floor rooms to the wounded Jewish fighters.

Zipporet Kohen-Raz, now a well-known Jerusalem artist, had come to the Old City with Esther, as part of the last group of teachers. Ostensibly entering as a youth leader for the Jewish Quarter children, she was immediately made an orderly in the hospital. She was there when Esther came to have her first wound bandaged, and then ran back to battle. Now, Esther was mortally wounded. Zipporet came to her stretcher, stroked her face and whispered, 'Yihyeh beseder' (It'll be OK). Esther stared back wide-eyed, and mumbled 'If you say so.'

Another of the medical orderlies was 17-year-old Yehudit Kahane. A graduate of evening first-aid courses and a volunteer with Magen David Adom, Yehudit had registered for National Service at the Schneller base on 12 April and had immediately been attached to an Old City convoy. She had reached the Misgav LaDach Hospital just before Passover, and was now assigned to evacuating the 119 wounded to the Armenian school. She recalls her difficulty carrying the stretchers over the rocky ground, and how they had to be lifted over walls at several points along the route. It was she who accompanied Esther on this last terrible journey, wiping her face to try and relieve her agony.

Shaar-Yashuv Cohen had suffered a leg wound in the final days of battle. A doctor had broken part of his cast, allowing him to hop on one leg to the Armenian school, an Arab Legion soldier on either side to ease the journey and help him up to the school's huge, high-ceilinged rooms on the top floor. He was placed alongside Esther's stretcher. A photo by *Time-Life* photographer John Phillips hangs from a wall of his Haifa home today, showing Shaar-Yashuv propped on his stretcher, and Esther lying unconscious nearby.

During the night, Arab Legion officers and Red Cross and UN representatives moved among the wounded, sorting them into evacuees and POWs. With only 39 genuine prisoners, Abdullah el Tal needed to boost his numbers: 51 of the wounded, including Shaar-Yashuv Cohen, were judged fit enough for captivity. Added to the 39 remaining fighters and the Jewish Quarter's male civilians, they brought the total number of POWs to 341. Dr Reiss, Rabbi Weingarten, his daughter Masha, nurses Chavah Kirshbaum and Malkah Shalit and two male nursing orderlies volunteered to go with the prisoners. When Abdullah el Tal saw the tiny force who had withstood the onslaught of his troops, he declared 'Had I known who I was up against with my battalion of trained soldiers, I would have come at you with sticks not guns.'

Towards morning, while most of the 119 wounded men and women in the Armenian school slept, Shaar-Yashuv hopped his way to the window. Below him, he saw the whole Jewish Quarter in flames. He could just make out the crumbling remains of the four ancient synagogues at the heart of a Quarter that had once been home to hundreds of Jewish families. The following day, Reuters Jerusalem correspondent Don Campbell would write: 'The scene is like Stalingrad or Berlin in May 1945. Roofless buildings, alleys waist-high in debris.' Several of the more lightly wounded joined Shaar-Yashuv at the window, and they began singing yearning patriotic songs of the return to Zion.

Their singing woke Esther, who pleaded for a painkiller. None remained, and she was offered a cigarette instead. 'No,' Shaar-Yashuv remembers her mumbling. 'No. Today it's Shabbat.' These were her last words. She lapsed into a coma shortly afterward.

When Adina and Ora the head nurse came to check on the wounded at 5.00 a.m., they found two of the female orderlies weeping next to a stretcher. 'Esther is dying,' they said. They had tried hard to save her, although the doctors had offered little hope. The lower part of her body had been paralysed since the explosion at the Alaloof. She had taken only liquids since she was hurt, and was in intense pain, making enormous efforts to suppress the moans that escaped her as she was evacuated to the Armenian school.

Adina stayed by the unconscious Esther:

> Esther lay quietly, her breathing very low. There were no more moans. Her face was calm, just as it was before she was wounded. Ora approached, looked at Esther and lifted the blanket to cover her face. It was all over, and with such cruel simplicity! I had no more strength. I rushed to the window and burst into tears. I do not know what I was crying for most. Was it for Esther's young life that had just ended so quietly, or for the terrible night that had just passed or was it just my own weakness? Ora asked me to control myself so that the Arabs should not see us crying. As I turned to leave the room, I met one of the Arab officers. He asked what had happened to the wounded girl lying there. I indicated by a shake of the head that she was dead and tried to hide my red eyes. He looked at me in silence and I am sure that he was sharing with me in my grief.

Chaim Safrai saw a lone covered stretcher in the corridor. Lifting the blanket, he found the body of his wife's dearest friend. A week later, he wrote to our parents:

> Mine was the privilege and the honour to have served with your daughter during the last battle in the Old City. All of

us who got to know her during those last 10 days of the fighting, have much to tell about Esther's brave and wonderful acts. She breathed her last in the early hours of Shabbat, Iyar 20, May 29 1948. May her soul rest among those of the everlasting and may Zion and its rebuilding be your comfort.

Esther was one month short of her 23rd birthday when she died. She was one of 39 Old City fighters who lost their lives, and like the others she was posthumously accepted as a soldier in the Israel Defence Forces. She was temporarily buried in a stone quarry in west Jerusalem, and transferred to the Mount Herzl military cemetery when it opened three years later. The rest of the dead were left behind in the mass Old City grave, until their reburial on the Mount of Olives in 1967, after the Six-Day War.

IDF archives preserve a handwritten note, numbered 627, sent on 5 June 1948, at 8.00 a.m. and received at 5.30 p.m. the same day. It reads:

> To: Manpower Branch. From: Netzach [Casualty Unit]. Please inform the owner of the Cailingold bookshop in Allenby Street, next to the Great Synagogue, Tel Aviv, that his granddaughter Esther, fell in the Old City in the last battle.

The news reached London on Sunday, 6 June, in the form of the 'Stop Press' announcement ('TWO LONDON GIRLS DIE IN BATTLE') that I had read on the train. Esther's own farewell reached us the following month:

> May 23, 1948
> Dear Mummy, Daddy and everybody
> If you do get this at all, it will be, I suppose, typical of all my hurried, messy letters. I am writing it to beg of you that, whatever may have happened to me, you will make the effort to take it in the spirit that I want and to understand that for myself I have no regrets. We have had a bitter fight,

I have tasted of Gehenem [Hell] – but it has been worthwhile because I am convinced that the end will see a Jewish State and the realisation of all our longings.

I shall be only one of many who fell [in] sacrifice, and I was urged to write this because one in particular was killed today who meant a great deal to me. Because of the sorrow I felt, I want you to take it otherwise – to remember that we were soldiers and had the greatest and noblest cause to fight for. God is with us I know, in his own Holy City, and I am proud and ready to pay the price it may cost to reprieve it. Don't think I have taken 'unnecessary risks' – that does not pay when manpower is short, but I did find the excitement I have always needed and have enjoyed it.

I hope you may have a chance of meeting any of my co-fighters who survive, if I do not, and that you will be pleased and not sad of how they talk of me. Please, please do not be sadder than you can help – I have lived my life fully if briefly, and I think that is the best way – 'short and sweet', very sweet it has been here in our own land.

I hope that you will enjoy from Mimi and Asher the satisfaction that you missed in me – let it be without regrets, and then I too shall be happy. I am thinking of you all, every single one of you in the family, and am full of pleasure at the thought that you will one day, very soon I hope, come and enjoy the fruits of that for which we are fighting.

Much, much love, be happy and remember me only in happiness.

Shalom and Lehitraot,

Your loving Esther.

Epilogue

Six thousand Israelis fell in the War of Independence, 1 per cent of the country's Jewish population. Of that number, 1,584 died in the battle for Jerusalem, and more than 2,000 more were wounded – a casualty list of close to 30 per cent of the fighting force on that front. From Esther's perspective, however, these people died to win an independent state for the Jewish people, and in that they succeeded, only a few short years after six million Jews had been put to death in Europe.

On 11 June 1948, the first truce between Jews and Arabs was declared. The guns fell silent and the young state could at last bring in refugees from Europe and acquire badly needed food, ammunition and heavy weapons. The truce lasted until 19 July, and among those who took advantage of it was our father, who reached Tel Aviv on 4 July. A permit from the IDF transport officer in Tel Aviv allowed him to travel to Jerusalem by military convoy on 5 July and remain there until 8 July, for the purpose of visiting his daughter's grave. The Moriah Battalion CO and officers at Schneller did all they could to help him; memos survive, requesting that he be given full cooperation.

'I hope you may have a chance of meeting any of my co-fighters who survive, if I do not, and that you will be pleased and not sad of how they talk of me,' Esther had written. Strenuous efforts were made for him to meet Esther's comrades-in-arms. Among them was Shulamit Velikovsky; he became very close to her and her family in America in the years ahead.

Father returned to Tel Aviv with Esther's prophetic last letter, given him by Chavah Leurer and Harry Levin, as well as a moving obituary from the *Ha'aretz* newspaper, which read in part:

239

Despite the fact that her wound had not healed, she ran out of the infirmary, snatched the weapon of a fallen colleague and took his place on the ramparts. Esther, who was physically very weak, was incredibly brave in spirit, very strong in her faith and stayed at her post until the end. With Sten gun in hand, she prevented the advance on the last stronghold which shielded the women and children, felling many among the charging enemy troops.

Three weeks later, *Ha'aretz* ran a second obituary on Esther, this one written by the young women who had served with her:

She was one of the first among us to volunteer for full-time service. She accepted each task gladly, guarding in the outposts and cooking for our group. When the girls were taken out of combat positions, she objected strongly. After filling a number of rear-echelon roles, she demanded to be sent to the Old City, and eventually succeeded in getting there. When the Legion began its heavy attacks, she went straight to the frontline positions, never flinching at the hail of shells and bullets, and bringing food and ammunition to the most exposed areas ... Her pure soul left us just as the Old City, which she came to defend, was going up in flames. Esther! You did not manage to receive very much from our Holy Land and you gave of your all, again and again. You served faithfully, you were our dearest colleague, always worrying about us and in the end, you sacrificed your life. We will remember you wherever we may go.

Harry Levin's tribute to Esther appeared in the May 1949 *London Zionist Review.* He wrote:

Duty, for Esther Cailingold, had a transcendent meaning. Whether in the kitchen or the firing line, on the air or in a first aid post, she always did her best, and tried to do more. She sought out the spheres where her service was most needed, and they were usually the most exposed. She clung to her ideals, which permeated her whole life, and gained the respect of all who knew her. A strong, faithful character and a gentle person.

Dr Avraham Laufer, head of the Old City Hadassah medical team during the last six weeks of the siege, wrote in the *Davar* newspaper of June 1949:

> When we returned home, we took with us the bodies of the two casualties who died in the Armenian School. They were the only ones who received a decent burial. One was a teacher, who had arrived the previous year from England, and who volunteered to go into the Old City. She was a girl who took charge of situations, and the toughest of the boys carried out her orders. She left the hospital after her first wound and later was brought in when the house which she was defending was blown up and her back was broken. All we could do was to ease her pain with a shot of morphine.

Our parents received a flood of letters from Esther's friends. Shulamit Velikovsky's ends:

> She herself chose to go to the heart of the Land of Israel. There she went out with a gun to meet and answer the fire and not wait for it at home. She did things because she felt they had to be done. She always wanted to be doing something essential. It was there in the Old City that she must have found that feeling of fulfillment. If you are as strong in character as your daughter would make us think, then try to find the strength to look at what Esther did from the standpoint not of one family, but of all the Jewish people, from the standpoint not of years, but of this generation of liberation, and many more that have been and are yet to come. I am sure you will be proud of your daughter who died while actively fighting, bringing liberation one step nearer to her downtrodden people. I love and admire Esther and this love and admiration includes you, her parents. She goes on living in all our hearts here.

Dina Schur wrote:

> You have lost your daughter, we have lost a wonderful friend and our nation has lost one of its very best children. Yet try to be comforted in the knowledge that, in her 22 years, Esther gave and received more love than most people experience even if they live to a ripe old age. In the short time that was given to her, she fulfilled all that God can demand from those who He puts on this Earth. She reached the highest standards possible of a human being. In her life and in her death she was an example to us all. She will live in us forever, and her story will be told to our children, if we ever get to that, and if not, we will know how to die, for she showed us the way – without fear or uncertainty, so that others may live. As long as we live, she has a place among us, and she made one for you too, her dear parents … I would willingly have given my life to save hers, and I want at least to try to make your heavy burden as light as possible. May God comfort you!

Yehudit (Ida) Safrai's letter spoke of Esther as a sister to her:

> Esther carried out her greatest wish. She fought courageously for her highest ideals. Passive obedience never satisfied her, so she sought urgent and important duties and fulfilled them with all the intelligence, earnestness and willpower of which she was capable. Her name is held in esteem by all the defenders of the Old City. Yet she sought no glory. She fought for her beliefs and she gave her all.

Rika Meidav remembers Esther

> as a shining star, a living ball of fire, a Biblical-type figure and an example of all those who gave their lives for the Land of Israel. She ran to save the Old City, to give of her all, to help. She indeed gave the highest sacrifice, her life. She was a wonderful person and I am proud that I knew her.

Fellow fighter Aharon Liron, writing in his diary in the Um el Jamil POW camp in Transjordan, described Esther Cailingold as

> a shining example to us all. We talked about her as we sat in our tents. She showed all of us the way with her stubborn bravery and her dedication. Several of the boys told me that after she was wounded on May 16, they saw her limping along at the end of the Street of the Jews and rushed to help her. She pushed them aside, pointed south and said, 'You're needed over there!' Although she was obviously still in pain and walked with a limp, she took over the machine-gun when necessary. In many of the attacks she was one of the first to move forward to meet the enemy, and always the last to retreat.

On 7 April 1949, recently released from a Jordanian POW camp, Moshe Rousnak wrote in his report to the Jerusalem District Command:

> I feel it is my duty to tell you about the late Esther Cailingold. She arrived in the Old City at the end of April 1948 with the last group of teachers, and was allotted to guard duties, as were all the other teachers. She stood at her post for a full two weeks. In the last stage of the battle, when most of the Jewish Quarter was already in enemy hands, Esther stood with a number of young fighters and bravely defended the last sector. During the fierce enemy attack, Esther was mortally wounded and died a short while later. Her death was a serious blow to all those who knew and admired her bravery and her gallant stand as a fearless fighter.

In his report to GHQ, Moshe Rousnak made special mention of Esther as worthy of commendation. The IDF High Command never responded, and none of the brave men or women who fought in the Old City received citations for bravery. Our family has always considered Moshe Rousnak's recommendation as Esther's citation.

Esther's memory is honoured in many ways. These include a forest planted in her name in Kibbutz Lavi, rooms and libraries named for her in children's homes and a scholarship fund at Yeshivat HaKotel in the Old City, where special prayers are said in her memory on Israel's annual Memorial Day, and a eulogy is delivered by *yeshiva* head Rabbi Hadari, whose wife Naomi was taught by Esther at Evelina. Esther's name is inscribed in the memorial cave in the Jewish Quarter, on the Machal memorial at Shaar Haggai, in the Haganah room at Beit Agron in Jerusalem and on the walls of the magnificent Armoured Corps Memorial at Latrun. In London, city of Esther's birth, her memory is perpetuated in a practical and permanent way in British Emuna's Esther Cailingold Group, which collects money to help needy children in Israel.

Ida (Yehudit) and Shulamit Velikovsky-Kogan have named their daughters Esther, and Mimi and I each have our Esties. All these little Esthers are now grown and have children of their own, and this new generation is producing a growing collection of term papers and matriculation projects about our brave sister.

'I am thinking of you all, every single one of you in the family, and am full of pleasure that you will one day, very soon I hope, come and enjoy the fruits of that for which we are fighting,' wrote Esther in her last letter. And that we did. Mimi married Gubby Haffner, I married Edna Lunzer, and we all settled in Israel, enjoying the fruits for which Esther and her comrades had fought and died. And I, my sons, daughter, nephews and nieces have all followed Esther into the Israel Defence Forces.

Nineteen years after Esther's death, Israel fought the Six-Day War and regained the Old City. By then, my father was seriously ill, and I went quickly to London, taking time only to go first to the Old City, kiss the ancient stones of the Western Wall and gaze on the ruins of the Jewish Quarter where my sister had died. I can still see father's face when I told him that I had come to London straight from the Western Wall. I think it was the first time in 19 years I had seen him really smile. He died two months later, and our mother finally joined us in Israel.

Fifty years on, Esther is still with me. As I make the 20-minute drive in my air-conditioned car through the new road-tunnels to visit my children and grandchildren at Efrat near the Etzion Bloc, I think of Esther's journeys on that same route to Kfar Etzion. When an Israeli F-15 jet fighter roars overhead, I think of the horrors of her last battle. I watch my grandchildren enjoying television and video, computers and CD-Roms, and think of the teenage runners between the outposts of Esther's time.

Israel 50 years on has five large universities and many more smaller ones. We have 747s and a world full of Israeli embassies. We have a whole system of high- and post-high school education, synthesising Torah and secular education. We have massive immigration: 240,000 people in 1949, within a year of the state's creation; and 199,000 in 1990, following the fall of the Soviet Union – in a country which the British claimed could not absorb more than 100,000 newcomers.

Hardest of all to believe are the peace agreements with Egypt and Jordan, the Rabin–Arafat and Netanyahu–Arafat hand-shakes, and even the fact that no shot has been fired in anger across the Syrian border in many years. This is what Esther fought for, and what can, in some way, compensate for her and the thousands of others who have given their lives for Israel. I'd like to think that Esther and all her fellow fighters are smiling at us, proud of our achievements and hopeful about our strides towards peace.

Esther's final request has been the hardest to fulfil – to 'be happy and remember me only in happiness'. Yet, in the midst of our grief, we have taken courage from her brave example, and learned to rejoice in the new generations growing up proud and free in our own land.

Bibliography

PERIODICALS

- *Davar**
- *Ha'aretz**
- *The Palestine Post*

UNPUBLISHED DOCUMENTS

- IDF Archives: documents relating to the battles on the Jerusalem front, November 1947 to May 1948*
- Moshe Erenwald, *The Jewish Quarter in Jerusalem's Old City in the War of Independence*, MA thesis*

BOOKS

- Argaman, Adina, *The Scroll of the Old City*, Maarachot, Tel Aviv, 1949*
- Ben Ari, Uri, *Follow Me*, Maariv Book Guild, Keter, Jerusalem, 1994*
- Ben-Gur, Elitzur, *Jerusalem Diary, 1948*, Ariel, Jerusalem, 1993*
- Churchill, Winston S., *The Second World War*, Cassell, London, 1948
- Gilbert, Martin, *The Boys*, Weidenfeld & Nicolson, London, 1996
- Gilbert, Martin, *Jerusalem in the 20th Century*, Chatto & Windus, London, 1996
- Glubb, John Bagot, *A Soldier with the Arabs*, Hodder & Stoughton, London, 1957
- Joseph, Dov, *The Faithful City*, Simon & Schuster, New York, 1960
- Levin, Harry, *Jerusalem Embattled*, Victor Gollancz, London, 1950

- Levy, Itzchak, *Jerusalem in the War of Independence*, Maarachot, Tel Aviv, 1986*
- Liron, Aharon, *The Old City of Jerusalem under Siege and in Battle*, Maarachot, Tel Aviv, 1986*
- Syrkin, Marie (ed.), *Golda Meir Speaks Out*, Weidenfeld & Nicolson, London and Jerusalem, 1973

LETTERS FROM FRIENDS AND COLLEAGUES

Sylvia Ball, née Rose
Joan Cooley, née Weiner
Miss Dalton
Betty Dawson, née Wake
Arieh Handler
Doris Haskell, née Rosenblatt
Shulamit Kogan, née Velikovsky
Etta Lerner

Harry Levin
Leatrice Levine, née Jacobs
Rika Meidav (*née* Menashe)
Geoffrey Paul, OBE
Moshe Rousnak
Yehudit Safrai, née Ida Gross
Dina Schur
Hannah Tannenbaum, née Faust

THE FOLLOWING PEOPLE KINDLY AGREED TO BE INTERVIEWED:

Ambassador Yehuda Avner
Rabbi Shaar-Yashuv Cohen
Rabbanit Naomi Hadari
Achia Hashiloni
Yehudit Jouran
Shulamit Kogan, née Velikovsky
Zipporet Kohen-Raz
Chavah Leurer

Hannah Lindenberg, née Goldschmidt
Rika Meidav (*née* Menashe)
Yehudit Nachman, née Kahane
Moshe Rousnak
Chaim Safrai
Yehudit Safrai, née Ida Gross
Daisy Ticho

* in Hebrew